Child Development

Perspectives in Developmental Psychology

M.D. Rutherford

STUDENT STUDY GUIDE

by Sandra Hessels

OXFORD

UNIVERSITY PRESS

OXFORD
UNIVERSITY PRESS

8 Sampson Mews, Suite 204, Don Mills, Ontario M3C 0H5
www.oupcanada.com

Oxford University Press is a department of the University of Oxford.
It furthers the University's objective of excellence in research, scholarship,
and education by publishing worldwide in

Oxford New York

Auckland Cape Town Dar es Salaam Hong Kong Karachi
Kuala Lumpur Madrid Melbourne Mexico City Nairobi
New Delhi Shanghai Taipei Toronto

With offices in

Argentina Austria Brazil Chile Czech Republic France Greece
Guatemala Hungary Italy Japan Poland Portugal Singapore
South Korea Switzerland Thailand Turkey Ukraine Vietnam

Oxford is a trade mark of Oxford University Press
in the UK and in certain other countries

Published in Canada by Oxford University Press

Library and Archives Canada Cataloguing in Publication

Rutherford, M. D.
Child development : perspectives in developmental psychology. Student study guide / M.D. Rutherford and Sandra Hessels.

ISBN 978–0–19–544482–7

1. Child psychology—Problems, exercises, etc.
2. Developmental psychology—Problems, exercises, etc.
3. Evolutionary psychology—Problems, exercises, etc.
I. Hessels, Sandra II. Title.
BF721.R877 2011 Suppl.   155.4   C2011-900263-9

Cover image: Oleksiy Maksymenko/Acclaim Images

Oxford University Press is committed to our environment. This book is printed on Forest Stewardship
Council certified paper, harvested from a responsibly managed forest.

Printed and bound in Canada
1 2 3 4 — 14 13 12 11

Contents

Introduction

This study guide is meant to enhance your understanding of M. D. Rutherford's *Child Development: Perspectives in Developmental Psychology*. Each chapter of the guide includes:

- Chapter Summary
- Learning Objectives
- Suggested Readings
- Study Questions
- Practice Tests

The chapter summaries and learning objectives provide a brief overview of the subject matter. They can be used as a first introduction and later as a quick recap.

The suggested readings are a mix of academic papers as well as books written for a popular audience. Some offer in-depth accounts of the topics outlined in the textbook and some are more tangential but they are all interesting. Be sure to check some of them out!

You will find a study question for practically every bit of information covered in the textbook—successful navigation of these questions points to a firm grasp on the material. The practice tests may be used as final tests of your retention of the material.

Use this study guide as a way of spending time with the concepts. Aim for a deep understanding. Write down your answers to the questions and always try to use your own words. Work with a classmate and teach each other—having to explain something to someone else is one of the best ways to consolidate learning. Teaching will also make you aware of the gaps in your own knowledge. Work for relatively short periods of time—don't cram everything into one session. If you give yourself enough time to go slowly, you'll learn the material effectively and you'll never feel overwhelmed.

I sincerely hope you find this study guide helpful and I hope your enthusiasm is sparked for this fascinating field of study. Good luck!

Sandra Hessels

Chapter 1
What is Developmental Psychology?

Chapter Summary

What Is Developmental Psychology?

The field of developmental psychology employs the scientific method to examine change across the lifespan. Developmental psychologists collect data and test hypotheses in attempts to describe and explain change. Developmental psychology encompasses a wide range of psychological processes and is related to many other branches of science.

What Is Development?

Development refers to changes throughout the life cycle. The union of a child's complete genome marks the beginning of his development, but it is important to remember that, long before that, natural selection evolved adaptations that conferred a reproductive advantage.

Why Study the Developmental Psychology of Children?

The study of developmental psychology is valuable in (at least) three ways: it provides insight into universal human nature; it sheds light on more complex adult psychological processes; and it is useful in real-world applications for interacting with children.

A Historical Look at Developmental Psychology and the Nature vs. Nurture Debate

Discussions and writings on child development long predate experimental research in the area. Early philosophers in the 4th century B.C.E. disagreed about the roles of nature and nurture: Plato was a *nativist* who believed that children are born with innate knowledge, and Aristotle was an *empiricist* who proposed that a newborn's mind is a blank slate waiting to be 'written on' by the environment.

In the 17th and 18th centuries, European philosophers continued the nature vs. nurture debate. John Locke, an empiricist, believed that all children were created equal and that knowledge was gained only by experience. Jean-Jacques Rousseau, a nativist, referred to children as 'noble savages' who, armed with an innate plan for development, should be free to explore on their own.

In 1877, Charles Darwin published an influential 'baby biography' detailing his observations of his son's development. In the late 19th and early 20th centuries, with university-supported research programs and the creation of academic journals in the field, developmental psychology began to thrive.

In the 1880s, G. Stanley Hall began the first psychology laboratory in the United States and 'founded' developmental psychology. Hall was interested in evolutionary theory and he applied evolutionary ideas to the study of developmental change. Hall introduced the *normative approach*, which involves comparing individual development to the averages of a large population. A student of Hall's, Arnold Gesell, furthered the use of the normative approach by making norms of developmental milestones available to parents and physicians.

The 'Father of Behaviourism', John B. Watson, was an empiricist in the extreme: he believed that all behaviour could be attributed to a series of simple associations made over time; cognition or thought was completely dismissed. Watson made important contributions to experimental design.

No other developmental psychologist had a greater impact on the field than Jean Piaget. In fact, the sub-field of cognitive development exists because of him. Piaget proposed that cognitive development occurs in stages. This theory was informed by the clinical method; he presented children with challenging tasks, asked questions, and assessed explanations.

Working in the Marxist Soviet Union, Lev Vygotsky emphasized the importance of cultural context on development. Vygotsky believed that adults play an important role in a child's cognitive development.

Nature and Nurture, Working Together to Make a Person

The nature vs. nurture debate has been pervasive in the history of developmental psychology and continues to inspire discussion. It is important to recognize, though, that *both* heredity and environment contribute to *all* traits and therefore the debate is fundamentally flawed.

An Evolutionary Perspective on Development

The developmental demands of the environment in which our ancestors evolved determined the function and design of the human mind; therefore, the study of developmental psychology greatly informs the field of evolutionary psychology.

The study of developmental psychology contributes to an understanding of how evolution works. Developmental psychologists can offer the following explanations to evolutionary psychologists: insight into how adults come into being; opportunities to examine how changes in the environment during development lead to changes in adults; an understanding of the interaction between genes and the environment; and information on non-adult adaptations.

Adaptationism and Functionality

Changes that confer fitness advantages slowly become universal in a population. Functional design improves by this natural selection of changes. Complex adaptations develop over many generations of such natural selection.

The Environment of Evolutionary Adaptedness

Natural selection solves adaptive problems in a particular environment. To understand the adaptations, it is necessary to know about the environment. Our hunter–gatherer ancestors lived and evolved in the *environment of evolutionary adaptedness* (*EEA*). The EEA of our ancestors included a great deal of variance. We have evolved to solve the adaptive problems of various environmental conditions.

Maladaptive Behaviour in the Modern World

Not all of our EEA-shaped behaviours are fitness-enhancing in our current environment. The scarcity of food in the EEA left us with an evolutionarily-determined preference for sugars, fats, and salts. An abundance of these in the modern world has allowed that preference to contribute to obesity. Dangerous things such as cars, guns, and electricity did not exist in the EEA, leaving us evolutionarily unequipped to fear them. Natural selection slowly builds psychological adaptations across generations, which leaves us as individuals vulnerable to changing environments.

Learning Objectives

After reading this chapter, you should be able to:

- Conceptualize developmental psychology and how it fits into the scientific spectrum (pp. 4–6)

- Learn what can be gained from studying the developmental psychology of children (pp. 6–7)

- Place developmental psychology in historical context by learning about the field's founders (pp. 7–14)

- Critique the nature vs. nurture question (p. 14)

- Examine the link between evolutionary psychology and developmental psychology (pp. 15–18)

- Identify how natural selection results in adaptations (pp. 18–21)

- Discuss how a mismatch between adaptations and the modern environment can result in maladaptive behaviour (pp. 21–24)

Suggested Readings

Dunier, M. (2009). Michael Apted's Up! series: Public sociology or folk psychology through film? *Ethnography, 10*, 341–345.

  This article is an interesting description of and comment on Michael Apted's Up! series of films. The same journal (the September 2009 issue of Ethnography) includes several other articles about the films, including an interview with Michael Apted.

Pinker, S. (2002). *The blank slate: The modern denial of human nature.* New York: Penguin Books.

  In this best-selling book, Pinker addresses many of the themes of Chapter 1.

Darwin, C. R. (1877). A biographical sketch of an infant. *Mind, 2*, 286–294.

  Darwin's seminal 'baby biography'

Watson, J. B. (1913). Psychology as the behaviorist views it. *Psychological Review, 20*, 158–177.

  This article is John B. Watson's diatribe against the study of consciousness and his appeal for strict objectivity in the science of psychology.

Study Questions

1. The film *7 Up!* tested the hypothesis that _____ were strong enough to determine a child's outcome at birth. Results were mixed.

What Is Developmental Psychology?

1. Developmental psychology is the scientific study of _____ across the human lifespan.

2. True or False: Developmental psychology is a science. Therefore, it is the responsibility of developmental psychologists to foster firm and definitive ideas and beliefs within the field.

3. _____ are educated guesses that can and should be tested.

4. What would be grounds for rejecting a hypothesis?

What Is Development?

1. Development begins when the _____ of a new individual is complete.

2. The egg and sperm are referred to as _____.

3. Define 'adaptation' (as it relates to the process of evolution).

Why Study the Developmental Psychology of Children?

1. Define 'species-typical environment'.

2. Why bother studying developmental psychology?

A Historical Look at Developmental Psychology and the Nature vs. Nurture Debate

1. Contrast the nativist and empiricist approaches to development with regard nature and nurture.

2. Who was a nativist and who was an empiricist? Match the belief system to the theorist listed below.

   a) John Locke   _____

   b) Plato   _____

   c) Jean-Jacques Rousseau   _____

   d) Aristotle   _____

3. Imagine you want to turn your child into the next great mathematician. If you were able ask John Locke for his advice, what might he tell you to do?

4. How did Rousseau propose treating the 'noble savages'?

5. A _____ is an intensive study describing the activities of an individual infant.

6. True or False: G. Stanley Hall is considered to be the founder of developmental psychology.

7. G. Stanley Hall began the first psychology laboratory in the United States at _____ University in the 1880s.

8. The _____ is idea that developmental changes parallel the species' changes through evolutionary time.

9. Computing averages that represent typical development reflects the _____.

10. John B. Watson's behaviourist perspective was rooted in _____'s discovery of _____ in dogs.

11. True or False: Watson assumed that humans were endowed with a large number of specific mechanisms that could associate any stimulus with any other stimulus, or with any response.

12. What did John B. Watson think of the study of cognition?

13. What did Watson conclude from his 'Little Albert' experiments?

14. John B. Watson's lasting contribution to developmental research was his insistence on _____.

15. How did Jean Piaget begin his career in developmental psychology?

16. Define 'genetic epistemology'.

17. What does it mean to say that Piaget's theory of cognitive development was a 'stage theory'?

18. True or False: Piaget's main concern in evaluating responses to cognitive challenges was whether the child's answer was right or wrong.

19. Piaget believed that young children were _____ bound, with very little pre-existing _____ structures.

20. Approaching an interview with a planned set of questions and an openness to follow up on areas of interest based on the child's responses is characteristic of the _____ method developed by Piaget.

21. Piaget's work didn't become influential in North America until the 1960s. Why not?

22. How were Lev Vygotsky's ideas influenced by historical context?

23. Who was more interested in the study of language, Piaget or Vygotsky?

24. True or False: Vygotsky agreed with Piaget that children progress through stages in a regimented order.

25. Define Vygotsky's notions of 'dialectical process' and 'zone of proximal development'.

26. True or False: The ideas of Lev Vygotsky became quite popular during his lifetime.

27. Match the developmental psychologist with his descriptor.

1.	Arnold Gesell	a)	founded the American Psychological Association
2.	Lev Vygotsky	b)	Father of Behaviourism
3.	G. Stanley Hall	c)	made normative information available to parents
4.	Jean Piaget	d)	greatest impact on the field of developmental psychology
5.	John B. Watson	e)	'social constructivist'

Nature and Nurture, Working Together to Make a Person

1. What would you say to someone who argued for a nature (or nurture) explanation of a trait?

An Evolutionary Perspective on Development

1. Evolutionary psychology is an approach that holds that being well informed about _____ and _____ will aid in understanding the function and design of the human mind.

2. Name two contributions of evolutionary psychology to developmental psychology.

3. Name four contributions of developmental psychology to evolutionary psychology.

4. True or False: Evolutionary psychologists are genetic determinists.

Adaptationism and Functionality

1. Before Darwin's theory, the common explanation for the complexities of the natural world was _____.

2. True or False: Natural selection is the only viable scientific explanation for adaptations.

The Environment of Evolutionary Adaptedness

1. 'EEA' stands for _____.

2. Imagine you time-travel backwards a few hundred years and you notice that most of the moths are white. Back in the present-day, you notice most of the moths are black. Given what you know about natural selection, what would you guess happened during the last few hundred years?

   (Set aside for the moment the fact that you would surely find more exciting things to do in your time-travelling than looking at moths!)

3. Based on our EEA, why would we humans have evolved to have a visual system that discriminates between red and green?

4. Evolutionary thinkers use the term _____ to refer to a shaping by natural selection such that reproductive success is maximized.

Maladaptive Behaviour in the Modern World

1. In ten words or less, why are fast cars and fast food so dangerous?

2. Why do humans like to eat sugars, fats, and salts?

3. Why don't humans crave fibre?

4. Why do humans fear snakes but not car accidents?

5. There is, to some extent, a mismatch between our evolutionary-determined behaviours and fitness in the modern world. Why?

6. Define 'generative entrenchment'.

Practice Test 1

1. Which of the following statements about the scientific method is true?
   a. It is used mostly in fields like biology and chemistry rather than psychology.
   b. There is a great deal of variability in how researchers define its principles (i.e. in how data is collected, analyzed, and used in making conclusions).
   c. It results in changes in ideas and beliefs over time.
   d. It is out-dated.

2. All of the following terms refer to the same thing *except* one. Which is different?

    a. gametes
    b. the genome
    c. the sex cells
    d. the sperm and the egg

3. Adaptations are _____ by natural selection.

    a. 'designed'
    b. 'invented'
    c. 'discouraged'
    d. 'experimented on'

4. Studying the development of language abilities in children is important because

    a. it provides insight into human nature in general.
    b. it may help us to explain complex language abilities in adults.
    c. it could help us to treat children with language disabilities.
    d. all of the above

5. Which of the following 'writes' on the 'blank slate' of empiricism?

    a. genes
    b. behaviours
    c. the environment
    d. biological processes

6. Abby believes that children have an innate understanding of the concept of time. Which philosopher would most strongly disagree?

    a. Plato
    b. Jean-Jacques Rousseau
    c. John Locke
    d. none of the above

7. Charles Darwin's 'baby biography' was useful because

    a. it was a highly-accurate depiction of an infant's development.
    b. it prompted some of the first careful observations of human development.
    c. it led to Darwin's theory of evolution.
    d. it proved that human children develop in the same way as other young animals.

8. The founder of developmental psychology is generally considered to be

    a. G. Stanley Hall.
    b. Jean Piaget.
    c. John Locke.
    d. Aristotle.

9. Arnold Gesell was the first to

   a. compute averages to represent typical development.
   b. apply evolutionary ideas to developmental psychology.
   c. use the term 'noble savages'.
   d. make normative information available to parents.

10. John B. Watson believed that all human behaviour was the result of

   a. cognitive processing.
   b. learned associations.
   c. a genetic program.
   d. a dialectical process.

11. Tyler has been reading about the prevalence of behaviourist ideas in the mid-1900s. He says that the field of developmental psychology would be better off if behaviourism had never been popular. What would you say in response?

   a. 'You're probably right'.
   b. 'You're wrong—the behaviourists were correct that development is all about learning'.
   c. 'I disagree—the behaviourists brought to the field an insistence on objective methods. That was probably just what psychology needed at the time (and continues to need)'.
   d. 'You're wrong—Jean Piaget was a behaviourist and he was the most influential developmental psychologist ever'.

12. Which of the following statements is *not* true regarding Piaget's theory of cognitive development?

   a. It is a stage theory.
   b. It was devised using the clinical method.
   c. It purports that experience gained from the environment is unimportant.
   d. It is an example of genetic epistemology.

13. Piaget and Vygotsky would have disagreed most on the influence of _____ on cognitive development.

   a. environmental factors
   b. social interaction
   c. genetics
   d. problem-solving

14. Vygotsky's zone of proximal development is defined by

   a. the tasks a child can complete with and without adult support.
   b. the tasks a child can complete before and after he has begun receiving a formal education.
   c. the tasks a child can complete with or without motivation to do well.
   d. the tasks a child can complete before and after he has learned to speak.

15. What would you say to someone who was trying to convince you of the importance of 'nature' over 'nurture' in learning to walk?

    a. 'You are correct that walking is more reliant on nature than nurture'.
    b. 'You are wrong—learning to walk is heavily influenced by environmental factors'.
    c. 'You may be right—opinions vary on whether nature or nurture is most important for motor development'.
    d. 'You are making a nonsensical argument—both nature and nurture are important for all abilities'.

16. A fitness advantage that makes individuals more likely to survive and reproduce is called a(n) _____.

    a. evolution.
    b. adaptation.
    c. adjustment.
    d. phenotypic determinant.

17. The environment of evolutionary adaptedness (EEA) refers to

    a. the environment that we currently live in.
    b. the environment that was ideally suited to the process of evolution.
    c. the environment in which natural selection took place.
    d. the environment of human beings in general.

18. Which of the following is a piece of the puzzle in explaining high rates of obesity in the modern world?

    a. Sugars, fats, and salts were scarce in the EEA.
    b. Foods high in fibre were scarce in the EEA.
    c. Food preferences vary considerably across generations.
    d. all of the above

19. We are still adapted to the EEA because

    a. our modern environment doesn't differ significantly from the EEA.
    b. there have been no major mutations since then.
    c. the evolution of human beings is effectively over.
    d. evolution is slow.

20. An evolution in human vision is extremely unlikely to happen anytime soon because

    a. it is a complex system and its development is reliant on many alleles.
    b. the environment is not important to vision.
    c. there is no behavioural manifestation of vision.
    d. human vision is perfect the way it is.

Practice Test 2

1. A hypothesis is

   a. an explanation of how development progresses.
   b. a belief about how development progresses.
   c. considered to be correct if there is a general consensus among researchers.
   d. irrelevant to the scientific method.

2. The environment that provides the features that the genome 'needs' for normal development is called the

   a. species-typical environment.
   b. niche environment.
   c. species-normative environment.
   d. evolutionarily-typical environment.

3. Plato and Aristotle

   a. didn't know each other.
   b. did not believe in disciplining children.
   c. were both empiricists.
   d. were on opposite sides of a nature–nurture debate.

4. Which of the following events did *not* happen in the late 19th and early 20th centuries?

   a. The first psychology laboratory in the United States was opened.
   b. Charles Darwin's theory of natural selection was inspiring an important early developmental psychologist.
   c. Academic journals about developmental psychology were emerging.
   d. all of the above happened

5. The normative approach involves

   a. allowing children to be responsible for their own development.
   b. treating all children equally in educational practices.
   c. comparing children to averages that represent typical development.
   d. carefully monitoring an individual child's development.

6. John B. Watson trained 'Little Albert' to fear white rats, providing an example of manipulating a child's behaviour by controlling

   a. a child's temperament.
   b. a stimulus and response pairing.
   c. the type of learning mechanism employed by the child.
   d. the behaviour of the rat.

7. Who created the field of cognitive development?

    a. G. Stanley Hall
    b. John Locke
    c. Lev Vygotsky
    d. Jean Piaget

8. Piaget's clinical method involves

    a. tallying up the number of correct and incorrect responses by a child.
    b. getting a child's response to a rigid set of interview questions.
    c. asking a child questions regarding his performance on a challenging task.
    d. a style of questioning that is no longer used by developmental psychologists.

9. How does evolutionary psychology contribute to developmental psychology?

    a. It helps clarify whether genetics or environment is more important for the development of a particular skill.
    b. It emphasizes the influence of genetics on development.
    c. It provides guidance for hypothesis testing.
    d. all of the above

10. Genetic determinism

    a. is the idea that a particular gene always leads to a particular phenotypic outcome.
    b. is commonly supported by evolutionary psychologists.
    c. provides an accurate explanation of how development works.
    d. all of the above

11. A consideration of developmental psychology is important for evolutionary psychologists for all of the following reasons *except*

    a. it provides insight into how an adult comes into being.
    b. it allows examination of how environmental changes during development lead to changes in the adult.
    c. focusing exclusively on adults means missing many interesting non-adult adaptations.
    d. it provides evidence for the special role of genes in determining behaviour.

12. Functional sub-components of an organism that were sculpted by natural selection are sometimes called

    a. organs.
    b. branches.
    c. genomes.
    d. modules.

13. If most bunnies in your part of the world have white fur, it is probably also true that

    a. a bunny mutation took place quite recently.
    b. the EEA has changed.
    c. the environment in your part of the world is often white.
    d. black bunnies are about to make a comeback.

14. Not all information that an individual will need in life could be coded in his genes. Why not?

    a. There was variance across conditions in the EEA.
    b. Genes don't always play a role in development.
    c. The number of adaptations that a species can acquire is limited.
    d. none of the above

15. We don't fear fast cars because

    a. they are not typically dangerous.
    b. natural selection does not apply to fears.
    c. our evolutionarily-determined attraction to speed and aesthetics outweighs any fear that they might inspire.
    d. there was no selection pressure in the EEA to create adaptations to them.

16. Natural selection shapes

    a. behaviours.
    b. the psychological processes that underlie behaviours.
    c. both *a* and *b*
    d. neither *a* nor *b*

17. A psychological adaptation that worked really well in the EEA

    a. works well in the current environment as well because the environment hasn't changed at all.
    b. works well in the current environment as well because it doesn't really matter if the environment changes.
    c. may be maladaptive in the current environment.
    d. is usually maladaptive in the current environment.

18. The spread of one mutation throughout an entire species is likely to take

    a. a few generations.
    b. about a hundred generations.
    c. hundreds or thousands of generations.
    d. millions of generations.

19. Progress brought on by evolution is thought to be _____ today than it might have been in the past.

    a. slower
    b. faster
    c. the same
    d. more important

20. _____ is a phenomenon that prevents development from evolving in radically different ways.

    a. Generative stability
    b. Generative entrenchment
    c. Generative permanence
    d. Generative ingraining

Study Questions: Answer Key

1. class influences (p. 3)

What Is Developmental Psychology?

1. changes (p. 4)

2. False—The scientific method functions to adjust ideas and beliefs over time. (p. 4)

3. Hypotheses (p. 4)

4. One could reject a hypothesis if
   - it is not supported by the results of experiments.
   - it is not consistent with what we know from other branches of science. (p. 4)

What Is Development?

1. genome (p. 6)

2. gametes (p. 6)

3. An adaptation is a trait that is designed and preserved by the process of natural selection because that trait confers a reproductive advantage in the environment in which it evolved. (p. 6)

Why Study the Developmental Psychology of Children?

1. The species-typical environment is the environment that provides the features that the genome needs or 'expects' in order to develop typically. (p. 6)

2. Consider the following in your response:
   - The study of developmental psychology informs our knowledge of universal human nature.
   - The components of psychological processes in children may provide clues to understanding adult psychological processes, which are often much more complex.
   - Developmental psychology can provide answers to practical questions about how to optimally nurture children.

   Of course, you may be able to think of other valid reasons to bother! (pp. 6–7)

A Historical Look at Developmental Psychology and the Nature vs. Nurture Debate

1. Answer:
   - A nativist believes that development is the result of innate (genetic) forces. Environment is not thought to be important in shaping the child. Nature over nurture.
   - An empiricist believes that a child comes into the world as a 'blank slate'; environment is all that is important for development. Nurture over nature. (pp. 7–8)

2. a) John Locke   Empiricist
   b) Plato   Nativist
   c) Jean-Jacques Rousseau   Nativist
   d) Atistotle   Empiricist (pp. 7–9)

3. Locke would make the following points:
   - All children are created equal, so you don't need to worry about whether *you* are hopeless at math!
   - Nurture is all-important. Environment is key. You should expose your child to mathematical principles and activities in order to fill that (initially blank) 'slate' with the appropriate knowledge.
   - Don't punish the child in the context of learning, as that may lead to an aversion to the material. (pp. 8–9)

4. Consider the following in your response:
   - Rousseau believed that the 'noble savages' (children) should be given as much freedom as possible
   - He proposed that children have inborn knowledge that is naturally revealed as they mature and so, until the age of 12, children's development is best facilitated by their own chosen activities and explorations. (p. 9)

5. baby biography (p. 10)

6. True (p. 10)

7. Johns Hopkins (p. 10)

8. theory of recapitulation (p. 10)

9. normative approach (p. 11)

10. Ivan Pavlov; classical conditioning (p. 12)

11. False—Watson believed that learning was accomplished by a *small* number of general-purpose mechanisms. (p. 12)

12. Watson believed
    - that psychologists should restrict themselves to examining observable behaviour.
    - that studying cognition was impossible (because thought is not behaviour) and scientifically uninteresting. (p. 12)

13. Watson's 'Little Albert' experiments concluded that by controlling the stimulus and response pairings that the child encounters, parents should be able to control the child's behaviour. (p. 12)

14. objective methods in experimental design (p. 12)

15. Jean Piaget
    - was hired to administer intelligence tests on school-aged children.
    - noticed both quantitative and qualitative differences in responses with age. (p. 12)

16. Genetic epistemology is a term coined by Piaget to refer to the process of cognitive development from birth through late adolescence. (p. 13)

17. According to Piaget
    - development was not smoothly continuous.
    - at any particular stage of development, children are limited to the skills characterized by that stage. When they reach the next stage, a whole new set of skills is available. (p. 13)

18. False—Piaget was more interested in how children thought than whether their answer was correct. (p. 13)

19. perceptually; cognitive (p. 13)

20. clinical (p. 13)

21. Piaget's work was not influential until the 1960s because
    - until then, behaviourism had a very strong hold on thinking in North America.
    - his terms and concepts were unfamiliar. (p. 13)

22. Consider the following in your response:
    - In the Marxist Soviet Union, there was great emphasis on culture, collectivism, and socialism.
    - Vygotsky's theory, accordingly, emphasizes the influence of culture and other people on a child's development. (p. 13)

23. Consider the following in your response:
    - Vygotsky was more interested in language.
    - Specifically, he was interested in the connection between language development and thought.
    - This also relates to Vygotsky's general emphasis on social interaction. (p. 13)

24. False—Vygotsky believed that the influence of culture was strong enough to disrupt the order of stages. (p. 13)

25. Vygotsky believed that much of a child's cognitive development resulted from the dialectical process of shared problem-solving between the child and an adult. Eventually the child internalizes the knowledge and thinking modeled by the adult.

    The zone of proximal development is defined by the range of tasks the child can complete with and without help from an adult. (p. 14)

26. False—Vygotsky's work was banned in his home country and was not translated into English until long after he died. (p. 14)

27. 1.   Arnold Gesell   c)   made normative information available to parents
    2.   Lev Vygotsky   e)   'social constructivist'
    3.   G. Stanley Hall   a)   founded the American Psychological Association
    4.   Jean Piaget   d)   greatest impact on the field of developmental psychology
    5.   John B. Watson   b)   Father of Behaviourism (pp. 10–14)

Nature and Nurture, Working Together to Make a Person

1.   Consider the following in your response:
     - Without nature, nothing develops; without nurture, nothing develops.
     - Every person (and their every trait) is a result of both nature and nurture.
     - Arguing for one over the other is like taking sides in a width/height argument on the determinants of area of a rectangle. (p. 14)

An Evolutionary Perspective on Development

1.   the process of evolution; the circumstances in which our ancestors evolved (p. 15)

2.   Evolutionary psychology
     - promotes research that is consistent with what is known about evolution by natural selection.
     - provides guidance in terms of hypothesis testing. (p. 15)

3.   Developmental psychology
     - provides insight into how an adult comes into being.
     - allows an opportunity to examine how changes during development lead to changes in the adult.
     - buffers evolutionary psychologists from accusations of 'genetic determinism'.
     - allows psychologists to study non-adult adaptations. (pp. 16–17)

4.   False—Evolutionary psychologists consider both genetic inheritance and the environment in explaining development. (p. 17)

Adaptationism and Functionality

1.   divine design/creationism (p. 18)

2.   True (p. 18)

The Environment of Evolutionary Adaptedness

1.   environment of evolutionary adaptedness (p. 20)

2.   Consider the following in your response:
     - It would be a pretty good bet that something happened in the environment to darken the landscape. Maybe changes in industrial practices resulted in soot that made tree bark darker.
     - White moths, which stand out to predators in such an environment, would be less likely than black moths to survive and reproduce (and spread their genes throughout the population). (p. 19)

3.   For hunter–gatherers in the EEA, spotting ripe (red) fruit in green foliage would have been important in gaining sustenance. (p. 20)

4.   strategy (p. 21)

Maladaptive Behaviour in the Modern World

1. We do not have evolutionary adaptations to deal with them. (pp. 21–22)

2. Humans like to eat sugars, fats, and salts because
   - in our EEA, food was often scarce.
   - sugar is a source of energy; fats help to maintain healthy hair and skin, cell functioning, and body temperature; and salts are necessary for nerve and cell function and regulating water content.
   - adaptations evolved to make us crave these things because we need them—people who would eat them whenever they got the chance were more likely to survive and reproduce.
   - In our modern environment, they are plentiful—our evolutionary-determined cravings have led to obesity. (p. 21)

3. In the EEA, commonly-eaten foods were very fibrous. We didn't need to crave fibre to get enough of it. (p. 21)

4. Humans fear snakes but not cars because
   - snakes existed (and were dangerous) in the EEA. A fear of snakes was adaptive and therefore fitness-enhancing.
   - cars did not exist in the EEA. (p. 22)

5. Consider the following in your response:
   - Natural selection can only shape the psychological processes that underlie behaviour, not behaviour itself. This leaves us vulnerable to changing environments.
   - Evolution is slow. Only about 10,000 years have passed since hunter–gatherer times—that is not long enough for potentially beneficial mutations to 'take'.
   - Evolution of complex adaptations is particularly slow because many mutations are involved.
   - Increasing complexity makes beneficial mutations less likely—the more complex an organism is, the less likely a random mutation will be beneficial. (pp. 22–24)

6. Generative entrenchment is a phenomenon that slows the evolution of developmental processes. Because early perturbations in development can have catastrophic effects later in development, random mutations that affect early development are unlikely to be beneficial. (p. 24)

Practice Test 1: Answer Key

1. c (p. 4)	6. c (pp. 8–9)	11. c (pp. 10–14)	16. b (p. 18)
2. b (p. 6)	7. b (p. 10)	12. c (p. 13)	17. c (pp. 19–20)
3. a (p. 6)	8. a (p. 10)	13. b (pp. 12–14)	18. a (p. 21)
4. d (p. 7)	9. d (p. 11)	14. a (p. 14)	19. d (p. 22)
5. c (p. 8)	10. b (p. 12)	15. d (p. 14)	20. a (p. 23)

Practice Test 2: Answer Key

1. b (p. 4)	6. b (p. 12)	11. d (pp. 16–17)	16. b (p. 22)
2. a (p. 6)	7. d (p. 12)	12. a (p. 18)	17. c (p. 23)
3. d (p. 7)	8. c (p. 13)	13. c (p. 20)	18. c (p. 23)
4. d (p. 10)	9. c (p. 15)	14. a (p. 21)	19. a (p. 23)
5. c (p. 11)	10. a (p. 17)	15. d (p. 22)	20. b (p. 24)

Chapter 2
Theories and Methods in Developmental Psychology

Chapter Summary

Piaget's Theory of Cognitive Development

As a testament to the length of his career and the breadth of topics he addressed, Jean Piaget remains the most influential researcher in developmental psychology. Piaget believed that development was discontinuous—after a period of unchanging skills, the child moves abruptly into a new stage, suddenly capable of more. Piaget's proposed four stages are as follows:

1. The sensorimotor stage
   - birth to age 2
   - limited to motor activity and physical interaction
   - six sub-stages

2. The preoperational stage
   - ages 2 to 7
   - rapid cognitive development in terms of language, memory, and pretend play
   - thinking is egocentric and concrete

3. The concrete operational stage
   - ages 7 to 11
   - beginning to understand symbols
   - thinking is less egocentric
   - understanding of concrete (but not abstract) operations

4. The formal operational stage
   - ages 12 to adulthood
   - fluent in use of symbols and abstract concepts
   - ability to make predictions and formulate hypotheses

Piaget believed that developmental change occurs by *assimilation* (interpreting new information in terms of previously understood knowledge), *accommodation* (changing existing knowledge to deal with new information), and *equilibration* (balancing assimilation and accommodation so as to maintain a stable understanding of the world, but still allow for development).

Radical advances in research methods have revealed that Piaget greatly underestimated the cognitive competence of infants and children. As well, change does not seem to occur in the discrete stages proposed by Piaget. Social and emotional contributions to development were also underestimated.

Associationism and Social Learning Theory

The *associationist perspective* encompasses learning theories. Adherents believe that development and learning are a result of a very few, very general-purpose learning mechanisms.

Learning by *classical conditioning* involves pairing a neutral stimulus (the conditioned stimulus) with an unconditioned stimulus that naturally elicits a response (the unconditioned response). Once the two stimuli are associated, the conditioned stimulus will elicit the response (the conditioned response) by itself.

John B. Watson, a behaviourist, used a white rat to demonstrate the power of conditioning on 'Little Albert's' fear response. Watson's ideas on child-rearing (strict discipline and regimented feeding schedules) had considerable influence in North America.

Using *operant conditioning*, behaviours become more or less likely as a result of reinforcers and punishers. B. F. Skinner took the idea of operant conditioning to a new level—he believed that a utopian civilization could be attained if child-rearing incorporated proper conditioning.

Albert Bandura, a proponent of *social learning theory*, emphasized the importance of imitation in learning, with adults providing models of behaviour.

Associationist and social learning theories are not without shortcomings. For one thing, not all variables (or associations) are created equal. It has become clear that learning mechanisms are much more specific than behaviourists once believed. As well, the ease with which we humans (children included) perceive similarity between objects and events (this perceived similarity is critical for learning mechanisms) is extraordinarily difficult to explain. Finally, learning theories are incomplete without reference to evolution since all learning mechanisms have an evolutionary history.

Developmental Systems Theory

According to this theory, the developing organism is more than the sum of its parts. All developmental resources (including DNA as well as a myriad of environmental components) interact in a complex system.

Claiming that environmental and biological factors interact in a complicated way is certainly true, but it is not an answer to the question of how development progresses. As well, developmental systems theorists do not acknowledge a special role for genes in development or evolution—this seems hard to reconcile with what we know about how evolution works.

Evolutionary Psychology

Darwin did not ignore psychology. Although he didn't get into specifics, he acknowledged that the theory of natural selection was relevant to psychology. Darwin also contributed his seminal 'baby biography' to the field of developmental psychology.

Ethology is the study of the fitness-enhancing behaviours shaped by natural selection. For example, Konrad Lorenz was a well-known ethologist who examined imprinting in birds. Ethological contributions to developmental psychology include the notion of critical periods as well as the idea of attachment to caregivers.

E. O. Wilson popularized *sociobiology*, the study of the biological basis (and evolutionary history) of social behaviour.

Evolutionary psychology applies to all sub-fields. *Modern evolutionary psychology* places emphasis on the EEA and the extent to which it matches (or doesn't match) our modern environment. Modern evolutionary psychologists also emphasize psychological processes over behaviour.

Methods of Developmental Psychology

Measuring change in children can be done *cross-sectionally* (different children at the same time) or *longitudinally* (same children at different times). A cross-sectional design is quicker and free of attrition and practice effects. Longitudinal designs have the advantage of measuring change within an individual and are free of cohort effects. The Concordia longitudinal study of aggression and withdrawal is one example. A *cross-sequential design* involves collecting data from more than one age group longitudinally. Although time-consuming and expensive, this approach has the advantages of both cross-sectional and longitudinal designs.

Experiments in developmental psychology may employ naturalistic observation in which data are collected in an everyday setting without manipulation from the experimenter. *Naturalistic observation* is high in external validity (it's very 'real') but there is very little control.

When it is impractical or unethical to manipulate variables, relationships can be assessed using a *correlational design*; however, a correlation cannot infer any causal relationship between the variables.

Causal relationships can be best determined by an *experimental design*. In a proper experiment, subjects are randomly assigned to conditions that reflect the independent variable(s), and dependent variables are measured.

Within- and Between-Subjects Design

An experimental design may be *within-subjects* (one group of participants are exposed to multiple experimental treatments) or *between-subjects* (multiple groups of participants are exposed to only one experimental treatment).

Techniques for Developmental Research

Developmental research has its own unique challenges. Children and, in particular, infants (who, of course, cannot verbalize) require specialized methods for assessing cognitive skills. The *preferential-looking paradigm* involves presenting an infant with two visual stimuli at the same time. A difference in looking time can indicate that the infant can discriminate between the stimuli. The *habituation paradigm* takes advantage of the fact that infants (like all humans) get bored with a repeated stimulus. After habituation, if the infant displays renewed interest when the stimulus changes, we have evidence of discrimination. The *violation of expectation paradigm* makes use of the idea that infants will look longer at events that they consider to be impossible. Again, by measuring looking behaviour, we can get a glimpse into infants' expectations of the world. *Non-visual psychophysical techniques* such as measures of heart rate, pupil dilation, skin conductance, sucking time, and, of course, brain activity, can also be informative.

Researchers strive for *reliability*—that is, getting results that can be repeatedly, consistently obtained under the same circumstances. *Validity* is also important, both internal (the study measures what it was intended to measure) and external (the results of the study can be generalized outside of the experiment itself).

All research conducted with human participants must be reviewed by an institutional review board. Research with children elicits unique ethical concerns and requires following extra-strict guidelines with regard to informed consent, the use of deception, the right to privacy, and the right to knowledge of results.

Learning Objectives

After reading this chapter, you should be able to:

- Identify the following four broad theoretical perspectives
  - Piaget's Theory of Cognitive Development (pp. 29–35)
  - Associationism and Social Learning Theory (pp. 35–39)
  - Developmental Systems Theory (pp. 39–41)
  - Evolutionary Psychology (pp. 42–35)

- Discuss the strengths and weaknesses of cross-sectional and longitudinal designs (pp. 45–49)

- Distinguish between correlational and experimental designs (pp. 49–50)

- Differentiate between testing within- or between-subjects (p. 50)

- Examine research techniques that can be employed with pre-verbal infants
  - the preferential-looking paradigm (p. 51)
  - the habituation paradigm (pp. 52–53)
  - the violation of expectation paradigm (p. 53)
  - non-visual psychophysical techniques (pp. 53–54)

- Appreciate the importance of experimental reliability and validity (pp. 55–56)

- Discuss the ethical considerations of conducting research on children (pp. 56–58)

Suggested Readings

Piaget, J. (2001). *The Language and Thought of the Child.* London: Routledge Classics.

Originally published in 1923, this book contains Jean Piaget's pioneering observations of the cognitive abilities of children.

Skinner, B. F. (1945, October). Baby in a Box, *Ladies Home Journal.*

This controversial article is B. F. Skinner's behaviourism-inspired revolutionary idea for child-rearing.

Wilson, E. O. (2004). *On Human Nature* (Rev. ed.). Cambridge, MA: Harvard University Press.

On Human Nature is a thought-provoking classic by the original sociobiologist.

Study Questions

Piaget's Theory of Cognitive Development

1. Piaget concluded that infants younger than 8 months lacked object permanence. What does this mean?

2. What would be a 'real-life' example of a situation in which an infant would demonstrate a lack of object permanence?

3. Baillargeon, Spelke, and Wasserman's (1985) experiment involving infants watching an impossible event provided evidence that 5-month-old infants have _____.

4. Much of contemporary cognitive developmental research has involved attempts to reply to _____'s claims.

5. Why was Piaget so influential in the field of developmental psychology?

6. True or False: Piaget viewed the development of the child as continuous, with gradual quantitative changes over time.

7. Match the following Piagetian stages with the corresponding age ranges.

   1. preoperational   a) 7 to 11 years
   2. formal operational   b) 2 to 7 years
   3. concrete operational   c) birth to 2 years
   4. sensorimotor   d) 12 years through adulthood

8. Match the following Piagetian stages with the corresponding descriptions of cognitive ability.

   1. preoperational   a) starting to be able to use symbols
   2. formal operational   b) interaction with the world is purely physical
   3. concrete operational   c) can perform mental operations on abstract qualities
   4. sensorimotor   d) able to logically problem-solve but only for concrete objects

9. Match the following sensorimotor sub-stage ages to the corresponding summaries.

   1. Birth to 1 month   a) novelty and exploration
   2. 1 to 4 months   b) mental representation
   3. 4 to 8 months   c) intentional behaviour
   4. 8 to 12 months   d) discovering procedures
   5. 12 to 18 months   e) exercising reflexes
   6. 18 to 24 months   f) developing schemes

10. Piaget put equal amounts of liquid in two containers and poured the liquid from one into a taller container. When asked which (if either) of the containers held more water, a child in the preoperational stage would say _____.

11. Define 'assimilation' (as Piaget defined it).

12. What would be an example of assimilation?

13. Define 'accommodation' (as Piaget defined it).

14. What would be an example of accommodation?

15. Define 'equilibration' (as Piaget defined it).

16. What are three shortcomings of Piaget's theory?

17. Why did Piaget under-estimate cognitive competence?

Associationism and Social Learning Theory

1. The associationist perspective covers _____ theories.

2. True or False: John Locke, if he were around today, would be a proponent of the associationist perspective.

3. In classical conditioning, a _____ stimulus becomes associated with a _____ stimulus.

4. Match the following classical conditioning terms with the corresponding descriptions.

   1. unconditioned stimulus (US)
   2. unconditioned response (UR)
   3. conditioned stimulus (CS)
   4. conditioned response (CR) stimulus

   a) something that follows the conditioned stimulus after training
   b) something that elicits a response after training
   c) something that elicits a response before training
   d) something that follows the presentation of the unconditioned

5. What is an example of classical conditioning that might happen in everyday life?

6. What were the US, UR, CS, and CR for Watson's 'Little Albert' experiment?

7. How could Watson have reversed the damage in Little Albert?

8. The above procedure for eliminating Little Albert's fear of the rat is an example of _____.

9. Summarize Watson's impact on child rearing.

10. True or False: Operant conditioning is most associated with Ivan Pavlov.

11. In operant conditioning, behaviours are a result of _____ and _____.

12. True or False: B. F. Skinner was moderate in his behaviourist beliefs.

13. What would Skinner advise you to do if your child has a temper tantrum?

14. Social learning theory was conceived by _____.

15. Social learning theorists have emphasized the role of _____ in socialization.

16. Summarize the shortcomings of associationist and social learning views.

Developmental Systems Theory

1. For complex systems (like the development of a human being), developmental systems theorists stress that the _____ is more than the _____.

2. True or False: According to developmental systems theorists, some developmental resources are more important than others.

3. What is the 'cornerstone' of developmental systems theorists' thinking?

4. Jake's parents would like him to play for the Toronto Maple Leafs when he grows up. Of course, it is impossible to predict whether or not that will happen. How would developmental systems theory explain why it is impossible to make such a prediction?

5. What are two shortcomings of the developmental systems theory?

Evolutionary Psychology

1. Name two key contributions by Charles Darwin to psychology.

2. Define 'ethology'.

3. Konrad Lorenz was an ethologist who studied _____ in birds.

4. Match the following individuals with their corresponding accomplishments.

   1. Irenaus   a) popularized the study of the biological basis and adaptive value of
      Eibl-Eibesfeldt   social behaviours
   2. John Bowlby   b) founder of human ethology
   3. E. O. Wilson   c) described the process of attachment in human infants

5. The study of the biological basis and adaptive value of social behaviours is called _____.

6. E. O. Wilson ran into considerable resistance in explaining his ideas about the evolutionary basis of human social behaviour. Why?

7. How does modern evolutionary psychology differ from earlier versions (i.e. ethology and sociobiology)?

Methods of Developmental Psychology

1. A _____-subjects design is used in comparing children of different ages in a cross-sectional design.

2. What are the advantages of using a cross-sectional design (note that these could also be framed as limitations of a longitudinal design)?

3. What are the disadvantages of cross-sectional design (note that these could also be framed as advantages of a longitudinal design)?

4. What is an example of a cohort effect?

5. A _____-subjects design is used in comparing children of different ages in a longitudinal design.

6. Why is selective attrition a big threat to interpreting the results of a study?

7. Why (specifically) might people show practice effects?

8. True or False: The well-known longitudinal study started by Jane Ledingham on aggression and withdrawal in children could have been done using a cross-sectional design instead.

9. How did the researchers conducting the Concordia longitudinal study guard against attrition?

10. According to Ledingham and Schwartzman, aggression in early childhood predicts _____ for both boys and girls and _____ and _____ for girls.

11. According to Ledingham and Schwartzman, withdrawal in early childhood predicts _____ and _____ for both boys and girls.

12. The current focus of the Concordia longitudinal study on aggression and withdrawal is _____.

13. What is a cross-sequential design?

14. A cross-sequential design is a combination of a _____ design and a _____ design.

15. Summarize the advantages of a cross-sequential design.

16. The downside of cross-sequential designs is that they are _____ and _____.

17. A study in which data are collected in everyday settings without experimental manipulation is _____.

18. What would be an example of a study in which you would be best to use naturalistic observation?

19. Natural observations are high in _____, low in _____, and completely lacking in _____.

20. What two things does a correlation coefficient reveal about the relationship between two variables?

21. True or False: In a correlational design, a researcher measures the effect of one variable on another.

22. Dr. Peace found a correlation between eating sugary foods and activity levels in children (the children who ate sugary foods had higher activity levels). What does this tell us about the relationship between eating sugary foods and activity level?

23. True or False: −.91 is a stronger correlation than .67.

24. Employing a/an _____ design is the best way to draw conclusions about causality.

25. True or False: Dr. Timleck tested two groups of subjects: one received the experimental manipulation and the other was a control group. To determine which subject was assigned to which group, she flipped a coin. Dr. Timleck used random assignment.

26. Researchers tested the effect of music lessons on IQ score. One group of children was given weekly piano lessons for a year. The other group had no exposure to music lessons. IQ was tested at the end of the year.

    a) What was the independent variable?

    b) What was the dependent variable?

Within- and Between-Subjects Design

1. With reference to timing and subject groups, explain the difference between a within-subjects and between-subjects design.

2. Match the design on the left with the design on the right.

    1. within-subjects   a) cross-sectional
    2. between-subjects   b) longitudinal

Techniques for Developmental Research

1. Imagine you are putting together an experimental test for young children. The children are verbal but quite young. What are some issues that you should keep in mind?

2. True or False: Dr. Anderson found that 6-month-old infants are capable of discriminating between x and y. Therefore, we can conclude that 5-month-old infants cannot discriminate between them.

3. Using the preferential-looking paradigm, if infants reliably look at one stimulus more than another, researchers infer that _____.

4. True or False: An experimenter using the preferential-looking paradigm is aware of which stimulus is on which side when observing infants' gaze direction.

5. Why are computers useful for measuring preferential-looking?

6. In addition to computers, another modern addition to the preferential-looking paradigm is the use of _____, which allows the researcher to detect _____.

7. Dr. Conrad presented images of triangles to baby Hayden. At first, Hayden looked intently at the triangles but after a while, he began to look away. Hayden is showing _____.

8. Dr. Conrad then shows Hayden images of circles and Hayden increases his looking time. This suggests that _____.

9. The violation of expectation paradigm assumes that infants will look longer at events that are _____.

10. Preferential-looking, habituation, and violation of expectation paradigms all measure _____.

11. What are some non-visual psychophysical techniques that may be used with infants?

12. Define 'reliability'.

13. The results of Dr. Honey's observational study were high inter-rater reliability but low on test–retest reliability. What does that really mean?

14. Define 'validity'.

15. _____ validity refers to generalizability outside of the research situation; _____ validity refers to how well the conditions of the study allow for measurement of the phenomenon of interest.

16. In order to be considered ethical, the _____ of the research must exceed the _____ to the participant.

17. What is an IRB?

18. Why is it crucial to have an ethics review for any experiment?

19. True or False: Because infants and young children are more resilient and they cannot speak up, the ethical guidelines for dealing with them are less stringent than the guidelines for adults.

20. How are the following ethical considerations dealt with when participants are infants or young children?
    a) Informed consent

b) Deception

c) Right to Privacy

d) Right to Knowledge of Results

Practice Test 1

1. Which of the following statements is *not* true regarding Piaget's theory of cognitive development?

   a. It proposes continuous change with age.
   b. It covers cognitive development from infancy through late adolescence.
   c. It has been tremendously influential in the field of developmental psychology.
   d. It does not allow for backtracking in the acquisition of abilities.

2. Which of the following is a correct match between sensorimotor sub-stage description and age?

   a. beginning of intentional behaviour, 4 to 8 months
   b. tool use starts, 12 to 18 months
   c. onset of mental representations, 8 to 12 months
   d. infant responds only with reflexes, 1 to 4 months

3. Which of the following is *not* a shortcoming of Piaget's cognitive developmental theory?

   a. Piaget greatly underestimated children's cognitive competence.
   b. Piaget did not address social and emotional contributions to development.
   c. Piaget's notion of stages is overstated.
   d. Piaget based his theory on observations he made over a short period of time (i.e. he did not work in the field for very long).

4. General learning theories and social learning theory in particular are a part of the _____ perspective.

   a. assimilation
   b. associationist
   c. conditioning
   d. integrationist

5. Something that elicits a behaviour before any training has taken place is called a

   a. conditioned response.
   b. unconditioned response.
   c. conditioned stimulus
   d. unconditioned stimulus.

6. B. F. Skinner's influence on child-rearing can be seen to this day in parents' use of

   a. corporal punishment.
   b. modeling good behaviour.
   c. 'time outs'.
   d. developmental systems.

7. The psychologist most associated with observational learning is

   a. B. F. Skinner.
   b. Charles Darwin.
   c. John B. Watson.
   d. Albert Bandura.

8. Imprinting is a psychological process important for

   a. visual development.
   b. attachment.
   c. language development.
   d. operant conditioning.

9. Using a cross-sectional design,

   a. there is only one group of participants.
   b. it is likely to take years to get the answer to a research question.
   c. it is not possible to examine changes within an individual.
   d. none of the above

10. The biggest problem with selective attrition is that

   a. the group of subjects remaining at the end of the experiment may be systematically different from the group that started the experiment.
   b. there are fewer subjects at the end of the experiment than at the beginning.
   c. participants may perform differently toward the end of the experiment because they are familiar with the testing methods.
   d. it is a time-consuming process.

11. A cross-sequential design

   a. involves testing within-subjects only.
   b. follows two or more groups longitudinally.
   c. is a cheap and easy way to answer research questions.
   d. is more vulnerable to the effects of selective attrition than a longitudinal design.

12. A study in which data are collected in everyday settings is called a(n)

   a. ecological observation.
   b. correlational examination.
   c. naturalistic observation.
   d. experimental design.

13. Which of the following is a strength of a correlational design?

    a. It can be a useful way to learn about something that can't be ethically manipulated.
    b. It allows for drawing conclusions about cause and effect.
    c. It may include numerous independent variables.
    d. It eliminates the effects of third variables.

14. A correlation coefficient is a number between _____ and _____.

    a. 0; +1.00
    b. -1.00; 0
    c. -1.00; +1.00
    d. -.10; +.10

15. Mrs. Eaton, a Grade 2 teacher, decides to conduct an experiment with her two classes. In one class, the students are given stickers for good behaviour. In the other class, they are given verbal praise for good behaviour. At the end of the week, Mrs. Eaton adds up the number of behavioural transgressions for each class and compares them. What is the dependent variable in this experiment?

    a. the stickers
    b. the verbal praise
    c. the stickers and verbal praise
    d. the number of behavioural transgressions

16. A within-subjects design is used for a _____ study and a between-subjects design is used for a _____ study.

    a. cross-sectional; longitudinal
    b. longitudinal; cross-sectional
    c. correlational; experimental
    d. experimental; correlational

17. Which of the following variables would require employing a between-subjects design?

    a. age
    b. income level
    c. education level
    d. gender

18. If a researcher finds evidence that children have developed a particular cognitive skill at a particular age, this does not give anyone the license to infer that the skill is absent before that age. Why not?

    a. Children are too unpredictable to allow for any solid conclusions.
    b. Children can only be tested using correlational designs which do not allow for many inferences.
    c. The methods used may not be sensitive enough to detect the cognitive skill in younger children.
    d. all of the above

19. The preferential-looking paradigm involves a(n) _____ choice on the part of the infant.

    a. binary
    b. auditory
    c. ethical
    d. timing

20. The violation of expectation paradigm relies on the idea that

    a. infants will look longer at events that are impossible.
    b. infants show changes in heart rate depending on what they are looking at.
    c. infants understand the concept of object permanence.
    d. infants can habituate to repeated stimuli.

21. Non-visual psychophysical techniques include all of the following *except*

    a. measuring pupil dilation.
    b. the violation of expectation paradigm.
    c. measuring sucking time.
    d. EEG recordings.

22. A measure of reliability that is particularly important for observational research is

    a. external reliability.
    b. internal reliability.
    c. inter-rater reliability.
    d. test–retest reliability.

23. Dr. LeBlanc is interested in memory performance. She has her subjects perform an experimental test of memory immediately before their final exam. Given the anxiety of the subjects, one would question this experiment's

    a. use of deception.
    b. validity.
    c. reliability.
    d. dependability.

24. In order to be considered ethical, the _____ must exceed the _____ .

    a. benefits to the participant; risks to society as a whole.
    b. aspirations of the experimenter; reluctance of the participant
    c. cost of the lack of knowledge; cost of the experiment
    d. benefits of the research; risks to the participant

25. All research conducted on human subjects must be reviewed by a(n)

    a. community review board.
    b. institutional review board.
    c. panel of scientists.
    d. government-designated committee.

Practice Test 2

1. Piaget's preoperational stage

    a. covers the period from 7 to 11 years of age.
    b. is associated with a decrease in egocentric thinking.
    c. is a time of rapid cognitive development.
    d. is composed of six sub-stages.

2. Equilibration is

    a. the process of interpreting new information in terms of previously understood theories.
    b. the process of balancing assimilation and accommodation to maintain a stable understanding of the world while allowing for development.
    c. the process of changing one's current theories to cope with new information.
    d. the process by which a child may develop new categories.

3. The thing that most prevented Piaget's findings from standing the test of time was

    a. his methodology.
    b. he fact that his observations were all made in only a few years.
    c. the fact that he didn't specify the detail of his theory.
    d. his theory only applies to infants.

4. For Pavlov's dogs, salivation was the

    a. unconditioned stimulus.
    b. unconditioned response.
    c. conditioned response.
    d. both *a* and *b*

5. John B. Watson's influence on child-rearing included the idea that

    a. parents should be affectionate with their children.
    b. children should be allowed to determine their own activities.
    c. children should be fed at regular intervals.
    d. misbehaving children should receive 'time outs'.

6. Molly, a 2-year-old child, likes to visit the toy store. After spotting a toy she really wants, Molly throws a tantrum because her father won't buy it for her. Which of the following is *not* a reinforcer for that behaviour?

    a. buying her the toy
    b. giving her some candy instead
    c. leaving the toy store immediately
    d. promising her that she will get the toy another day

7. Unlike its predecessors, social learning theory focused on

   a. punishments.
   b. personality and social development.
   c. cognitive development.
   d. evolutionary principles.

8. Which of the following is a valid criticism of associationist and social learning views?

   a. It is unclear how a child knows when two objects or events are similar.
   b. They rely too heavily on evolutionary theories.
   c. They insist that no component of the developmental system be credited with a special role
   d. all of the above

9. Developmental systems theory proposes that

   a. observational learning is most important.
   b. genes play a special role in development.
   c. the whole of a complex system is more than the sum of its parts.
   d. environment plays a special role in development.

10. Which of the following statements is true of Charles Darwin?

    a. He did not foresee the application of his theory of natural selection to the field of psychology.
    b. He contributed to the field of developmental psychology by publishing his 'baby biography'.
    c. He detailed specific connections between evolution and developmental psychology.
    d. He invented the field of ethology.

11. The phenomenon of critical periods was discovered by

    a. ethologists.
    b. behaviourists.
    c. E. O. Wilson.
    d. Jean Piaget.

12. Which of the following questions would be most relevant to the study of sociobiology?

    a. How do children learn to associate words with objects?
    b. How do punishers decrease the likelihood of a behaviour?
    c. How do genes affect physical characteristics?
    d. How has human aggression been shaped by natural selection?

13. Modern evolutionary psychologists differ from their predecessors in that they

    a. have narrowed their focus to certain sub-fields of psychology.
    b. place more emphasis on the modern environment.
    c. place more emphasis on the environment of evolutionary adaptedness.
    d. none of the above

14. Which of the following is a drawback of a longitudinal design?

    a. practice effects
    b. attrition
    c. time-consuming
    d. all of the above

15. The Concordia longitudinal study has revealed that

    a. aggression in early childhood predicts academic trouble in adolescence—but only for boys.
    b. highly aggressive children tend to outgrow the aggression as they get older.
    c. early measures of withdrawal predict poor academic achievement in adolescence.
    d. early measures of aggression in girls is associated with lower rates of teen pregnancy.

16. A correlation coefficient indicates the _____ and _____ of a relationship.

    a. cause; strength
    b. direction; strength
    c. direction; power
    d. trend; power

17. Dr. Bleile's experiment includes an experimental group and a control group. When subjects show up to participate, Dr. Bleile lets them decide which group they would like to be part of. Dr. Bleile will not be able to draw causal conclusions from her results because of a lack of

    a. random assignment.
    b. dependent variables.
    c. planned assignment.
    d. reliability.

18. The independent variable is controlled by the

    a. subjects.
    b. experimental setting.
    c. experimenter.
    d. any or all of the above

19. Modern additions to the preferential-looking paradigm include

    a. computer screens to presentation.
    b. programs to counterbalance stimuli presentation.
    c. eye-tracking devices.
    d. all of the above

20. Using a habituation paradigm, _____ indicates that the infant detected a difference.

    a. expectation violation
    b. dishabituation
    c. unhabituation
    d. habituation

21. Using _____, Baillargeon et al. (1985) demonstrated that infants understand object permanence at a younger age than Piaget proposed.

    a. habituation
    b. non-visual techniques
    c. the violation of expectation paradigm
    d. the preferential-looking paradigm

22. Marco, a 4-month-old infant, is staring attentively at a toy mobile rotating above him. His heart rate decreases. Marco is probably _____ the mobile.

    a. interested in
    b. afraid of
    c. ignoring
    d. surprised by

23. Reliability refers to the extent to which the results are

    a. ethical.
    b. valid.
    c. generalizable
    d. repeatable.

24. The extent to which the research measures generalize the intended factor outside of a research situation is referred to as

    a. internal validity.
    b. test–retest validity.
    c. general validity.
    d. external validity.

25. All of the following are ethical standards for conducting research *except*

    a. right to informed consent.
    b. right to an attorney
    c. right to anonymity.
    d. right to confidentiality.

Study Questions: Answer Key

Piaget's Theory of Cognitive Development

1. Object permanence refers to an understanding that an object continues to exist even when it can no longer be observed directly. (p. 31)

2. An infant might demonstrate a lack of object permanence in the following situations:
   - If something covers a toy she is looking at, the infant may look away as if the toy has disappeared.
   - If you hide your face behind your hands and then suddenly reveal it, the infant may be surprised and delighted. For this reason, peek-a-boo is a very popular game among infants who are just learning object permanence. (p. 31)

3. a representation of objects, even when the objects are out of sight

   (results using refined methodology suggested that Piaget overestimated the age of acquiring object permanence) (p. 29)

4. Jean Piaget (p. 30)

5. Piaget was influential because
   - he was active in the field for a long time (almost 60 years).
   - his work covered a very broad age range (from infancy to late adolescence).
   - he incorporated a broad range of topics into his theories (e.g. understanding of physical properties, time, language, numbers, the perspectives of others). (p.30)

6. False—Piaget's theory was a stage theory. He believed that the child spends a period of time in one stage with a stable set of skills and then moves quite suddenly to a different stage with an array of new skills suddenly available. He believed that there was no back-tracking or skipping of stages. (p. 30)

7. 1. preoperational   b) 2 to 7 years
   2. formal operational   d) 12 years through adulthood
   3. concrete operational   a) 7 to 11 years
   4. sensorimotor   c) birth to 2 years (p. 31)

8. 1. preoperational   a) starting to be able to use symbols
   2. formal operational   c) can perform mental operations on abstract qualities
   3. concrete operational   d) able to logically problem-solve but only for concrete objects
   4. sensorimotor   b) interaction with the world is purely physical (p. 31)

9. 1. Birth to 1 month   e) exercising reflexes
   2. 1 to 4 months   f) developing schemes
   3. 4 to 8 months   d) discovering procedures
   4. 8 to 12 months   c) intentional behaviour
   5. 12 to 18 months   a) novelty and exploration
   6. 18 to 24 months   b) mental representation (p. 32)

10. the taller container held more (p. 32)

11. Assimilation involves interpreting new information in terms of previously understood theories and knowledge. (p. 33)

12. An infant may apply a sucking scheme used while eating to other things that can be put in his mouth (e.g. his thumb, a toy). This is one example of assimilation, but there are millions of others—think of another one! (p. 33)

13. Accommodation involves changing one's current theory, understanding, or knowledge in order to cope with new information. (p. 33)

14. An infant may discover that not all animals with four legs and a tail fit into the same category as the family dog—some are cats, some are horses, etc. This is one example of accommodation, but there are millions of others—think of another one! (p. 33)

15. Equilibration is the process of balancing assimilation and accommodation in order to maintain a stable understanding of the world while still allowing for development. (p. 33)

16. Three shortcomings of Piaget's theory are as follows:
    - He underestimated the cognitive competence of infants and children.
    - The stage model is overstated.
    - He underestimated the importance of social and emotional contributions. (pp. 34–35)

17. Piaget underestimated cognitive competence because
    - he relied on too heavily on children's ability to explicitly *report* their understandings.
    - his tasks were difficult and conservative in how the answers could be interpreted. (p. 34)

Associationism and Social Learning Theory

1. learning (p. 35)

2. True—Locke was an empiricist who believed that behaviour results from experiences. This fits with the associationist perspective's focus on learning theories. (p. 35)

3. neutral; psychologically meaningful (p. 35)

4.

1. unconditioned stimulus (US)	c)	something that elicits a response before training
2. unconditioned response (UR)	d)	something that follows the presentation of the unconditioned stimulus
3. conditioned stimulus (CS)	b)	something that elicits a response after training
4. conditioned response (CR)	a)	something that follows the conditioned stimulus after training

(p. 36)

5. The sour taste of lemon juice (US) in your mouth causes you to salivate (UR). Just seeing a lemon (CS) may cause you to salivate (CR). Try this trick with your little brother: pair the sound of a bell with lemon juice in his mouth—you can have him drooling at the sound of the bell alone. This is one example, but there are millions of others—think of another one! (p. 36)

6. US: loud startling noise
   UR: fear of the noise
   CS: the white rat
   CR: fear of the rat (p. 36)

7. Watson could have paired the white rat with a positive stimulus (candy, for example). He could have given Little Albert a treat every time Albert saw the rat. After repeated pairings, Albert would begin to associate the rat with the positive experience of getting the treat and would (hopefully!) get over his fear. (p. 36)

8. systematic desensitization (p. 37)

9. Watson advocated strict discipline, a regimented feeding schedule, and minimal affection. (p. 37)

10. False—Pavlov's experiments with dogs led to the discovery of *classical* conditioning. (p. 37)

11. reinforcers; punishments (p. 37)

12. False—Skinner was an extreme behaviourist. He believed that *every* behaviour was the result of conditioning. (p. 37)

13. Skinner would tell you
    - that a child might act disruptively 'just to get attention'.
    - that giving the child attention may make the unwanted behaviour more likely.
    - to pay no attention to the disruptive behaviour (this is the basis of 'time outs'). (p. 38)

14. Albert Bandura (p. 38)

15. imitation/observational learning (p. 38)

16. Consider the following in your response:
    - Any two variables are not equally easily associated (and these views can't account for that).
    - It is unclear how children know when two objects/events are similar (and that ability is key to such views).
    - Proponents of these views cannot ignore evolution (since learning rules has an evolutionary history). (pp. 38–39)

Developmental Systems Theory

1. whole; sum of its parts (p. 39)

2. False—developmental systems theorists regard all resources as equally important. (p. 39)

3. The cornerstone of developmental systems theorists' thinking is that developmental influences are bi-directional throughout levels of the hierarchy—influences on development affect *and* are affected by other influences. (p. 40)

4. Consider the following in your response:

    - Developmental systems theory (DST) proposes that everything affects everything else, making development far too complex to make specific predictions.

    - Further complicating attempts at predictions is the theory's proposal that small initial changes early on can have very large and far-reaching effects. (p.41)

5. Two shortcomings of the developmental systems theory are

    - it doesn't actually answer the complex question of development.

    - it insists that no component of the system (genes included) be credited with a special role in development or evolution. (p. 41)

Evolutionary Psychology

1. Charles Darwin
    - wrote a 'baby biography' that was innovative in the field of developmental psychology.
    - suggested the application of the ideas of natural selection to psychology. (p. 42)

2. Ethology is the study of fitness-enhancing behaviours that were shaped by natural selection. (p. 42)

3. imprinting (p. 42)

4. 1. Irenaus Eibl-Eibesfeldt   b) founder of human ethology

   2. John Bowlby   c) described the process of attachment in human infants

   3. E. O. Wilson   a) popularized the study of the biological basis and adaptive value of social behaviours (p. 43)

5. sociobiology (p. 43)

6. E. O. Wilson ran into resistance because
   - it was the late 1970s and the behaviourists' belief that all human behaviours could be manipulated by learning was still the prevailing view.
   - people were averse to the idea that their *actions* were the product of natural selection. (pp. 43–44)

7. Modern evolutionary psychology differs because
   - there is more of an emphasis on the EEA.
   - there is now an explicit consideration of psychology. (pp. 44–45)

Methods of Developmental Psychology

1. between (p. 45)

2. The advantages of using a cross-sectional design are as follows:
   - It's quick.
   - There is no attrition (no loss of participants over time).
   - There are no practice effects (because the task is completed only once). (p. 45)

3. The disadvantages of using a cross-sectional design are as follows:
   - It doesn't measure change within individuals.
   - It may suffer from cohort effects. (p. 45)

4. An example of a cohort effect might include the following:
   - A teaching method may be used for Grade 2 students one year and not the next.
   - A parenting practice may have been popular in the 1980s and not the 1990s.
   - There are, of course, many, many others—think of another one! (p. 45)

5. within (p. 46)

6. Selective attrition is a threat for the following reasons:
   - Attrition refers to subjects dropping out of the experiment—a few people dropping out may not seem like a big deal.
   - The big problem is that it may be selective—the participants who decide to drop out may be meaningfully different from the ones who decide to stay in.
   - For example, it could be the ones who perform more poorly on the measure or who have less interest in the study who drop out.
   - This means that the later group of subjects will be systematically different from the earlier group
   - This jeopardizes the researcher's ability to draw valid conclusions. (p. 47)

7. People might show practice effects because
   - they know better how the test works.
   - they remember previous answers.
   - they are more comfortable with the setting and the researcher. (p. 47)

8. False—The researchers were interested in the stability of aggression and withdrawal characteristics *within* individuals. (p. 47)

9. The researchers helped prevent attrition by focusing on the most geographically stable demographic group in Canada: the Francophone community of Montreal. These subjects were relatively unlikely to move away (a major cause of attrition). (p. 48)

10. academic trouble in adolescence; previous sexual behaviour; teen pregnancy (p. 48)

11. academic trouble in adolescence; low self-esteem in adolescence (p. 48)

12. intergenerational transfer of traits (because the participants' children are now participating as well) (p. 48)

13. A cross-sequential design involves studying different-aged groups at the same time, once initially and then after a set period of time, in order to observe age-related changes. (p. 48)

14. cross-sectional; longitudinal (p. 48)

15. A cross-sectional design
    - allows the researcher to study the passage of time and individual differences.
    - buffers against the effects of selective attrition.
    - allows the researcher to assess cohort effects. (pp. 48–49)

16. time-consuming; expensive (p. 49)

17. naturalistic observation (p. 49)

18. Naturalistic observation is best for examining anything in which it is essential that the participants act naturally (e.g. normal play activities of young children). (p. 49)

19. generalizability; experimental control; random assignment (p. 49)

20. A correlation coefficient reveals
    - whether the relationship between the variables is positive or negative.
    - how strong the relationship is. (p. 50)

21. False—In a correlational design, a researcher observes the relationship between two variables but can conclude nothing about the effect of one on the other. (p. 50)

22. Dr. Peace's study reveals the following:
    - It tells us that sugary foods and activity level are positively correlated (as one increases, so does the other).
    - It doesn't tell us anything about what causes what.
    - It may be that eating those foods caused more activity; it may be that children who were more active were more likely to eat those foods; it may be that both are affected by a third factor. (p. 49)

23. True—The strength of a correlation is indicated by the number (–/+ doesn't matter for strength). (p. 50)

24. experimental (p. 50)

25. True—Group assignment was random. If there are differences between the two groups, Dr. Timleck can be confident (assuming she did other things correctly) that her manipulation caused the differences between groups. (p. 50)

26. a) music lessons or not

    b) IQ score (p. 50)

Within- and Between-Subjects Design

1. Answer:
    - A within-subjects design involves taking measurements of the same group of subjects at Time 1 and Time 2.
    - A between-subjects design involves taking measurements of different groups of subjects. (p. 50)

2. 1. within-subjects   b) longitudinal
     2. between-subjects   a) cross-sectional (p. 50)

Techniques for Developmental Research
1. Some issues to keep in mind are
   - the test needs to capture and hold their interest.
   - the task needs to be made clear to them. (p. 51)

2. False—Just because 5-month-old infants haven't been proven to do so yet doesn't mean they never will (creating sensitive tests for infants is challenging). (p. 51)

3. the infants can tell the difference between the two (p. 51)

4. False—It is important that the experimenter not know which stimulus is on which side so as not to have an expectation that may bias judgments. (p. 51)

5. Computers are important because
   - presenting the stimuli on a computer screen means that each subject will see the same stimuli, under the same lighting conditions, and for the same duration.
   - the order of stimuli can be easily counterbalanced. (p. 51)

6. eye-tracking technology; where exactly the infant is looking (p. 52)

7. habituation to triangles (p. 52)

8. Hayden can tell the difference between triangles and circles (p. 53)

9. impossible (pp. 51–53)

10. eye direction (pp. 44–46)

11. Some non-visual psychophysical techniques are
   - changes in heart rate, pupil dilation, skin conductance
   - sucking time
   - measures of brain activity (e.g. EEG) (pp. 53–54)

12. Reliability refers to consistency in repeated measures of the same variable using the same measurement method. (p. 55)

13. This means that
   - observers agreed in their assessments of what was being observed (high inter-rater).
   - separate administrations of the test did not produce the same results (low test–retest). (p. 55)

14. Validity is the extent to which a measuring technique measures the attribute that it is designed to measure. (p. 55)

15. External; internal (p. 55)

16. benefits; risks (p. 56)

17. An IRB is
   - Institutional Review Board
   - a panel of objective and knowledgeable individuals who determine whether the benefits of a particular research project exceed the risks.
   - a group that may make suggestions to the researcher or, in some cases, deny permission to conduct the experiment. (p. 56)

18. Consider the following in your response:
    - Funding agencies require the review for releasing funds to a researcher.
    - Scientific journals require the review before findings can be published.
    - As well, the assessment of the IRB provides objective opinions that will help the researcher act ethically—something any moral human being would strive for. (p. 56)

19. False—Infants and children are less able to comprehend the risks and benefits of the research and they may be more vulnerable to stressors. For those reasons (and others), researchers dealing with infants and children must follow stricter guidelines than those dealing with adults. (p. 56)

20. a) Informed consent
    - Researchers must explain what will happen so that the child can understand and must receive consent from the child.
    - The parent/guardian must also provide consent (only parent/guardian in the case of an infant).
    b) Deception
    - The participant needs to be debriefed after the experiment is over.
    - It is important that the participant feel ok about the experiment before she leaves.
    c) Right to privacy
    - The experimenter must protect participants' identity—there must be complete anonymity and confidentiality.
    d) Right to knowledge of results
    - If the child participant so desires, the researcher must provide the results of the study in a way that the child can understand them.
    - If the research involves a beneficial therapy and the child is in the control group, she has a right to the beneficial treatment if available. (pp. 57–58)

Practice Test 1: Answer Key

1. **a** (p. 30)	8. **b** (p. 42)	15. **d** (p. 50)	22. **c** (p. 55)
2. **b** (p. 31)	9. **c** (p. 45)	16. **b** (p. 50)	23. **b** (p. 55)
3. **d** (pp. 34–35)	10. **a** (p. 47)	17. **d** (p. 50)	24. **d** (p. 56)
4. **b** (p. 35)	11. **b** (p. 48)	18. **c** (p. 51)	25. **b** (p. 56)
5. **d** (p. 36)	12. **c** (p. 49)	19. **a** (p. 51)	
6. **c** (p. 38)	13. **a** (p. 49)	20. **a** (p. 53)	
7. **d** (p. 38)	14. **c** (p. 50)	21. **b** (p. 53)	

Practice Test 2: Answer Key

1. **c** (p. 31)	8. **a** (pp. 38–39)	15. **c** (p. 48)	22. **a** (pp. 53–54)
2. **b** (p. 33)	9. **c** (p. 39)	16. **b** (p. 50)	23. **d** (p. 55)
3. **a** (p. 34)	10. **b** (p. 42)	17. **a** (p. 50)	24. **d** (p. 55)
4. **d** (pp. 35–36)	11. **a** (p. 42)	18. **c** (p. 50)	25. **b** (pp. 57–58)
5. **c** (p. 37)	12. **d** (p. 43)	19. **d** (p. 51)	
6. **c** (p. 38)	13. **c** (pp. 44–45)	20. **b** (p. 52)	
7. **b** (p. 38)	14. **d** (p. 47)	21. **c** (p. 53)	

Chapter 3
The Basics: Evolution, Genes, and Conception

Chapter Summary

A Modern Understanding of Evolution

Gregor Mendel discovered that the mechanism of inheritance (the gene) is particulate. Charles Darwin proposed the theory of evolution by natural selection. Together, these contributions form the modern synthesis, the foundation for our modern understanding of evolution.

Darwin's Problem: Blending Inheritance

In Darwin's time, the accepted view of inheritance was that it was fluid—inherited 'stuff' blends together and averages. This doesn't fit with the theory of natural selection because blending would dilute advantageous traits. The novel, beneficial effects of mutations could never spread through the population.

Mendelian Inheritance

Mendel's experiments with pea plants helped him puzzle out the properties of inheritance. He discovered that what was inherited was particulate, that each individual carries two copies of the particulate units (one from each parent), and that units were dominant or recessive.

Chromosomes, Genes, and Alleles

Chromosomes are located in the nucleus of each cell. Each chromosome is comprised of a large DNA helix containing thousands of genes. Defining 'gene' is surprisingly difficult; for our purposes, a *gene* is a functional piece of DNA that remains across a large number of generations, potentially long enough play a part in natural selection. An *allele* is a variant of a gene (for example, there are blue eye alleles and brown eye alleles) that may occupy a particular location on a chromosome. Once an allele has become universal, it is called a gene. When there are two or more possible alleles, they are a source of variation in the population.

Evolutionary Processes

Mutations (spontaneous errors in DNA) are actually quite common. A mutation in a somatic cell will not amount to much of anything. A mutation in a sex cell (egg or sperm) can be passed to the next generation and may therefore play a part in evolution.

Alleles passed from parent to offspring are selected randomly. This can cause changes in gene frequency (*genetic drift*), particularly in very small populations with an isolated gene pool (the *founder effect*). Changes in gene frequency (a reduction in genetic diversity) can also be caused by a population *bottleneck*, a drastic reduction in the population for at least one generation.

Adaptations, By-Products, and Noise

In addition to producing adaptations, natural selection produces *by-products*, traits that 'tagged along' with adaptations (e.g. we have belly buttons not because they are adaptive themselves but because they are left over from the adaptive umbilical cord), and noise from random effects that were not selected for.

A trait may also come to be used for something other than its adapted purpose, a phenomenon known as *exaptation*.

What Does DNA Do Anyway?

DNA can replicate itself. It can also be transcribed (by way of *messenger RNA*) into proteins that have many functions in our bodies. The shape, and therefore function, of proteins is determined by DNA as well as environmental factors. A single gene may have effects on more than one phenotypic trait. This phenomenon, called *pleiotropy*, explains how a gene with a detrimental effect can get selected for (it may also have a beneficial effect).

Interactionism: The Bidirectional Influences of Developmental Resources

There is a consensus among developmental theorists on interactionism: development is the result of an interaction between genes and environment. The specific examples described in the textbook help to illustrate how the interaction actually works.

Meiosis, Conception, and Pregnancy

Genetic material from the mother's egg and the father's sperm combines to form the *zygote*. Eggs and sperm are produced by *meiosis*, a process of cell division that produces cells containing 23 unpaired chromosomes. During meiosis, separate chromosomes exchange sections of DNA (a process referred to as crossover). This creates brand new, unique chromosomes.

When a zygote divides within the first few days of conception, the result will be *monozygotic twins* with identical genomes. When more than one egg is released by the mother during ovulation and each egg is fertilized by a different sperm, the result will be *dizygotic twins*, each with its own genome. Monozygotic twins may or may not share an amniotic sac and a placenta depending on when the zygote divides. Monozygotic twins are not truly identical—non-identical prenatal environments, developmental noise, and strategic specialization can lead to differences.

The phases of pregnancy are referred to as the germinal (conception to second week), embryonic (third to eighth week), and fetal (eighth week on) periods. The placenta, umbilical cord, amniotic sac, and amniotic fluid function to support the embryo/fetus.

Summary of the germinal period:
- zygote results from conception
- rapid cell division
- ends with conceptus implanting in uterine wall

By the end of the embryonic period
- facial features and body parts (e.g. fingers and toes) are recognizable;
- central nervous system has formed;
- all internal organs are present and developing;
- sexual differentiation has started;
- the embryo moves by itself.

By 28 weeks

- the fetus may be well developed enough to survive on its own;
- the eyes are open and the auditory system is functioning;
- brain development is on par with a newborn;
- the fetus' most important job is to grow bigger.

The placenta has unrestricted access to the mother's blood supply and provides the fetus with oxygen and nutrients. It also removes carbon dioxide and waste from the fetus.

During the first trimester, women often have a strong aversion to certain types of foods (morning sickness). It seems that morning sickness helps to protect the developing fetus from foods that may be contaminated during this integral time of organ development and the development of the central nervous system. Pregnant women tend to be better than non-pregnant women at recognizing that a male face is unknown to them and they have been shown to express greater negativity toward unknown people. These differences may be adaptive in protecting the fetus from people who may bear harmful pathogens.

Brain Development

Neurons transmit information in the brain. Information is received from other neurons via the *dendrites* and an electrical impulse travels down the axon to the synapse.

The brain is the fastest growing organ, reaching 90 per cent of its adult weight by age 6. Almost all neurons are produced by 18 weeks gestation. Some move actively (using a chemical attraction) to a particular destination and some are pushed by other cells. Individual neurons gradually develop complexly-branching dendrites. Myelination (which continues into adolescence) encases axons in an insulating myelin sheath.

Synaptogenesis is the process of creating synapses between neurons, allowing for trillions of connections in the brain. Many neural connections are unused and eventually lost through *synaptic pruning*. Excess synaptogenesis followed by synaptic pruning provides a great deal of plasticity in the brain.

The two hemispheres of the brain are somewhat different. They control opposite sides of the body. As well, the left hemisphere tends to be specialized for language and the right for spatial abilities. This specialization continues throughout childhood.

Learning Objectives

After reading this chapter, you should be able to:

- Explain how Charles Darwin and Gregor Mendel developed an understanding of evolution (pp. 65–69)

- Define the building blocks of heredity: chromosomes, genes, and alleles (pp. 69–72)

- Discuss the role of mutations in evolution (pp. 72–73)

- Discuss the roles of genetic drift, founder effects, and bottlenecks in evolution (pp. 73–75)

- Differentiate between three products of evolution (adaptations, by-products, and noise) and one extra twist (exaptations) (pp. 76–78)

- Examine the functions of DNA (pp. 78–83)

- Consider the interaction between genes and the environment in development (pp. 83–87)

- Describe the process of meiosis (pp. 87–91)

- Differentiate between monozygotic and dizygotic twins (pp. 91–93)

- Trace the progression of prenatal development through pregnancy (pp. 93–95)

- Examine the role of the placenta (pp. 95–96) and evolutionary adaptations (pp. 96–97) in pregnancy

- Outline early brain development (pp. 97–99)

Suggested Readings

Darwin, C. (1911). *On the origin of species by means of natural selection.* London: Hurst.

Often cited but unread by many, Darwin's description of his theory of evolution is well worth reading.

Caspi, A., Sugden, K., Moffitt, T. E., Taylor, A., et al. (2003). Influence of life stress on depression: Moderation by a polymorphism in the 5-HTT gene. *Science, 301*, 386–389.

The original paper described in the section titled 'Genetic Susceptibility to Depression?' It is a fairly challenging (though short!) read. In addition to learning more details about Caspi et al.'s findings, it provides a glimpse of how genes and environmental factors are discussed in scientific writing.

Scarr, S., & McCartney, K. (1983). How people make their own environments: A theory of genotype → environment effects. *Child Development, 54*, 424–435.

This article proposes Scarr's theory that genotypes direct experience (niche-picking).

Study Questions

A Modern Understanding of Evolution

1. The discoveries of Charles Darwin and Gregor Mendel are together known as the _____.

2. Darwin's contribution was _____.

3. Mendel's contribution was _____.

Darwin's Problem: Blending Inheritance

1. Specifically, what problem of Darwin's did Mendel solve?

2. Define 'mutation'.

Mendelian Inheritance

1. Gregor Mendel is sometimes called The Father of _____.

2. Summarize Mendel's findings in breeding tall and short pea plants.

3. What were Mendel's four conclusions?

Chromosomes, Genes, and Alleles

1. What does a chromosome do most of the time?

2. True or False: Defining what a gene is has been more difficult than defining what a chromosome is.

3. Define 'gene'.

4. What is an example of an allele?

5. Once an allele is universal, it becomes a(n) _____.

6. True or False: Very few alleles in the human genome have become universal.

Evolutionary Processes

1. True or False: Mutations are rare. They don't happen to most people.

2. A mutation only really matters (i.e. it is only involved in natural selection) if _____.

3. DNA is made up of _____ nucleotides.

4. Why are there no centaurs?

5. Define 'genetic drift'.

6. Martha's Vineyard, an island in Massachusetts, has an unusually high population of deaf people. This is an example of _____.

7. The Toba catastrophe theory proposes that roughly 70,000 years ago, the human population was reduced to about 15,000 individuals. The resulting lack of genetic diversity would be called a _____.

8. If you were the all-powerful, supernatural decider of everything, what could you do to get rid of blue eyes in human beings?

Adaptations, By-Products, and Noise

1. The process of evolution leads to adaptations; it also leads to _____ and _____.

2. Bones are white because calcium (which is white) was naturally selected for its strength. The fact that bones are white is an example of _____.

3. Define 'noise' (in evolutionary terms).

4. What is the rule for distinguishing between evolutionary adaptations, by-products, and noise?

5. Bird feathers originally evolved to provide warmth. Subsequently, they have come to be used in flight. This is a classic example of _____.

What Does DNA Do Anyway?

1. DNA stands for _____.

2. What are two special functions of DNA?

3. Two strands of DNA zip together to form a _____.

4. Define 'genome'.

5. A DNA double helix looks like a _____.

6. The chromosome molecule is made up of complimentary strands of chemicals. The two strands are _____-bonded to each other and the bases within each strand are _____-bonded to each other.

7. What are the four types of bases in a DNA double helix?

8. These four bases are, together, referred to as _____.

9. Before replicating itself, a DNA molecule _____.

10. Proteins are sequences of _____.

11. DNA is transcribed into _____, which is translated into _____.

12. How does transcription work?

13. What environmental factors can affect the shape of a protein (and, therefore, its function)?

14. True or False: Most of the genome's DNA is not transcribed.

15. Genes really don't do much. All they do is store the information that _____.

16. High testosterone levels are associated with prostate cancer in middle-age men. Because they are also associated with higher fertility in young men, they tend to get a 'free ride' into middle-age. This is an example of _____.

Interactionism: The Bidirectional Influences of Developmental Resources

1. True or False: Modern developmental psychologists can be roughly divided into nativists and empiricists.

2. The transporter gene for the neurotransmitter serotonin is _____, meaning that a person gets one of two possible alleles.

3. The serotonin transporter gene codes for a protein that helps regulate _____.

4. Summarize the relationship between the serotonin transporter gene and the risk of depression.

5. True or False: Social status can affect gene expression.

6. An example of an environmental effect on gene expression in humans is _____.

7. Sandra Scarr's _____ theory proposes that, to some extent, a child determines his environment.

8. According to Scarr, in early childhood, the child who shows a great deal of interest in something may evoke a response in his parents. This produces _____ relationship.

9. According to Scarr, in later childhood, the child has the autonomy to quite actively control his environment and pick his niche. This produces _____ relationship.

10. The textbook outlines two possible ways to talk about a gene–environment interaction. What are they?

Meiosis, Conception, and Pregnancy

1. Define 'zygote'.

2. In humans, the zygote lasts for _____.

3. The process by which eggs and sperm are produced is called _____.

4. True or False: Humans are 'haploid'.

5. Match the following phases of meiosis with the corresponding descriptions.

    1. Meiosis I   a) produces two haploid daughter cells

                             b) produces four daughter cells

    2. Meiosis II   c) includes crossover

                             d) reductive division

                             e) results in a chromotid that is ready to pair up in mating

6. What would happen if all cells could divide only by mitosis (i.e. what if there was no such thing as meiosis)?

7. Define 'crossover' (during meiosis).

8. Crossover results in _____.

9. Why might potential parents choose to employ alternative technologies in fertility?

10. IVF stands for _____.

11. At a sixth-year assessment, the parents of children conceived via alternative fertility methods were warmer, more responsive to their children, and more emotionally involved with their children than parents of control children (conceived naturally). This is a correlation. How might the relationship be explained?

12. Match the following twin types with the corresponding descriptions.

    1. monozygotic twins

    2. dizygotic twins

    a) more closely related than ordinary siblings
    b) somewhat heritable
    c) accounts for about 1 in 285 births
    d) more likely with older mothers

13. True or False: Fraternal twin births are more common in the United States than Canada.

14. Monozygotic twins who share a _____ are more similar than those who did not on measures such as IQ.

15. Why are conjoined twins sometimes referred to as 'Siamese' twins?

16. Two individuals are never identical. How does the case of Chang and Eng prove that?

17. How and why do monozygotic twins become different?

18. Match the following periods of prenatal development with the corresponding timeframes.

    1. germinal
    2. embryonic
    3. fetal

    a) eighth week after conception until birth
    b) first two weeks after conception
    c) third to eight week after conception

19. The _____ is the link between the embryo/fetus and the placenta.

20. Prenatal development is cephalocaudal, meaning that features near the _____ develop sooner than the rest of the body.

21. The conceptus implanting into the uterine wall marks the end of _____.

22. Match the following amounts of time after conception with the corresponding descriptions.

    1. 2 to 6 weeks   a) may be well developed enough to survive outside of the womb
    2. 8 weeks   b) recognizably human face
    3. 7 to 12 weeks   c) central nervous system develops
    4. 28 weeks   d) external genitalia develop

23. After 28 weeks, the biggest job of the fetus is to _____.

24. True or False: If the timing of birth were predicted based on the relative maturity at birth in other primates, humans would be expected to be born at around 6 months of gestation.

25. The limiting factor in the duration of the gestational period is the conflict between _____ and _____.

26. What is a placenta and what does it do?

27. True or False: The development of the placenta relies on the genome of the mother, not the fetus.

28. In evolutionary terms, 'morning sickness' could be called _____.

29. True or False: Women who experience morning sickness are less likely to have a miscarriage than women who do not.

30. Pregnant woman have been shown to express increased _____ toward unknown people compared to non-pregnant women. This reflects another _____ in pregnancy that may have developed to protect the fetus.

Brain Development

1. A mature human brain has _____ neurons.

2. How are dendrites and axons are involved in transmitting information through a neuron?

3. The junction between neurons is called a _____.

4. At age 3, the brain is _____ of adult weight and the body is _____ of adult weight.

5. What is produced almost completely between the third and eighteenth weeks after conception?

6. At peak, how many new neurons are produced per minute?

7. How do migrating neurons get to their proper destination?

8. Neuronal migration is complete by _____ of gestation.

9. Dendrites can become extremely complex with a myriad of branches. This process of branch formation, called _____, increases the neuron's capacity to form connections with other cells.

10. What is myelination and what effect does it have?

11. Define 'synaptogenesis'.

12. The developmental timeline for synaptogenesis differs for different _____.

13. True or False: Synaptic pruning, a process during which synaptic density decreases as synaptic connections are lost, is usually a symptom of brain malfunctioning.

14. An initial excess of neurons that is sculpted by experience is thought to provide a great deal of _____.

15. Match the following brain hemispheres with the corresponding descriptions.

1. left
    a) processes sensory information from and sends motor commands to the left side of the body

    b) thought to be more involved in spatial thinking and visual imagery

2. right
    c) processes language information (usually)

    d) processes sensory information from and sends motor commands to the right side of the body

16. True or False: Hemispheric specialization starts in early childhood.

Practice Test 1

1. The pairing of Charles Darwin's theory of evolution by natural selection and Gregor Mendel's discovery of the particulate nature of genes is known as

    a. blended inheritance.
    b. the modern synthesis.
    c. adaptive design.
    d. particulate evolution.

2. Which of the following statements is *not* true of a chromosome?

   a. It can be seen under a microscope.
   b. It is composed of a large DNA helix.
   c. It is located in the nucleus of the cell.
   d. It contains millions of genes.

3. A gene is

   a. a transcribed sequence on a chromosome.
   b. a functional sequence of DNA that functions as a unit of natural selection.
   c. ten letters of a chromosome.
   d. none of the above—there is no single undisputable definition

4. Centaurs (part human, part horse) do not exist because

   a. they would be poorly-designed organisms.
   b. nature has not yet selected the genes that exist for centaur formation.
   c. this design does not exist as a possibility and natural selection can only select among possibilities.
   d. non-centaur genes are dominant.

5. Genetic drift

   a. occurs because selection of alleles is random.
   b. is more likely to have effects in large populations than small populations.
   c. causes deleterious changes in the genome.
   d. all of the above

6. Which of the following would be an example of a population bottleneck?

   a. A mother with both brown eye and blue eye alleles passes the blue eye allele to 9 out of her 10 children.
   b. Brown fur in rabbits becomes prevalent due to a changing landscape.
   c. A massive flood wipes out all but 10,000 people, none of whom have (or carry an allele for) cystic fibrosis.
   d. none of the above

7. If a trait cannot reasonably be classified as an adaptation or a by-product of evolution, what is it called?

   a. an exaptation
   b. variability
   c. a pleiotrope
   d. noise

8. An exaptation occurs when

    a. a feature did not arise as an adaptation for its present role but was subsequently co-opted for that function.
    b. genetic diversity is lost.
    c. there is a shift in gene frequency as a result of a founder situation.
    d. an adaptive feature carries with it another feature that is neutral for survival.

9. Which of the following statements is *not* true of DNA?

    a. It can replicate itself.
    b. It is present in the nucleus of sex cells but not somatic cells.
    c. Its function is to transcribe proteins.
    d. It stands for deoxyribonucleic acid.

10. A codon is

    a. a type of messenger RNA.
    b. a protein.
    c. a triplet of nucleotides.
    d. an amino acid chain.

11. In one species of fish that has been studied, rank in the social hierarchy affects expression of the gene that codes for

    a. neurotransmitter production.
    b. body size.
    c. number of fins.
    d. sex hormone receptors.

12. Scarr's niche-picking theory can be best summed up in which of the following ways?

    a. The child acts according to a genetic blueprint.
    b. The child to some extent determines his environment.
    c. The child's family makes a causal contribution to the child's development.
    d. The child is passive.

13. Which of the following statements is *not* true of a human zygote?

    a. It lasts for about two weeks.
    b. It is a single cell.
    c. It has a full compliment of genetic material.
    d. It exists during the germinal period.

14. Humans are diploid, meaning that each cell has two copies of each

    a. gene.
    b. chromosome.
    c. chromatid.
    d. sex cell.

15. Meiosis is *not*

    a. the reason all children of a pair of parents are not identical.
    b. the process by which sex cells are produced.
    c. a process that results in paired chromosomes.
    d. a process that involves reductive division.

16. In vitro fertilization is the process of

    a. injecting sperm directly into the uterus.
    b. combining egg and sperm in a laboratory.
    c. implanting the conceptus into the uterine wall.
    d. injecting sperm into the vagina.

17. Which of the following statements is true about twins?

    a. There are more monozygotic twins than dizygotic twins.
    b. They are always more closely genetically related than ordinary siblings.
    c. They are more common in younger mothers.
    d. none of the above

18. People who share identical genomes are likely to be different anyway. Why?

    a. strategic behaviour
    b. environmental differences
    c. developmental noise
    d. all of the above

19. At _____ weeks, the fetus *may* be well developed enough to survive on its own.

    a. 16
    b. 20
    c. 28
    d. 38

20. In the last few weeks of prenatal development, the primary goal of the fetus is to

    a. prune synaptic connections.
    b. coordinate organ functioning.
    c. learn to see.
    d. get bigger.

21. The development of the placenta relies on the genome of

    a. the fetus.
    b. the mother.
    c. the fetus and the mother in combination.
    d. neither the fetus nor the mother.

22. The textbook cites research that suggests that, compared to non-pregnant women, pregnant women have better memory for

    a. foods consumed.
    b. male faces.
    c. names.
    d. facial expressions.

23. Neuronal production is mostly complete by

    a. 18 weeks after conception.
    b. 24 weeks after conception.
    c. birth.
    d. age 2.

24. Which of the following statements is true of synapse density?

    a. It peaks at about 5 years of age.
    b. It peaks in the prefrontal cortex earlier than in the visual cortex.
    c. It is a function of the growth of axons and dendrites.
    d. It is a determinant of neuronal migration.

25. Which of the following is *not* a good match?

    a. left hemisphere of the brain—controls the right side of the body
    b. right hemisphere of the brain—more active for language processing
    c. right hemisphere of the brain—receives sensory information from the left side of the body
    d. right hemisphere of the brain—more active for visual imagery

Practice Test 2

1. Which of the following statements is *not* one of Mendel's conclusions about heredity?

    a. Each parent makes a heritable contribution to the offspring.
    b. Inherited matter blends together.
    c. Genes may be dominant or recessive.
    d. Each individual carries two copies of the heritable matter.

2. A universal allele is called a

    a. gene.
    b. locus.
    c. genome.
    d. chromosome.

3. Mutations

    a. are rare—they do not occur in most people.
    b. are a potential mechanism of natural selection *if* they occur in a somatic cell.
    c. are best described as spontaneous changes in chromosomes.
    d. have random outcomes.

4. The prevalence of Usher syndrome in southern Louisiana is an example of

    a. natural selection.
    b. a population bottleneck.
    c. the founder effect.
    d. an exaptation.

5. A belly button is an evolutionary

    a. exaptation.
    b. noise characteristic.
    c. adaptation.
    d. by-product.

6. DNA

    a. is present in the nucleus of animal but not plant cells.
    b. makes up the genome.
    c. determines outcomes.
    d. acts in mysterious ways.

7. Which of the following is *not* a type of DNA base?

    a. leucine
    b. cytosine
    c. thymine
    d. adenine

8. If a trait increases fertility *and* leads to cancer, then it can be said that the cancer is a _____ effect.

    a. phenotypic
    b. polymorphic
    c. pleiotropic
    d. pirotropic

9. Which of the following views is most prevalent in contemporary developmental psychology?

    a. nativism
    b. empiricism
    c. interactionism
    d. all three are popular

10. Which of the following statements best describes the relationship between the serotonin transporter gene and depression?

   a. The presence of the serotonin transporter gene is associated with a greater risk of depression.
   b. The presence of the longer serotonin transporter gene was more important than the presence of stressful environmental factors in predicting depression.
   c. The presence of the longer serotonin transporter gene was more important than the presence of stressful environmental factors in predicting depression.
   d. The presence of the shorter serotonin transporter gene and stressful environmental factors are, together, associated with a greater risk of depression.

11. A study cited in the textbook identified 209 genes that were expressed differently in

   a. lonely and non-lonely people.
   b. tall and short people.
   c. extroverted and introverted people.
   d. dominant and submissive people.

12. The result of Meiosis I is _____ cell(s).

   a. one haploid
   b. two haploid
   c. one diploid
   b. two diploid

13. The result of Meiosis II is _____ cell(s).

   a. 1
   b. 2
   c. 4
   d. 8

14. Which of the following is a significant source of genetic diversity?

   a. meiosis
   b. founder situations
   c. genetic drift
   d. crossover

15. Vicki and Anik are dizygotic twin girls. Which of the following is true?

   a. They have the same genome.
   b. They are more likely than average to have grandchildren who are dizygotic twins.
   c. They are more likely than average to give birth to monozygotic twins.
   d. They shared a placenta in the womb.

16. The membrane that forms the placenta is called the

    a. chorion.
    b. blastocyst.
    c. conceptus.
    d. uterus.

17. An example of cephalocaudal development is that

    a. the brain develops sooner than the heart.
    b. the torso develops sooner than the arms.
    c. the fingers develop sooner than the toes.
    d. the eyes develop sooner than the ears.

18. By 12 weeks after gestation, the fetus

    a. can move.
    b. may swallow amniotic fluid.
    c. may practice breathing.
    d. all of the above

19. The placenta does *not*

    a. invade the uterine wall.
    b. allow the mother's blood vessels to constrict.
    c. act in a parasitic way.
    d. provide oxygen to the fetus.

20. Pregnant women experience morning sickness because

    a. researchers have not yet developed a cure.
    b. pregnant women tend to eat unusual foods.
    c. it is an adaptive way to protect the fetus.
    d. the immune system reacts to the fetus as a foreign object.

21. How many neurons does a mature human brain have?

    a. thousands
    b. millions
    c. billions
    d. trillions

22. A fibre designed to receive a signal in a brain cell is called a

    a. dendrite.
    b. axon.
    c. neuron.
    d. synapse.

23. A 3-year-old child is typically at roughly _____ per cent of his adult body weight and _____ per cent of his adult brain weight.

   a. 20; 100
   b. 20; 80
   c. 50; 50
   d. 40; 60

24. Myelination increases

   a. the arborization of dendrites.
   b. the rate of synaptogenesis.
   c. hemispheric specialization.
   d. the efficiency of electrical transmission.

25. The human brain is surprisingly good at recovering from injury as long as the injury occurs

   a. after myelination is complete.
   b. before hemispheric specialization.
   c. while there is a surplus of synaptic connections.
   d. after the age of 2 or 3.

Study Questions: Answer Key

A Modern Understanding of Evolution

1. modern synthesis (p. 64)

2. the theory of evolution by natural selection (p. 64)

3. the discovery of the particulate nature of genes (p. 64)

Darwin's Problem: Blending Inheritance

1. Consider the following in your response:
   • Darwin believed (as most did at the time) that inherited material from parents was fluid—that contributions blended together—meaning that traits would average
   • This was a problem for Darwin because blending would dilute advantageous traits and mutations would disappear.
   • Mendel's discovery of particulate inheritance (no blending) solved the problem. (p. 65)

2. A mutation is a spontaneous error in creating a true replica in the process of DNA replication, resulting in a novel sequence. (p. 66)

Mendelian Inheritance

1. Modern Genetics (p. 68)

2. Answer:
    - Mendel used purebred tall and short plants, cross-pollinating tall with short.
    - He then bred the second generation among themselves.
    - Blended inheritance would have predicted that tall and short would produce medium and that the second generation mediums would produce more mediums.
    - Instead, Mendel found that the first generation were all tall and the next generation was roughly 75 per cent tall and 25 per cent short. (pp. 68–69)

3. Mendel's four conclusions are the following:
    1. Inherited matter is particulate rather than fluid.
    2. Each individual carries two copies of the particulate units of inheritance (genes, as we refer to them now).
    3. The offspring receives one copy of the heritable particle from each parent.
    4. The heritable particles are passed on intact (unchanged by the contribution of the other parent). They can, however, influence the expression one another. (p. 69)

Chromosomes, Genes, and Alleles

1. Most of the time, chromosomes are neatly gathered up in the nucleus of each cell, waiting to be involved in replication or transcription. (p. 69)

2. True—A chromosome is one clear-cut molecule. A gene could potentially be defined many different ways. (p. 69)

3. A gene is a functional sequence of DNA that remains across a large number of generations, potentially for long enough for it to function as a significant unit of natural selection.

    (Note that this is a definition that will work for our purposes; it is not the only possible definition of a gene.) (p. 70)

4. The following are examples of alleles:
    - There are alleles associated with blue eyes and alleles associated with brown eyes (in humans).
    - There are alleles associated with smoothed surfaces and alleles associated with wrinkled surfaces (in pea plants).
    - There are different alleles for any kind of characteristic that varies between individuals. (p. 71)

5. gene (p. 71)

6. False—About two thirds of alleles are essentially universal. (p. 71)

Evolutionary Processes

1. False—Mutations are quite common. Estimates for humans range from 30–175 per lifetime. (p. 72)

2. it occurs in a sex cell (p. 72)

3. four (p. 72)

4. There are no centaurs, not because it wouldn't be a good design, but because natural selection can only select among the designs that arise. Evolution cannot be driven in a particular direction. (pp. 72–73)

5. Genetic drift is the change in gene frequency that results from the fact that genes passed from parent to offspring are selected randomly. (p. 73)

6. the founder effect (p. 73)

7. population bottleneck (p. 75)

8. To get rid of people with blue eyes, you might consider the following:
   - Getting rid of people with blue eyes would be a bit complicated because you wouldn't be able to tell from looking at an individual's eye colour whether or that they have blue eye alleles (some people with brown eye alleles—and therefore brown eyes—have blue eye alleles as well).
   - With a knowledge of alleles, you could exterminate or make infertile anyone with blue eye alleles.
   - This would effectively get rid of not just everyone who has blue eyes but anyone who could have offspring with blue eyes.
   - This would create a bottleneck and the blue alleles would be lost forever. (p. 75)

Adaptations, By-Products, and Noise

1. by-products; noise (p. 76)

2. a by-product of evolution (p. 76)

3. Noise in natural selection is comprised of random effects that were not selected for. Not all traits are selected for or against by natural selection. Because they are inconsequential, neutral traits may become somewhat prevalent. (p. 77)

4. There really isn't a rule for distinguishing between adaptations, by-products, and noise—sometimes the distinction is unclear; however, an adaptation, compared to the other two, tends to be more efficient, economical, precise, and reliable. (p. 77)

5. an exaptation (p. 77)

Adaptations, By-Products, and Noise

1. deoxyribonucleic acid (p. 78)

2. Two special functions of DNA are that
   - it can replicate itself.
   - it can be transcribed, resulting in a protein. (p. 78)

3. double helix (p. 78)

4. A genome is an individual's complete genetic endowment, all of the individual's DNA. (p. 80)

5. twisted ladder (p. 80)

6. weakly; strongly (p. 80)

7. A (adenine)
   C (cytosine)
   G (guanine)
   T (thymine) (pp. 80–81)

8. nucleotides (p. 81)

9. 'unzips' (splits down the middle) (p. 81)

10. amino acids (p. 81)

11. messenger RNA; proteins (p. 81)

12. The following is an outline of the process of transcription:
    - The DNA molecule unzips so that the template strand is exposed.
    - Nucleotides pair up with the template strand and create a single mRNA strand.
    - Each of the bases in the DNA bonds with an available complimentary mRNA nucleotide.
    - The new mRNA molecule is 'read' three nucleotides at a time and the triplet (a codon) is matched with the corresponding amino acid.
    - Amino acids are attached, one by one, until the protein is complete. (p. 82)

13. Factors that can affect the shape of a protein include
    - local pH
    - temperature (p. 82)

14. True (p. 82)

15. codes for proteins (p. 82)

16. pleiotropy (p. 83)

Interactionism: The Bidirectional Influences of Developmental Resources

1. False—Everyone agrees on interactionism, that development is an interaction between genes and the environment. (p. 83)

2. polymorphic (p. 84)

3. the amount of serotonin that gets into neurons (and therefore how serotonin affects the neurons) (p. 84)

4. Answer:
    - There are two types of the serotonin transporter genes—one short, one long.
    - The shorter allele is associated with a greater risk of depression but only if the person is exposed to a major stressor/trauma in childhood.
    - This is an example of a gene–environment interaction. (pp. 84–85)

5. True—Burmeister et al. (2007) found that an individual fish's rank in the social hierarchy affects the expression of the gene that codes for androgen and estrogen receptors. The higher the rank, the more receptors are produced by DNA. More receptors lead to more dominant behaviour. (p. 85)

6. loneliness (one study identified 209 genes that were expressed differently in lonely versus non-lonely people) (p. 86)

7. niche-picking (p. 87)

8. an evocative gene–environment (p. 87)

9. an active gene–environment (p. 87)

10. The two possible ways to talk about a gene–environment interaction are as follows:
    - You can statistically identify contributions to the variance in the population (heritability).
    - You can ask *how* genes and the environment are employed in the *development* of a given trait. (Note that these are both valid questions but they should be distinguished from one another.) (p. 87)

Meiosis, Conception, and Pregnancy

1. The zygote is the fertilized egg, still in the single-cell stage. (p. 87)

2. four days (p. 87)

3. meiosis (p. 89)

4. False—Humans are 'diploid', meaning that each cell has two copies of each chromosome. (p. 89)

5. 1. Meiosis I   d) reductive division
                   a) produces two haploid daughter cells
                   c) includes crossover
   2. Meiosis II   b) produces four daughter cells
                   e) results in a chromotid that is ready to pair up in mating (pp. 89–91)

6. If meiosis did not exist, each generation would have twice the genetic material as the previous generation. (p. 89)

7. Crossover occurs when a pair of homologous chromosomes (for example, one from the maternal grandmother and one from the maternal grandfather) pair up and exchange sections of DNA. (p. 89)

8. a brand new, never-before-seen chromosome (p. 89)

9. People might employ alternative technologies in fertility if
   - they are gay or lesbian.
   - a single woman wishes to be a mother.
   - the male member of a couple does not produce sufficient, viable sperm.
   - the female member of a couple has trouble conceiving or maintaining a pregnancy. (p. 90)

10. in vitro fertilization (p. 90)

11. Consider the following in your response:
    - Maybe using alternative fertility methods caused the parents to be that way.
    - Maybe being that way made these people more likely to seek out a way to have a child when natural methods didn't work.
    - Maybe there are other factors involved (e.g. perhaps both are related to socioeconomic status). (p. 90)

12. 1. monozygotic twins   c) 1 in 285 births
                           a) more closely related than ordinary siblings
    2. dizygotic twins   b) somewhat heritable
                           d) more likely with older mothers (p. 91)

13. True—Try to think of some reasons why that might be the case! (p. 91)

14. placenta (p. 92)

15. Conjoined twins are sometimes referred to as 'Siamese twins' because
    - the most well-known set of conjoined twins were Chang and Eng.
    - Chang and Eng were from Thailand, which was then called Siam.
    - people from Siam were known as 'Siamese'. (p. 93)

16. To support the claim that two individuals are never identical, consider the following:
    - Chang and Eng were monozygotic, conjoined twins. They shared the same genome, the same prenatal environment, and the same environment after birth.
    - Despite the fact that their genetic and environmental influences were as similar as they could possibly be, Chang and Eng had very distinct personalities. (p. 93)

17. Monozygotic twins become different for the following reasons:
    - There are some differences that reflect developmental noise—differences that cannot be accounted for by either genetics or environment.

- As well, twins are likely to find some strategic advantage to being unique individuals and therefore strive for specialization. (p. 93)

18. 1. germinal   b) first two weeks after conception
    2. embryonic   c) third to eight week after conception
    3. fetal   a) eighth week after conception until birth (p. 93)

19. umbilical cord (p. 94)

20. head (p. 94)

21. the germinal period (p. 95)

22. 1. 2 to 6 weeks   c) central nervous system develops
    2. 8 weeks   b) recognizably human face
    3. 7 to 12 weeks   d) external genitalia develop
    4. 28 weeks   a) may be well developed enough to survive outside of the womb
    (pp. 94–95)

23. grow bigger (p. 95)

24. False—Humans would be expected to be born at around 18 months of gestation (we are born early). (p. 95)

25. the mother's pelvis size; the infant's brain growth (p. 95)

26. The placenta
- is a highly–vascularized, spongy organ.
- carries oxygen and nutrients through it and into the fetus, and carbon dioxide and wastes are removed. (p. 95)

27. False—It's the genome of the fetus. (p. 95)

28. an adaptation in pregnancy (p. 96)

29. True—Morning sickness is understood to be a mechanism that protects the developing fetus. (p. 96)

30. negativity; adaptation (pp. 96–97)

Brain Development

1. over 100 billion (p. 97)

2. Answer:
- Dendrites receive electrical signals from nearby neurons.
- Axons conduct electrical signals from the cell body to the axon terminals. (p. 97)

3. synapse (p. 97)

4. 80 per cent; 20 per cent (p. 97)

5. neurons (p. 97)

6. 250,000 (pp. 97–98)

7. Neurons migrate in the following way:
- Neurons are produced near the centre of the brain.
- Some are passively pushed outwards by new cells that were created after them.
- Other neurons seek their destination using a chemical attraction between the migrating neuron and the target. (p. 98)

8. 7 months (p. 98)

9. arborization (p. 98)

10. Myelination has the following effects:
    - The process of myelination encases the axons of neurons in a myelin sheath.
    - The myelin sheath acts as an insulator and allows efficient transmission of electrical impulses. (p. 98)

11. Synaptogenesis refers to the growth of synapses between neurons. (p. 98)

12. parts of the brain (e.g. synaptogenesis peaks the visual cortex years before it peaks in the prefrontal cortex) (p. 98)

13. False—Synaptic pruning is a normal (and quite important) part of development. (p. 98)

14. plasticity (p. 98)

15. 1. left

    d) processes sensory information from and sends motor commands to the right side of the body

    c) processes language information (usually)

  2. right

    a) processes sensory information from and sends motor commands to the left side of the body

    b) thought to be more involved in spatial thinking and visual imagery (p. 99)

16. False—Hemispheric specialization continues through infancy and childhood but it appears to starts earlier (before birth). (p. 99)

Practice Test 1: Answer Key

1. **b** (p. 64)	8. **a** (p. 77)	15. **c** (p. 89)	22. **b** (p. 96)
2. **d** (p. 69)	9. **b** (p. 78)	16. **b** (p. 90)	23. **a** (p. 98)
3. **d** (p. 70)	10. **c** (p. 81)	17. **d** (p. 91)	24. **c** (p. 98)
4. **c** (pp. 72–73)	11. **d** (p. 85)	18. **d** (p. 92)	25. **b** (p. 99)
5. **a** (p. 73)	12. **b** (p. 86)	19. **c** (p. 95)	
6. **c** (p. 75)	13. **a** (p. 87)	20. **d** (p. 95)	
7. **d** (p. 77)	14. **b** (p. 89)	21. **a** (p. 95)	

Practice Test 2: Answer Key

1. **b** (p. 69)	8. **c** (pp. 82–83)	15. **b** (p. 91)	22. **a** (p. 97)
2. **a** (p. 71)	9. **c** (p. 83)	16. **a** (p. 91)	23. **b** (p. 97)
3. **d** (p. 72)	10. **d** (p. 84)	17. **a** (p. 94)	24. **d** (p. 98)
4. **c** (p. 74)	11. **a** (p. 86)	18. **d** (p. 95)	25. **c** (p. 99)
5. **d** (p. 76)	12. **b** (p. 89)	19. **b** (p. 95)	
6. **b** (p. 80)	13. **c** (p. 91)	20. **c** (p. 96)	
7. **a** (pp. 80–81)	14. **d** (p. 89)	21. **c** (p. 97)	

Chapter 4
Nature, Nurture, and Development

Chapter Summary

Understanding Nature and Nurture

The *standard social science model* (*SSSM*) summarizes the common view of human nature in recent decades. This model assumes that the mind has no initial content, that biology is irrelevant to human culture, and that the human mind has only a few general learning mechanisms.

All traits are the product of a complex interplay between genes and environmental influences; therefore the nature vs. nurture question is nonsensical.

Causality

It is overly simplistic to attribute an outcome to a *cause*. Outcomes have *causes*. In addition to multiple causes, outcomes are made possible by non-causal factors. Psychological experiments are aimed at isolating the contribution of a single cause. Human intuition leads us to seek a single cause for an event (the fallacy of exclusive determinism). While useful in everyday life, scientists should guard against this intuitive limitation and acknowledge that events, artifacts, and organisms have multiple causes.

Heritability

It is important to interpret the *heritability statistic* correctly. It is *not* an indicator of how much a trait was caused by genes and the environment respectively. Rather, the heritability statistic indicates how much variation in the human population can be accounted for statistically by differences in genes or the environment. Calculating this statistic does not require a good understanding of how development occurs and the value of this statistic does not imply much about how development occurs.

The Heritability Statistic

Francis Galton introduced the idea that psychological traits and characteristics might be inheritable. Among his lasting contributions to the field: using twins to estimate heritability, regression analysis, and the correlation statistic. The heritability statistic is a modification of the correlation statistic.

IQ Heritability as an Example

IQ is somewhat unique in the realm of developmental testing in that the approach to its study has always been ideographic rather than normative. In the early 1900s, Binet and Simon created an intelligence test with the aim of predicting children's success in school. Since then, IQ tests have been continually refined and standardized. The Stanford–Binet Intelligence Scale and the Wechsler tests are examples of current IQ tests. Both are intended for use with children and both focus on skills that are relevant for school performance.

IQ scores are associated with academic and professional achievement, bolstering confidence in their validity; however, they are not perfect predictors. Similarly, IQ scores show a fair bit of stability over time but they are not perfectly stable.

Estimates of heritability can be calculated by comparing the concordance among closely-related people to the concordance among less closely-related people. More specifically, family studies of intelligence examine concordance of IQ across known genetic relatedness. The relationship between IQ and genetic relatedness is strong but not perfect. Adoption studies examine concordance of IQ between children and their adoptive- and biologically-related family members. The concordance between children and their biologically-related family members tends to be stronger than with their adoptive families. Twin studies compare monozygotic twins to dizygotic twins, taking advantage of the difference in shared genome between the two types. The concordance between monozygotic twins tends to be higher than between dizygotic twins. Family, adoption, and twins studies all have specific limitations and none have provided much of an explanation for *how* intelligence develops.

The heritability statistic must be calculated over a large population to avoid skewing, especially for rare traits. As well, the trait must vary across the population otherwise, there is no variance to attribute to genes (or anything else). The heritability statistic measures variance in the expressed trait and not variance in genes or environment. This is a practical matter; at this point, variance in the expressed trait is the only thing we know *how* to measure. The heritability statistic varies across groups. It may change depending on the location, historical time period, or age of the population.

Knowledge of how intelligence develops cannot be gained from the heritability statistic; however, longitudinal studies have revealed environmental factors in the home (related to parenting styles, among other things) that are associated with IQ. Ethnic groups differ on IQ scores. These differences may be explained by ethnic differences in economic status and attitudes about education. As well, IQ tests may have an inherent cultural bias in terms of content and communication style.

Wrapping Up Heritability: What It Is Not

Heritability does not indicate how much of a trait comes from genes or from the environment. It does not indicate whether a trait is unchangeable (and, in fact, it can be artificially manipulated). It does not indicate whether a trait is inherited.

Facultative Adaptation

Learning is obviously influenced by the environment, but that's not to say that evolution or biological influences do not play a role. In fact, learning mechanisms are themselves naturally selected adaptations.

Facultative adaptations increase fitness by allowing for adjustments to a particular environment. They are adaptations that are designed to respond to possible environments in the EEA. For example, an individual's exposure to sunlight would have varied in the EEA. The ability to suntan protected any individual who needed it. More complex psychological facultative adaptations exist for such things as language learning and parental investment.

When an aspect of the environment is stable over many generations, it is more efficient for an organism to rely on the information in the environment rather than storing it in the genome. The ability to remain flexible to changing aspects of the environment is also an advantage.

There are two broad classes of learning mechanisms: experience-expectant and experience-dependent. Experience-expectant learning produces changes in the brain in response to stimuli that all members of the species experience in a species-typical environment. There is often a critical period for this type of learning, a specific time period during which this learning can take place. For example, in order for vision to be normal (for the brain to 'learn how to see'), an individual must be exposed to visual stimuli early on. Experience-dependent learning produces changes in the brain in response to individual, specific information. Learning to speak English, for example, involves exposure to English words. Experience-dependent learning is not restricted to critical periods.

The relationship between a specific environmental factor and a measurable phenotypic expression is referred to as a norm of reaction. A specific environmental setting will lead not to one specific phenotype but to a range of possibilities.

There Are Many Types of Learning

Learning mechanisms allow for learning (quite obviously). These mechanisms have been designed by natural selection. How we learn (which mechanism) depends on what we are learning. Further, the effects of the environment depend on learning mechanisms. Clearly, one general-purpose learning mechanism would be insufficient to support our myriad of abilities.

Prepared Learning

Contrary to the ideas of John B. Watson and B. F. Skinner, the human mind does not seem to be equally open to *any* association. Garcia and Mineka found that rats will avoid food that was followed by nausea but not food that was followed by an electric shock. Because of conditions in the EEA, rats are prepared to make the association between food and nausea but not food and shocks. Humans are also more prepared to learn some associations over others. For example, many of us associate danger (and, therefore, fear) with snakes but few associate danger with cars.

Learning Objectives

After reading this chapter, you should be able to:

- Understand the basics of the standard social science model (pp. 106–107)
- Recognize the false dichotomy of nature vs. nurture (pp. 107–109)
- Examine the nature of causality (pp. 109–110)
- Conceptualize heritability and the heritability statistic (pp. 111–115)
- Explore heritability using IQ as an example (pp. 116–124)
- Consolidate your knowledge of heritability by reviewing what it is *not* (pp. 124–128)
- Appreciate the flexibility and environmental responsiveness provided by facultative adaptations (pp. 128–132)
- Differentiate between experience-expectant and experience-dependent learning (pp. 132–134)
- Discuss the environment–phenotype norm of reaction (pp. 135–136)
- Think about the complexity of learning mechanisms and the questions that could be asked about them (p. 136)
- Explain how organisms are 'prepared' to learn (pp. 137–139)

Suggested Readings

Plomin, R., DeFries, J. C., & Fulker, D. W. (2006). *Nature and Nurture During Infancy and Early Childhood*. New York: Cambridge University Press.

This book explains the development of individual differences by looking at the interaction of heredity and environment.

Skinner, B. F. (1948). *Walden Two*. Indianapolis, IN: Hackett Publishing Company.

B. F. Skinner outlines his fictional modern utopia, created by knowledge of human behaviour.

Garcia, J., Kimeldorf, D. J., and Koelling, R. A. (1955). Conditioned aversion to saccharin resulting from exposure to gamma radiation. *Science, 122,* 157–158.

This short paper describes Garcia's ground-breaking findings with rats.

Study Questions

Understanding Nature and Nurture

1. What killed Henry Ziegland, the dynamite or the bullet?

2. SSSM stands for _____.

3. What is the SSSM?

4. Which are assumptions of the SSSM?

5. The SSSM acknowledges two types of learning: _____ and _____.

6. What does it mean to say that the SSSM includes an assumption of associationism?

7. What would you estimate are the relative contributions of genes and environment to the trait of creativity?

Causality

1. True or False: One outcome has one cause.

2. Define the 'fallacy of exclusive determinism'.

Heritability

1. True or False: A heritability statistic tells you the percentage of a trait that was caused by heredity.

2. True or False: The heritability statistic gives us an idea of whether or not a medical condition is treatable.

3. Robert Plomin, who is quoted in the textbook, does *not* say that height is due more to genetic contribution than to an environmental contribution. What does he say instead (about height)?

4. True or False: In order to calculate the heritability statistic, you must first have some understanding of how development progresses.

5. Humidity and temperature account for variance in snowflake formation. What does that tell us about how snowflakes are formed?

The Heritability Statistic

1. Galton concluded that nature was a greater contributor to 'eminence' than nurture because _____.

2. Galton's (above) conclusion is suspect because _____.

3. Galton created _____ analysis, which allows for estimating the relationship between various measures.

4. The _____ statistic was modified to create the heritability statistic.

5. Define the 'heritability statistic'.

6. What is the mathematical formula for the heritability statistic?

IQ Heritability as an Example

1. As a developmental psychologist, how might you use the heritability statistic?

2. How has the purpose of intelligence testing been different from the purpose of other types of developmental testing?

3. What was Binet and Simon's original goal in measuring intelligence?

4. Besides Binet and Simon, who was another very early intelligence tester?

5. What are two commonly-used current IQ tests?

6. The scores on the WPPSI-III and the WISC-IV are sub-divided into four scales. What are they?

7. Outline some evidence for the validity of IQ scores.

8. The correlation between Stanford–Binet IQ scores and academic performance is in the range of
_____.

9. True or False: Measures of IQ are very stable over time.

10. True or False: The correlation of IQ scores at ages 6 and 12 is lower than the correlation of IQ scores at ages 6 and 9.

11. Miguel has an extremely high IQ score at the age of 10. What, in general, would you predict about what Miguel will be like at the age of 40?

12. In family studies of intelligence, IQ is compared across known _____.

13. In ten words or less, what do family studies tell us about IQ and genetic relatedness?

14. Family studies alone can be hard to interpret. Why?

15. Adoption studies compare the correlation of a trait between _____ to the correlation of the trait between _____.

16. True or False: Rob grew up with an adoptive family. His adoptive family members have relatively low IQ scores. His biological family members have relatively high IQ scores. Based on general findings from adoption studies, we would predict that Rob's IQ is relatively low.

17. What are some things to keep in mind about adoptions that may complicate findings from adoption studies?

18. Dr. Tsang collected IQ scores for monozygotic and dizygotic twins. She found that the correlation for monozygotic twins is .90 and for dizygotic twins is .50. What is the calculated heritability?

19. Comparing monozygotic to dizygotic twins can help disentangle _____ and _____.

20. The heritability statistic must be calculated over a large population because _____.

21. True or False: Negligible variance in the trait of interest would result is a high heritability statistic.

22. Keep in mind: the heritability statistic measures variance in the _____. There is no practical way to measure variance in _____ or _____.

23. True or False: The correlation of IQ between siblings raised together is lower than the correlation of IQ between monozygotic twins raised apart.

24. Why might the calculated heritability of IQ differ across different studies?

25. In infancy, the heritability of IQ is _____ than in adolescence.

26. As environments become more uniform, heritability _____.

27. Longitudinal studies have examined the relationship between home environment characteristics and children's IQ scores. What environmental factors have been shown to be important?

28. Using the Carolina Abecedarian Project as your model, how would you go about providing educational resources to low SES groups of children (in order to increase IQ scores and educational achievement)?

29. Why might there be differences in IQ scores between ethnic groups?

Wrapping Up Heritability: What It Is Not

1. True or False: When heritability of a trait is 100 per cent, we know that there are no environmental circumstances that can affect development of that trait.

2. What three things does the heritability statistic not tell you?

3. What is an example of a trait in which the heritability statistic is very high but environmental influences can have dramatic effects?

4. What is an example of an inherited trait with a very low heritability statistic?

5. True or False: Adaptations have a very low heritability.

6. Define a 'human universal'.

7. What are some examples of human universals?

8. Underlying those behavioural universals is a(n) _____.

9. The skin colour thought experiment described in the textbook is meant to demonstrate that _____.

Facultative Adaptation

1. What's the problem with talking about learning as if it is an alternative to biological processes?

2. Define 'facultative adaptations'.

3. Facultative adaptations evolved because of _____ in the EEA.

4. What are some examples of facultative adaptations?

5. The level of parental investment one experiences in early childhood signals to the developing child which _____ will be the most fruitful strategy.

6. What are the advantages of being born cognitively immature but equipped with learning mechanisms?

7. Explain how our reliance on the environment may be necessary given the limitations of our nervous system.

8. What does it mean to say that we can 'store information' in the environment?

9. What is an example of an environmental cue that humans rely on?

10. Match the following types of adaptations with the corresponding descriptions.

   1. facultative
   a) those that develop when they become functional in the current environment

   2. obligate
   b) those that develop reliably as long as the individual is developing in a species-typical environment

11. Define 'experience-expectant learning mechanism'.

12. What are some examples of experience-expectant learning?

13. Define 'experience-dependant learning mechanism'.

14. What are some examples of experience-dependant learning?

15. Match the following types of learning with the corresponding descriptions.

   1. experience-expectant learning
   a) varies a great deal between individuals

   b) largely universal

   c) reliant on idiosyncratic environment

   2. experience-dependant learning
   d) continues throughout the lifespan

   e) relies on what the genome 'expects'

   f) critical period

16. Some forms of learning can *only* take place during a _____.

17. A time period during which a specific kind of learning most easily takes place is referred to as a
_____.

18. Researchers speculate that in order to develop the ability to perceive and pursue mealworms, a chick must be able to _____.

19. The chick–toe phenomenon described above is an example of _____.

20. What happens if a cat is completely deprived of visual stimuli to one eye early in life?

21. What brain differences have been found between rats reared in a complex, interesting environment and rats reared in a simple, deprived environment?

22. Behaviourally, the rats reared in complex environments were better at _____.

23. What brain differences have been found between violinists/cellists and other musicians?

24. Compared to matched control subjects, those who can read _____ have more cortical cells dedicated to one hand.

25. Define 'norm of reaction'.

26. Norms of reaction can vary dramatically from one _____ to another.

27. What's stopping us from mapping out all the norms of reaction in humans?

There Are Many Types of Learning

1. Asking how much of a trait is innate and how much is learned is of limited interest. The textbook outlines some more interesting questions that we may ask about learning. What are they?

Prepared Learning

1. How would John B. Watson have explained prepared learning?

2. What was the theme of B. F. Skinner's books (e.g. *Walden Two, Beyond Freedom and Dignity*)?

3. John Garcia's and Susan Mineka's research suggests that the mind is not a _____.

4. Garcia found that a rat seemed to develop an aversion to a food if two things were true. What were the two things?

5. How could you explain this food aversion learning in rats with reference to the EEA?

6. The food aversion learning in rats is an example of _____.

7. The learned associations of Garcia's rats were surprising in terms of number of exposures because _____.

8. The learned associations of Garcia's rats were surprising in terms of delay time because _____.

9. True or False: When Garcia paired sweetened water with an electric shock, the rats learned to avoid the sweet water.

10. In ten words or less, why are some associations relatively easily learned?

11. Through observational learning, monkeys can be trained to fear a _____ but not a _____.

12. Similar to monkeys, humans are more likely to develop phobias to _____ stimuli.

Practice Test 1

1. Who/what killed Henry Ziegland?

    a. his ex-girlfriend's brother
    b. the bullet
    c. the dynamite
    d. all of the above and none of the above

2. SSSM stands for

    a. standard statistical sociology model.
    b. social science statistics model.
    c. scientific selection set model.
    d. standard social science model.

3. What portion of the trait of extroversion is attributable to experience and what portion is due to genetics?

    a. It's about 50:50.
    b. Since extraversion is a psychological and not a physical trait, it is reasonable to assume that environment plays a larger role than genetics.
    c. This is not a reasonable question.
    d. none of the above

4. Experiments

    a. are aimed at determining the single cause of an event.
    b. use statistics to isolate the contribution of a particular cause of an event.
    c. attempt to determine the non-causal factors involved in an event.
    d. are aimed at determining how many causes underlie an event.

5. The snowflake analogy described in the textbook is meant to illustrate that

    a. much can be learned from examining snowflakes.
    b. outcomes are always the result of many factors.
    c. a complete understanding of an outcome can be derived from knowledge of *which* factors contribute to the outcome.
    d. we may understand *which* factors contribute to an outcome without understanding *how* the outcome occurs

6. Heritability =

    a. $$\frac{V(genes)}{V(genes) + V(environment) + V(g*e)}$$

    b. $$\frac{V(environment)}{V(genes) + V(environment) + V(g*e)}$$

    c. $$\frac{V(genes)}{V(environment) + V(g*e)}$$

    d. $$\frac{V(environment)}{V(genes) + V(g*e)}$$

7. The study of intelligence has always differed from other developmental topics in that it has been

    a. correlational.
    b. associationist.
    c. normative.
    d. ideographic.

8. Which of the following is *not* a current IQ test?

    a. WPPSI-III
    b. Stanford–Binet Intelligence Scale
    c. WECH-II
    d. WISC-IV

9. The Wechsler test of intelligence includes four scales that include all but one of the following:

    a. use of logic
    b. processing speed
    c. perceptual reasoning
    d. working memory

10. The heritability of IQ

    a. decreases with age.
    b. increases with age.
    c. increases and then decreases with age.
    d. is the same across ages.

11. Heritability =

    a. (correlation between monozygotic twins – correlation between dizygotic twins)/2
    b. (correlation between monozygotic twins + correlation between dizygotic twins)/2
    c. (correlation between monozygotic twins – correlation between dizygotic twins) x 2
    d. (correlation between monozygotic twins + correlation between dizygotic twins) x 2

12. Which of the following statements is *not* true regarding IQ correlations?

    a. Correlations between siblings raised apart are higher than between adoptive siblings.
    b. Correlations between monozygotic twins raised apart are higher than between dizygotic twins raised together.
    c. Correlations between dizygotic twins raised together are higher than between siblings raised together.
    d. Correlations between adoptive siblings are higher than between adoptive parents/adoptive children.

13. A longitudinal study described in the textbook listed risk factors associated with declines in IQ. All of the following were listed *except*

    a. lack of affection from the mother.
    b. being an only child.
    c. authoritarian parenting.
    d. unemployed head of household.

14. Which of the following have low heritability estimates?

    a. adaptations
    b. number of fingers and toes
    c. human universals
    d. all of the above

15. Standardizing the environment such that everyone is exposed to a very small range of environment types will lead to

    a. more variance overall.
    b. genetic variance
    c. high heritability.
    d. low heritability.

16. Speaking of traits as either 'evolved' or 'learned' ignores the fact that

    a. psychological mechanisms are never the result of evolution.
    b. learning is always secondary to evolution.
    c. the two act in opposition.
    d. learning mechanisms are designed by natural selection.

17. Which of the following is *not* an example of experience-expectant learning?

   a. skilled fingering in violinists.
   b. vertical/horizontal line perception in cats
   c. mealworm detection in chicks
   d. language comprehension in humans

18. Language learning is aided by the fact that

   a. all the necessary information is provided by the genome.
   b. very young children orient selectively to faces.
   c. genes and environment do not interact in complicated ways.
   d. there is no critical period for language abilities.

19. Experience-dependent learning

   a. involves a critical period.
   b. involves mechanisms that optimize the relationship between one's brain and one's idiosyncratic environment.
   c. is necessary for normal brain development to result.
   d. relies on environmental cues that remain unchanged over generations.

20. Which of the following is *not* an example of experience-dependant learning?

   a. learning the alphabet
   b. learning to walk
   c. learning to ride a bike
   d. learning to skeet shoot

21. It is necessary to talk of norms of reaction because

   a. there are many types of learning.
   b. psychologists take a normative approach to the study of human characteristics.
   c. there is no one-to-one relationship between an environmental factor and its phenotypic effect.
   d. none of the above

22. Garcia noticed that rats developed an aversion to food if

   a. the rat ate the food just after being exposed to radiation and the food had been eaten by the rat in the past.
   b. the rat ate the food just prior to being exposed to radiation and the food had been eaten by the rat in the past.
   c. the rat ate the food just after being exposed to radiation and the food was previously unknown to the rat.
   d. the rat ate the food just prior to being exposed to radiation and the food was previously unknown to the rat.

23. Garcia's rats learned to associate food with nausea after

    a. a single exposure.
    b. several exposures.
    c. many exposures.
    d. zero exposures.

24. How did Mineka's monkeys learn to fear a boa constrictor?

    a. They were classically conditioned.
    b. They were rewarded for displaying fear of the snake.
    c. They watched a video of another monkey displaying fear of the snake.
    d. They were bitten by a snake.

25. Garcia's and Mineka's findings with rats and monkeys were quite devastating to

    a. the blank slate view of development.
    b. cognitive psychologists.
    c. proponents of nurture over nature.
    d. geneticists.

Practice Test 2

1. All of the following are assumptions of the SSSM *except*

    a. biology is irrelevant to human behaviour and psychology.
    b. there are only a few, very general learning mechanisms.
    c. the human mind is a mostly blank slate at birth.
    d. it is impossible to identify a single cause of an event.

2. The fact that we have a strong intuition that we should be able to identify a single cause for any event is referred to as

    a. the fallacy of exclusive determinism.
    b. the single cause hypothesis.
    c. the fallacy of single causes.
    d. the causal myth.

3. Which of the following statements is *not* true about Sir Francis Galton?

    a. He was the first to use the terms 'nature' and 'nurture' with regard to development.
    b. He concluded that environmental factors were more important to development than heredity.
    c. He was Charles Darwin's cousin.
    d. He made lasting contributions to the realm of statistical analysis.

4. If the heritability of introversion is .47, then

    a. 47 per cent of the trait of introversion is controlled by the genotype.
    b. 53 per cent of the trait of introversion is environmentally-determined.
    c. the proportion of variance in introversion that is attributable to genetic differences among individuals is .47.
    d. both *a* and *b*

5. The heritability statistic was created by modifying the _____ statistic.

    a. correlation
    b. mean
    c. regression
    d. standard deviation

6. The heritability estimate is best used for

    a. pinpointing developmental causes.
    b. determining trait stability.
    c. examining the role of genetics.
    d. providing clues for testing a hypothesis.

7. The modern enterprise of measuring intelligence started

    a. in the United States.
    b. early in the last century.
    c. for the purpose of testing army recruits.
    d. as a way to identify gifted children.

8. Which of the following statements is true about IQ scores?

    a. The relationship between IQ measured at one point in childhood and IQ measured at another point in childhood is weak.
    b. They are positively correlated with adult occupational status.
    c. The correlation of IQ scores between first cousins is higher than the correlation of IQ scores between grandparents and grandchildren.
    d. There is a greater concordance of IQ scores between adoptive family members than biologically-related family members.

9. As environments become less uniform, heritability

    a. becomes unstable.
    b. remains the same.
    c. decreases.
    d. increases.

10. Which of the following statements is true regarding IQ correlations?

    a. Correlations between first cousins are about the same as between grandparents/grandchildren.
    b. Correlations between parent/child are higher than between siblings.
    c. Correlations between ages 12 and 18 are higher than between ages 12 and 9.
    d. Correlations between ages 3 and 12 are higher than between ages 3 and 9.

11. In order to calculate the heritability statistic,

    a. there must be an interaction between genes and the environment.
    b. there must be appreciable variance in the trait.
    c. it is necessary to focus on a small population.
    d. none of the above

12. All of the following were discussed in the textbook as possible explanations for differences in IQ scores between different ethnic groups *except*

    a. differences in parents' attitudes toward education.
    b. economic differences.
    c. genetic differences.
    d. differences in access to medical care.

13. Results from the Carolina Abecedarian Project indicate that

    a. educational resources may help improve IQ scores but only for high SES groups.
    b. interventions to improve IQ scores are only effective if the intervention continues throughout childhood.
    c. interventions to improve IQ scores should start in infancy.
    d. educational resources are unlikely to have much of an impact on IQ scores.

14. Heritability does *not* tell us

    a. whether a trait is inherited.
    b. whether a trait is treatable.
    c. whether a trait is immutable
    d. all of the above

15. Which of the following is *not* example of a facultative adaptation?

    a. eye colour
    b. skin calluses
    c. suntanning
    d. language learning

16. We humans are born cognitively immature but equipped with learning mechanisms. That is a good thing for all of the following reasons *except*

    a. We are unable to 'store information in the environment'.
    b. We use regularities in the environment to make development more efficient.
    c. We don't overload our genome with the responsibility of directing the creation of billions of neuronal synapses.
    d. We are able to adjust to changes in the environment.

17. Forms of learning that take place most easily at a certain time are said to have a(n)

    a. ideal phase.
    b. sensitive period.
    c. receptive phase.
    d. critical period.

18. Language learning involves

    a. experience-expectant learning.
    b. experience-dependant learning
    c. both *a* and *b*
    d. neither *a* nor *b*

19. Experience-expectant and experience-dependant learning may also be referred to as

    a. plasticity.
    b. heritability.
    c. interactionism.
    d. specified learning.

20. Mapping out the norms of reaction

    a. is a necessary precursor to learning about development.
    b. is pointless.
    c. has already been done for most human traits.
    d. would be costly and time-consuming.

21. Which of the following is a false dichotomy?

    a. learned vs. innate
    b. nature vs. nurture
    c. biology vs. culture
    d. all of the above

22. B. F. Skinner wrote books for a non-scientific audience that encouraged people to think that _____ could be used to create a utopia.

   a. genetics
   b. modern advances in the understanding of psychology
   c. natural selection
   d. facultative adaptations

23. Garcia's rats could learn to associate _____ with a red light.

   a. an electric shock
   b. nausea
   c. anything
   d. nothing

24. Prepared learning is the result of

   a. frequent pairings of stimuli.
   b. evolutionary history.
   c. a norm of reaction.
   d. practice.

25. The take-home message from Garcia's and Mineka's work with rats and monkeys is that

   a. the mind is (initially) a blank slate.
   b. experience-expectant learning is more important than experience-dependant learning.
   c. some associations are learned more easily than others.
   d. you shouldn't work with rats and monkeys.

Study Questions: Answer Key

Understanding Nature and Nurture

1. What killed Henry Ziegland?
   - The point of this story is that this is an unanswerable question.
   - The bullet without the dynamite wouldn't have killed him and the dynamite without the bullet wouldn't have killed him. One was not more important than the other.
   - In the same way, nature and nurture both contribute to development. It is not a matter of one or the other. (p. 105)

2. standard social science model (p. 106)

3. The SSSM
   - is a summary of current thoughts about human nature.
   - includes the assumptions that underlie more undergraduate curriculum and popular press reports on human issues. (p. 106)

4. The assumptions of the SSSM include the following:
   - The human mind is more or less a blank slate at birth.
   - Biology is irrelevant to human behaviour and psychology.
   - There are not many *specific* learning mechanisms but rather very few, very *general* learning mechanisms. (p. 106)

5. classical conditioning; operant conditioning (p. 106)

6. Associationism proposes that learning happens by associating one stimulus with another or by associating a behaviour with a reward or punishment. This is part of the learning assumption of the SSSM. (pp. 106–107)

7. Consider the following in your response:
   - This is not a reasonable question.
   - A change in genes would change the outcome. A change in environment would also change outcome. Since both are important, it makes no sense to ask which is *more* important. (p. 108)

Causality

1. False—Any outcome always has multiple causes. (p. 109)

2. The fallacy of exclusive determinism refers to the fact that we have a very strong intuition that we should be able to identify a single cause for any event. (p. 110)

Heritability

1. False (p. 111)

2. False—The heritability estimate, whether high or low, is not an indication of treatability. (p. 111)

3. Robert Plomin says that *differences* in height among individuals are due more to *differences* in genes among individuals than *differences* in environmental input among individuals. This is a crucial distinction. (p. 112)

4. False (p. 112)

5. Knowledge of variation in snowflakes really doesn't tell us much at all about how snowflakes are formed. In the same way, an estimate of variation that can be statistically accounted for by differences in genes (i.e. heritability) does not give an *understanding* of development. (pp. 112–113)

The Heritability Statistic

1. people who had reached eminence were likely to be related to each other (p. 114)

2. he made no attempt to control for environmental factors (p. 115)

3. regression (p. 115)

4. correlation (p. 115)

5. The heritability statistic is the estimate of the proportion of the measured variance in a trait among individuals in a given population that is attributable to genetic differences among those individuals. (p. 115)

6. $\text{Heritability} = \dfrac{V(\text{genes})}{V(\text{genes}) + V(\text{environment}) + V(g*e)}$ (p. 114)

IQ Heritability as an Example

1. Probably the best use of the heritability statistic is to help provide clues as to what hypotheses might be worth testing. (p. 116)

2. The purpose of intelligence testing has been different in the following ways:
    *   Unlike other types of developmental testing, the purpose of intelligence testing has been to measure differences between individuals.
    *   The approach to intelligence testing has been 'ideographic' rather than normative. (p. 116)

3. They created the Binet–Simon Intelligence Test to identify French schoolchildren who needed special/remedial education. (p. 116)

4. The US Army embraced intelligence testing for recruits for World War I. (p. 116)

5. Two commonly-used current IQ tests are
    *   the Stanford–Binet Intelligence Scale (derived from the Binet–Simon test).
    *   the Wechsler tests. (p. 116)

6. The four scales on the WPPSI-III and the WISC-IV are
    *   verbal comprehension
    *   perceptual reasoning
    *   working memory
    *   processing speed (p. 117)

7. Consider the following in your response:
    *   The Stanford–Binet is correlated with academic performance.
    *   Intelligence tests correlate with adult occupational status. (p. 117)

8. .50–.60 (p. 117)

9. False—They are only somewhat stable over time. (p. 117)

10. True—The correlation diminishes as the age interval increases. (p. 117)

11. Based on Miguel's IQ score,
    *   it is somewhat likely (though certainly not definite) that he will have done well academically and professionally.
    *   it is somewhat likely (though certainly not definite) that he will still have a high IQ score. (p. 117)

12. genetic relatedness (p. 117)

13. There is a strong but imperfect relationship between them. (p. 117)

14. Family studies can be hard to interpret because families share not only genes but environmental aspects such as education and economic circumstance. (p. 118)

15. adopted children and their adoptive parents; biologically related family members living in different households (p. 118)

16. False—In general, findings indicate that there is a greater concordance of IQ scores between biologically-related than adoptive relatives. (p. 118)

17. Consider the following in your response:
    *   Adoption agencies tend to match adoptive children with adoptive parents on a number of factors.
    *   Adoptive families are kind of a special group—not everyone has the motivation or socio-economic status to adopt. (p. 118)

18. $(.90–.50) \times 2 = .80$ (p. 119)

19. shared genes; shared environments (p. 119)

20. the results from a small group would be skewed, especially for rare traits (p. 120)

21. False—Negligible variance would render the heritability statistic meaningless. There would be no variance to attribute to genes or any other source. (p. 120)

22. expressed trait; genes; environmental factors (p. 120)

23. True (pp. 120–121)

24. Consider the following in your response:
    - In addition to methodological differences, the heritability of IQ is different in different populations.
    - Population variables that may affect IQ heritability include location, historical time period, and age group. (p. 120)

25. lower (p. 120)

26. rises (p. 121)

27. Lower IQ scores are associated with
    - unemployed head of household
    - mother with no high school diploma
    - four or more children in the family
    - absent father
    - authoritarian parenting
    - unusually high maternal anxiety
    - poor mental health of mother
    - lack of affection from mother
    - little effort by parents to contribute to intellectual development
    - extremely severe or extremely lax discipline

    Higher IQ scores are associated with
    - parental emphasis on intellectual acceleration
    - consistent discipline (p. 122)

28. To increase IQ scores and educational achievement of low SES groups of children,
    - start early (in infancy).
    - deliver intensive intervention through daily educational activities.
    - continue the intervention for a significant period of time (five years or more). (p. 123)

29. There may be differences in IQ scores between different groups because
    - there may be economic differences between groups.
    - there may be differences in parents' attitudes toward education between groups.
    - there may be bias in the IQ tests in terms of content and communication style. (pp. 123–124)

Wrapping Up Heritability: What It Is Not

1. False—There could still exist environmental circumstances that would affect development of the trait. (p. 124)

2. Things the heritability statistic does not tell you are
    - how much of a trait comes from genes or from the environment;
    - whether a trait is immutable;
    - whether a trait is inherited. (p. 124)

3. Phenylketonuria is highly heritable but a change diet (an environment factor) can completely prevent any disability. (p. 125)

4. Consider the following in your response:
   - Number of fingers and toes is certainly inherited but the heritability statistic for that trait is very low.
   - There is very little variance in the total number of fingers and toes, and most of variance is due to environment (e.g. accidents, etc.) (p. 126)

5. True—Natural selection lowers variability (e.g. non-white rabbits are quickly eaten by predators in the snow). (p. 127)

6. A human universal is a trait or characteristic that you would find in any human group on earth. (p. 128)

7. All human groups on earth
   - are social
   - live in groups
   - have status and hierarchy within groups
   - have and observe rules regarding politeness and etiquette
   - live in families
   - exchange gifts
   - etc. (p. 128)

8. evolved cognitive adaptation (p. 128)

9. heritability can be artificially manipulated (p. 128)

Facultative Adaptation

1. The problem is that learning mechanisms are designed by natural selection and are, therefore, adaptations themselves. (pp. 128–130)

2. A facultative adaptation is one that is designed to respond to specific cues in the environment, thus preparing organisms for the varying conditions that were possible in the EEA. (p. 130)

3. variance (p. 130)

4. Some examples of facultative adaptations are
   - calluses on hands and feet as a result of friction on the skin
   - a suntan in response to the skin's exposure to ultraviolet radiation (p. 130)

5. life-cycle strategy (early development and reproduction or abstinence until marriage) (pp. 130–131)

6. Consider the following in your response:
   - It can be more efficient not to burden the genome with things that are always there in the environment.
   - Circumstances change and it is good to be able to adjust to the changes. (p. 131)

7. Consider the following in your response:
   - In our brains, here are billions and billions of connections between neurons.
   - Our genome (composed of only about 30,000 genes) just doesn't have the resources to control everything. (p. 131)

8. To say that information can be 'stored in the environment' means that if some aspect of the environment is constant across many generations, it makes sense for the organism to rely on the information in the environment rather than taking up precious genetic space. (p. 131)

9. An environmental cue that humans rely on is the sun, which rises and sets predictably (and always has). We use this for calibrating internal schedules. (p. 131)

10. 1. facultative   a) those that develop when they become functional in the current environment
    2. obligate   b) those that develop reliably as long as the individual is developing in a species-typical environment (pp. 131–132)

11. An experience-expectant learning mechanism is one that is designed to respond to species-typical environmental input, usually during a critical period, in order for normal brain development to result. (p. 133)

12. Some examples of experience-expectant learning are
    • learning a language
    • learning to walk (p. 133)

13. An experience-dependant learning mechanism is one that responds to individual, specific information. (p. 134)

14. Some examples of experience-dependant learning are
    • learning a specific language
    • learning algebra (p. 134)

15. 1. experience-expectant learning   f) critical period
                                          b) largely universal
                                          e) relies on what the genome 'expects'

    2. experience-dependant learning   d) continues throughout the lifespan
                                          a) varies a great deal between individuals
                                          c) reliant on idiosyncratic environment

    (pp. 132–134)

16. critical period (p. 133)

17. sensitive period (p. 133)

18. see his own toes (p. 133)

19. experience-expectant learning (p. 133)

20. Consider the following in your response:
    • The cat will be blind in that eye.
    • Each eye needs visual stimulation during the critical period to learn to see. (pp. 133–134)

21. The rats raised in the complex environment had
    • more neuronal dendritic extensions
    • more synapses on each neuron
    • more synapses overall
    • thicker cortex (p. 134)

22. learning new things later in life (p. 134)

23. Consider the following in your response:
    - Violinists and cellists use their left hands to manipulate strings.
    - They have
        - more cortical cells in the brain area controlling the left hand.
        - more cortical cells in the brain area receiving sensory information from the left hand. (p. 134)

24. Braille (p. 134)

25. Norm of reaction describes the relationship between a specific environmental factor and a measurable phenotypic expression. (p. 135)

26. genotype (p. 135)

27. We have not mapped out all the norms of reaction in humans because
    - although such research could, it would be costly and time-consuming.
    - there would be ethical concerns. (p. 135)

There Are Many Types of Learning

1. Some interesting questions we can ask about learning include the following:
    - What is the design of the child's mind that allows it to learn?
    - How do particular learning mechanisms learn?
    - What content is needed for learning?
    - What input is needed for learning?
    - What are the effects of manipulating the inputs within the range of naturally-occurring circumstances?
    - What are the effects of manipulating the input outside of that range? (p. 136)

Prepared Learning

1. Consider the following in your response:
    - He couldn't have really explained prepared learning.
    - Watson believed that all associations were equally likely and prepared learning suggests that they are not. (p. 137)

2. In his books, Skinner encouraged the idea that modern advances in the understanding of psychology could be used to create a utopian world by controlling the behaviour of the population. (p. 137)

3. blank slate (p. 137)

4. Garcia found that rats avoided food that
    - the rat ate just prior to being exposed to (nausea-inducing) radiation.
    - was previously unknown to the rat. (pp. 137–138)

5. In the EEA, experiencing nausea after eating usually meant that something was poisonous and should be avoided in the future. (p. 138)

6. prepared learning (p. 138)

7. the associations were made *very* quickly (after a single exposure) (p. 138)

8. the associations were made despite an unusually long delay between the stimuli (p. 138)

9. False—Rats seem to be prepared to learn about taste aversion from nausea (not an electric shock). (p. 138)

10. Those associations were important in our evolutionary history. (p. 139)

11. snake; flower (pp. 138–139)

12. evolutionarily relevant (p. 139)

Practice Test 1: Answer Key

1. **d** (p. 105)
2. **d** (p. 106)
3. **c** (p. 108)
4. **b** (p. 110)
5. **d** (pp. 112–113)
6. **a** (p. 114)
7. **d** (p. 116)

8. **c** (p. 116)
9. **a** (p. 117)
10. **b** (p. 120)
11. **c** (p. 119)
12. **a** (pp. 118–119)
13. **b** (p. 122)
14. **d** (p. 126)

15. **c** (p. 128)
16. **d** (pp. 128–129)
17. **a** (p. 133)
18. **b** (p. 134)
19. **b** (p. 134)
20. **b** (p. 134)
21. **c** (p. 135)

22. **d** (pp. 137–138)
23. **a** (p. 138)
24. **c** (pp. 138–139)
25. **a** (p. 139)

Practice Test 2: Answer Key

1. **d** (p. 106)
2. **a** (p. 110)
3. **b** (pp. 114–115)
4. **c** (p. 115)
5. **a** (p. 115)
6. **d** (p. 116)
7. **b** (p. 116)

8. **b** (pp. 117–118)
9. **c** (p. 121)
10. **a** (p. 118)
11. **b** (p. 120)
12. **c** (pp. 123–124)
13. **c** (p. 123)
14. **d** (p. 124)

15. **a** (p. 130)
16. **a** (p. 131)
17. **b** (p. 133)
18. **c** (pp. 132–134)
19. **a** (pp. 132–134)
20. **d** (p. 135)
21. **d** (p. 136)

22. **b** (p. 137)
23. **a** (p. 138)
24. **b** (p. 138)
25. **c** (p. 139)

Chapter 5
Perceptual Development

Chapter Summary

The Function of Perception: Adaptive Behaviour

We don't always perceive the *truth* about the world. In fact, our visual system, for example, *constructs* the things that we see. The function of perception is to allow us to behave adaptively in the world (this doesn't always require absolute faithfulness to reality).

Because our mental processes are automatic, we are unable to appreciate their complexity. This is referred to as *instinct blindness*. Seeing colours, for example, is completely effortless and so we tend to take it for granted.

Things that we find interesting or beautiful are not inherently so. Our visual system has been designed by natural selection, and the things that we find to be interesting and beautiful are things that convey information that increases reproductive success.

Early Competencies and Interests

The world presents an information overload and we must deal with the barrage of stimuli. The developing infant must have mechanisms for orienting to developmentally relevant information. Faces provide a wealth of social information and are favourite visual targets for young infants.

Prenatal Perceptual Development

Development of the senses begins in the womb. Vision lags behind the other senses because there is very little visual sensation in utero. The fetus does hear sounds that are internal and external to the mother. A newborn will even adjust his sucking behaviour in response to a reward of listening to his mother's voice (DeCasper & Fifer, 1980) or of hearing a familiar story that was read to him prenatally (DeCasper & Spence, 1986).

A fetus can touch and feel things. A fetus can taste and smell flavours in the amniotic fluid. In fact, it has taste preferences (it prefers sweet flavours) and it can, through exposure, develop taste preferences that show themselves in infancy.

Postnatal Perceptual Development

Teller acuity cards can be used to test infant preferences as an assessment of visual discrimination and, hence, acuity. Visual acuity in a newborn is quite poor (20/600), partly because of undeveloped fovea. Over the first six months, vision improves dramatically (to 20/40) partly due to myelination and specialization in the visual cortex and to improved focusing skill.

Newborns can distinguish between green and red and white but they cannot make colour discriminations as adults do. With maturation of cone photoreceptors, colour vision is nearly adult-like by 4 months of age.

The *visual cliff paradigm* involves placing infants on a glass-topped box that appears to have a steep drop-off. It is clear from their reactions that infants as young as 6 months old perceive depth. Fearful reactions to the perceived drop-off are associated with an experience of self-propelled locomotion. Nonfearful reactions (i.e. decreased heart rate in reaction to the deep side) are evident much earlier than 6 months and suggest that depth perception develops earlier than fear of falling.

Newborns can detect motion and can track moving objects. By 3 months, infants make smooth eye movements to track motion and expect objects to move according to trajectories.

Newborns' hearing, though not as sensitive as adults, is quite well developed. Infants are more sensitive to high-pitched noises and less sensitive to low-pitched noises compared to adults. Newborns and infants are particularly responsive and sensitive to speech sounds.

From birth, infants are sensitive to touch. Many early reflexes (e.g. rooting, sucking, grasping, Babinski) occur in response to touch stimuli. As well, newborns react to temperature changes and pain.

Taste and smell function from birth. Infants prefer sweet tastes and smells. They respond to other tastes and smells with distinctive facial expressions. Newborns prefer the smell of human milk over all other smells. Infants demonstrate numerous smell preferences (e.g. the smell of their mothers' breast milk over that of strangers, the smell of a lactating woman over a non-lactating woman).

Intermodal Perception

Early on, infants are able to coordinate information from multiple perceived modalities (e.g. an infant recognizes by sight a pacifier that has been in his mouth). This *intermodal perception* suggests that infants have internal representations of objects and events.

Constancies

The same object can project very different images on our retinas depending on variables such as distance and illumination. Our visual system is able to perceive constancy despite this. Infants show evidence of size, shape, and brightness constancy very early on (within two months) and colour constancy by 4 months of age.

The Nobel Prize-Winning Work of Hubel and Wiesel: Experience-Expectant Development

By recording the activity of single cells in the visual cortex of cats, Hubel & Wiesel distinguished between *simple cells* (that respond to either horizontal or vertical lines) and *complex cells* (that receive input from simple cells and integrate information).

Hubel and Wiesel also studied the development of *ocular dominance columns*, columns of neurons in the visual cortex that respond to input from one of the eyes. Ocular dominance columns do not exist in newborns. They form as a result of pruned connections between the retina and the visual cortex over the first couple of months. Normal development of ocular dominance columns is dependent on visual experience during a critical period. That is, it is an experience-expectant process.

The force of nature in visual development shows itself in a predictable pattern of alternating left-eye/right-eye dominant columns. Nature, though, works together with nurture: visual deprivations in the environment permanently change the visual system.

Visual Deprivation and Development in Humans

Hubel & Wiesel's work was with cats but we have learned a great deal about visual deprivation and development in humans by examining cases of visual restoration. Both Michael May and Sidney Bradford, who lost their sight very early in life and regained it much later, had deficits in depth perception, facial perception, and object recognition.

No one would intentionally deprive a human infant of sight in order to study visual development; however, children born with cataracts (and therefore obstructed vision) provide the opportunity for a *natural experiment*. From natural experiments, we have learned that humans who were visually deprived early in life perform significantly worse on face recognition tasks even though the cataracts were removed early and they subsequently had unobstructed vision. Further, they show deficits in holistic face processing. This is particularly interesting, as holistic face processing doesn't typically develop until around the age of 6 (long after the period of visual deprivation). *Sleeper effects* such as this reveal that early experience can set up neural architecture that underlies much later perceptual abilities.

Associationist Accounts of Visual Development

Early empiricists seem to have been instinct-blind to perception. They took perception for granted and offered no explanation for its development. Contemporary associationists propose that perceptual systems are built by simple learning mechanisms and unconscious statistical analyses of past experience. They argue that the purpose of perception was to allow the individual to behave in useful ways. Associationists are somewhat unclear as to why the individual may rely only on information they have encountered in his lifetime. The associationist view is also hard-pressed to explain some perceptual phenomena (e.g. critical periods, sleeper effects).

Learning Objectives

After reading this chapter, you should be able to:

- Appreciate how our perceptual system adaptively *constructs* our perceived reality (pp. 146–151)

- Explain how infants' interests have adaptive value (pp. 151–153)

- Discuss the degree of perceptual development that takes place before birth (pp. 153–157)

- Trace the early (postnatal) development of vision (pp. 157–162), hearing, touch, taste (pp. 162–163), and smell (p. 164)

- Describe how sense modalities combine in intermodal perception (p. 164)

- Summarize the nature and development of visual constancy for size (pp. 165–166), shape (pp. 166–167), brightness, and colour (pp. 167–168)

- Outline the ground-breaking work of Hubel & Wiesel (pp. 168–171)

- Examine the repercussions of early visual deprivation (pp. 171–174)

- Assess and critique how associationists explain visual development (pp. 174–176)

Suggested Readings

Gregory, R. L., & Wallace, J. G. (1963). Recovery from early blindness: A case study. *Experimental Psychology Society Monographs, No. 2.* Cambridge, UK: Cambridge University Press.

This is a fascinating case study of Sidney Bradford. The paper was reproduced in 2001 and is available on Richard Gregory's website:
http://www.richardgregory.org/papers/recovery_blind/recovery-from-early-blindness.pdf

BBC News. (February, 2008). *Calls to ban 'anti-teen' device.*

This interesting article is about a campaign calling for 'The Mosquito' to be banned from shopping centres on the grounds that it unfairly discriminates against young people. The article can be found on the BBC website: http://news.bbc.co.uk/2/hi/uk_news/7240180.stm

Hubel, D. H., & Wiesel, T. N. (2005). *Brain and visual perception: The story of a 25-year collaboration.* Oxford, UK: Oxford University Press.

This book is the story of the collaboration between Hubel and Wiesel. Included are reprints of their most important publications.

Study Questions

1. Michael May was blinded at a young age and regained his sight more than 40 years later. Cases like May's teach us about _____.

The Function of Perception: Adaptive Behaviour

1. True or False: We perceive the world as it truly is.

2. What is the function of perception?

3. Larger animals are able to hear _____ frequency sounds and smaller animals are able to hear _____ frequency sounds.

4. Why does an animal's size affect the frequency of sounds it can hear?

5. Loomis and colleagues had people estimate the distance to a landmark. What did they find?

6. What conclusions would you draw from Loomis' research?

7. When physically fatigued, people will judge hills as steeper than they would otherwise. Why would that make sense evolutionarily?

8. Define 'instinct blindness'.

9. What are some specific examples of instinct blindness?

10. True or False: Human faces are inherently beautiful.

11. If we saw the objective truth about visual stimuli, our perception of a movie would be _____.

Early Competencies and Interests

1. What was William James referring to as a 'blooming, buzzing confusion'?

2. _____ are necessary to allow the perceptual system to deal with relevant information.

3. Infants look at face-like images longer than they look at scrambled facial features or other images. Why are they so interested in faces?

4. An infant's favourite part of the face is the _____.

5. True or False: Newborns prefer a direct gaze to an averted gaze.

6. Raj, a 6-month-old infant, can see his father's eyes and head turning. The car that his father is looking toward is in Raj's field of vision. Raj is able to _____.

7. In terms of their scan path for a face, what is the difference between 1- and 2-month-old infants?

Prenatal Perceptual Development

1. True or False: Learning starts at birth.

2. _____ is the least developed sense at birth.

3. Why is (above) the least developed sense?

4. What can a fetus hear (prenatally)?

5. DeCasper & Fifer found that newborns could alter their sucking behaviour in order to _____.

6. How did DeCasper & Fifer show that postnatal preferences are affected by prenatal experiences?

7. Before birth, the fetus can hear the mother's intonation and stress patterns. We know this because _____.

8. People start to lose the ability to hear the highest pitches at the age of _____.

9. Why do people gradually lose the ability to hear high pitches?

10. Shop owners may use _____, which emit loud, high-pitched sounds, to discourage loitering by teens and young adults.

11. How do we know that a fetus can touch and feel things?

12. The _____ exposes the fetus to the flavours and tastes of the food that the mother has recently eaten.

13. Imagine that you are the doctor of a patient who is pregnant. You are concerned about the amount of amniotic fluid in the amniotic sac—there is just barely enough. You don't want the fetus drinking any of it. What would you do?

14. If you had a group of pregnant women eat sardines every day for the last month of pregnancy, what would you predict about their children's later attitudes toward sardines?

15. True or False: The fetus experiences smell.

Postnatal Perceptual Development

1. A newborn infant can see at 20 feet what a normal adult can see at _____ feet.

2. A newborn is able to see (in focus) things that are 20 cm from the eye. Why is this distance significant?

3. Lack of development in the _____ in young infants makes inspection of fine detail impossible.

4. _____ cards measure infant visual acuity by assessing preference between cards presented side-by-side.

5. Why don't newborns have adult-like vision?

6. Infants don't have adult-like colour vision until 4 months; however, newborns can distinguish between _____ and _____.

7. Why can newborns make such limited colour distinctions?

8. Gibson & Walk placed infants on the shallow side of a 'visual cliff' and had their mothers call them over to the deep side. How did 6- to 14-month-old infants react?

9. Fear of the visual cliff is associated with experience with _____.

10. Kittens whose only experience with movement in a non-darkened room was movement that was controlled by *another* kitten differed from kittens that controlled movement themselves. How?

11. What can be concluded from this kitten experiment?

12. When an object approaches her face, a 1-month-old infant is likely to _____.

13. True or False: When a 2-month-old is placed on the deep side of visual cliff, his heart rate is likely to increase.

14. True or False: Depth perception comes before fear of falling.

15. A 12-month-old child will cross the deep side of the visual cliff if his parents are _____ but not if the parents _____.

16. True or False: Newborns prefer stationary objects to moving objects.

17. If an object that is moving from left to right disappears behind a screen, a 3-month-old infant will _____.

18. A newborn prefers to listen to _____ over pure tones.

19. The quietest sound that a newborn can hear is _____ times as intense as the quietest sound an adult can hear.

20. True or False: Infants hear low-pitched sounds better than high-pitched sounds.

21. On what part of the body does the sense of touch develop earliest?

22. Match the following early reflexes to the corresponding descriptions.

1. rooting	a) closes hand to grasp what's there
2. sucking	b) infant sucks what is placed in mouth
3. grasping	c) in response to stroking sole of foot, toes fan out and foot twists
4. Babinski	d) infant turns toward touch on the cheek

23. Outline some evidence suggesting that exposure to pain as a newborn can have long-lasting effects.

24. Newborns prefer _____ tastes. They show adult-like facial expressions to _____ and _____ tastes. They are neutral to _____ tastes.

25. Newborns prefer the smell of _____ over all other smells.

26. True or False: Bottle-fed infants prefer the smell of formula over the smell of a lactating woman.

27. True or False: Infants will reliably turn toward a breast pad from their own mother on the second day after birth.

28. Match the following approximate ages to the corresponding developmental milestones.

   1. 1 month   a) adult-like colour vision is achieved
   2. 2 months   b) depth perception develops with self-locomotion
   3. 3 months   c) 20/40 vision is achieved
   4. 4 months   d) adult-like acuity is achieved
   5. 6 months   e) tracks a moving object smoothly and accurately
   6. 9 months   f) look mostly at the outline of faces
   7. 5 years   g) ocular dominance columns have just developed

Intermodal Perception

1. Define 'intermodal perception'.

2. True or False: Piaget rejected the idea of intermodal perception.

3. True or False: Associationists have difficulty explaining intermodal perception.

Constancies

1. Define 'constancy' (as it relates to visual perception).

2. What is an example of constancy?

3. True or False: If two objects are the same size, we will always see them as the same size.

4. How did Slater and colleagues test for size constancy in infants?

5. As early as _____, infants show evidence of brightness constancy.

6. As early as _____, infants show evidence of colour constancy.

7. True or False: There is a one-to-one relationship between light wavelength and perceived colour.

8. True or False: Colour constancy does not work in all artificial lighting situations.

The Nobel Prize-Winning Work of Hubel and Wiesel: Experience-Expectant Development

1. True or False: David Hubel is from Canada.

2. In ten words or less, what did Hubel & Wiesel discover about simple cells in the visual system?

3. Define (Hubel & Wiesel's) 'complex cells'.

4. Define 'ocular dominance column'.

5. True or False: Ocular dominance columns exist in the visual cortex of the newborn.

6. Hubel & Wiesel were interested in the visual system of humans but their experiments could not be ethically performed on humans. They used _____ instead.

7. True or False: Ocular dominance columns form as a result of new connections between the retina and the visual cortex.

8. In reference to above: How do we know this?

9. Define 'synaptic pruning'.

10. How is the development of the visual system an experience-expectant process?

11. The visual system has a great deal of early plasticity. This is potentially of great benefit to _____.

Visual Deprivation and Development in Humans

1. Both Michael May and Sidney Bradford lost their sight at an early age and regained it much later in life. What were some of their visual limitations (after 'regaining sight')?

2. True or False: Sidney Bradford was able to read the time from a clock immediately after his operation.

3. Michael May had a lack of activation in the _____, the part of the brain that usually responds to faces.

4. Define 'natural experiment'.

5. Maurer and colleagues were able to learn about the development of face perception because of a natural experiment involving _____.

6. What did Maurer and colleagues learn about face perception from their natural experiment?

7. Define 'sleeper effect'.

8. Define 'holistic face processing'.

9. Maurer and colleagues found that individuals who had cataracts removed in the first year of life later showed deficits in holistic face processing. What was most surprising about this finding?

10. According to Maurer and colleagues, sleeper effects may arise because '_____'.

Associationist Accounts of Visual Development

1. Classic empiricists had a bad case of _____ in that they took perception as a given and overlooked its development.

2. How would an associationist explain size constancy?

3. According to an associationist, the percept generated is the one that _____.

4. Associationists are committed to a _____ view of perception.

5. What are some phenomena related to perceptual development that would present a challenge to someone who believed in general-purpose learning mechanisms?

6. A baby who survives an encounter with a tiger might very well learn to stay away from tigers in the future; however, an empiricist who suggests that that's all there is to it is leaving out a great deal of complexity. What is the empiricist leaving out?

Practice Test 1

1. The function of perception is

   a. to allow us to appreciate the beauty in the world.
   b. to aid us in surviving and reproducing.
   c. to make the world accessible to thought.
   d. to enable us to see the world as it really is.

2. Perception of speech sounds is a complicated matter. Failing to recognize the impressiveness of our feat of understanding speech sounds is an example of

   a. a perceptual instinct.
   b. auditory blindness.
   c. language insight blindness.
   d. instinct blindness.

3. In order for the perceptual system to attend to, select, and use developmentally relevant information, _____ is/are necessary.

   a. orienting devices
   b. general-purpose learning mechanisms
   c. social input
   d. habituation

4. Maurer and Salapatek (1976) found that 1-month-old infants, when looking at a face, spent more time looking at

   a. the mouth.
   b. the eyes.
   c. the outline of the face.
   d. none of the above. They scanned the entire face without focusing on any part in particular

5. The least developed of the senses at birth is

   a. hearing.
   b. vision.
   c. touch.
   d. smell.

6. DeCasper and Spence (1986) found that newborns preferred a story that had been read to them prenatally to an unfamiliar story. This demonstrates that

   a. there is no learned vs. innate dichotomy.
   b. 'environment' begins at birth.
   c. it doesn't make sense to categorize things as 'influenced by the environment' or 'develops before birth'.
   d. it is always quite clear which elements in the environment are important for development.

7. Compared to a control group, infants whose mothers drank carrot juice regularly during the end of their pregnancy

   a. showed no effect of carrot juice exposure.
   b. were averse to the smell of carrots.
   c. consumed less carrot-flavoured cereal.
   d. showed fewer negative facial expressions to carrot-flavoured cereal.

8. The visual system resides in the _____ of the brain.

   a. temporal cortex
   b. occipital cortex
   c. parietal cortex
   d. subcortical area

9. Visual acuity for a newborn is roughly

   a. 20/40.
   b. 20/100.
   c. 20/300.
   d. 20/600.

10. The _____ is the central part of the retina and is dense in photoreceptors.

   a. fovea
   b. lens
   c. visual cortex
   d. cornea

11. Which of the following statements is *not* true regarding infant colour vision?

   a. Newborns can see only black and white.
   b. Infants prefer saturated colours.
   c. Colour vision developed throughout infancy and into childhood.
   d. Photoreceptors develop at different rates.

12. Whether or not an infant displays fear of the deep side of the visual cliff depends on

   a. whether he has depth perception.
   b. whether he has moved around by himself.
   c. how his parent reacts to the visual cliff.
   d. all of the above

13. Dmitri is 4 months old. A toy car is moving from right to left and disappears behind a curtain. How would you expect Dmitri to react?

   a. He will look at the spot where the car disappeared.
   b. He will look to the left of the curtain.
   c. He will look at the curtain.
   d. He will look away altogether.

14. Which of the following statements is *not* true regarding newborn hearing?

   a. They prefer voices over other sounds.
   b. A sound must be four times louder for an infant to hear it (compared to an adult).
   c. They don't hear high-pitched sounds as well as adults.
   d. Their auditory system is quite well developed.

15. Reliable responses to touch stimuli in newborns are referred to as

   a. preferences.
   b. reflexes.
   c. conditioned responses.
   d. discriminations.

16. Over their first 4 months, there is a shift in infants' responses to _____ tastes.

    a. salty
    b. sweet
    c. bitter
    d. sour

17. Which of the following will a baby who is fed formula prefer?

    a. the smell of a lactating woman
    b. the smell of a non-lactating woman
    c. the smell of formula
    d. the baby will have no preference

18. Which of the following statements is *not* true regarding developmental milestones?

    a. Shape constancy is achieved by 2 months.
    b. Adult-like colour vision is achieved by 4 months.
    c. Acuity reaches 20/40 by 4 months.
    d. Colour constancy is achieved by 4 months.

19. In infants, an example of intermodal perception is

    a. recognizing that his mother is the same whether she is standing near or far away
    b. recognizing that air temperature can feel warm or cold.
    c. recognizing that speech sounds are different than music.
    d. recognizing the banana he saw before it went into his mouth is what tastes like banana.

20. Our visual system perceives constancy despite differences in

    a. modularity.
    b. projections on the retina.
    c. objective size.
    d. preferences.

21. Brightness and colour constancy involve dealing with tremendous changes in

    a. light wavelength.
    b. orientation.
    c. size.
    d. frequency.

22. Hubel & Wiesel's ground-breaking work on visual development took place mostly in the

    a. 1940s.
    b. 1960s and 1970s.
    c. 1980s and 1990s.
    d. the last decade.

23. Hubel & Wiesel called visual cortex cells that respond preferentially to either horizontal or vertical lines _____ cells.

   a. easy
   b. minimal
   c. simple
   d. regular

24. What happens when a kitten is deprived of visual input to the left eye?

   a. The ocular dominance columns that would be devoted to the left eye do not process information at all. This setup is permanent.
   b. The ocular dominance columns that would be devoted to the left eye do not process information at all. This setup changes when the left eye starts receiving visual input.
   c. The ocular dominance columns that would be devoted to the left eye process information from the right eye instead. This setup reverses itself when the left eye starts receiving visual input.
   d. The ocular dominance columns that would be devoted to the left eye process information from the right eye instead. This setup is irreversible.

25. Cases such as Michael May and Sidney Brandford are more informative with regard to

   a. genetic influences.
   b. holistic face processing.
   c. critical periods.
   d. visual scanning.

Practice Test 2

1. The fact that there is a discrepancy between peoples' ability to correctly judge distance when asked to report it and when asked to walk it blindfolded demonstrates

   a. that motion perception functions more efficiently than vision.
   b. the existence of instinct blindness.
   c. that the function of perception applies to behaviour rather than knowledge.
   d. none of the above

2. We humans are interested in looking at _____ over just about anything else because _____.

   a. faces; they provide a great deal of social information
   b. faces; by objective measures, they are aesthetically pleasing
   c. man-made objects; they have been designed to appeal to us
   d. man-made objects; they provide a great deal of useful information

3. When watching a movie, we perceive motion. This demonstrates that

    a. our visual system is designed to see motion as interesting.
    b. our visual system constructs the things that we see.
    c. motion detection is innate.
    d. experience dictates perception.

4. What did DeCasper and Fifer's experiments examining newborn hearing preferences required the infant to do?

    a. Habituate to a sound.
    b. Look in the direction of a preferred sound.
    c. Display distinctive facial expressions.
    d. Alter their sucking frequency.

5. If the amniotic fluid is sweetened,

    a. the fetus will develop an aversion to sweet tastes.
    b. the fetal heart rate will increase.
    c. the fetus will drink more of it.
    d. fetal movement will cease.

6. Acuity reaches adult levels around the age of

    a. 6 months.
    b. 2 years.
    c. 5 years.
    d. 10 years.

7. All of the following are true of newborn vision *except*

    a. the visual cortex is not fully developed.
    b. acuity is constant across a wide range of distances.
    c. the lens is inflexible.
    d. eye movements are smooth.

8. Teller acuity cards rely on _____ to test acuity.

    a. motion detection
    b. preferences
    c. peripheral vision
    d. depth perception

9. Which of the following colours are newborns least sensitive to?

    a. blue
    b. black
    c. red
    d. green

10. Sam is 8½ months olds and has started crawling. Julie is 8½ months old and is not yet crawling. According to a study described in the textbook, what is likely to be a difference between Sam and Julie?

   a. Julie will express fear of the visual cliff and Sam will not.
   b. Sam will smoothly move his eyes to track a moving object and Julie will not.
   c. Sam will prefer to watch moving objects and Julie will prefer to watch stationary objects.
   d. Sam will perform better at object retrieval tasks that require depth perception.

11. Stroking the bottom of an infant's foot will cause the toes to fan out and the foot to twist. This is called the _____ reflex.

   a. Galant
   b. rooting
   c. pedal
   d. Babinski

12. When tested between 4 and 6 months of age, boys who had not been anaesthetized during circumcision showed _____ than boys who had been anaesthetized during circumcision.

   a. a greater sensitivity to temperature
   b. a stronger grasping reflex
   c. a more intense pain response
   d. none of the above

13. Chen, a 1-week-old infant, is presented with a chocolate smell. How is he likely to react?

   a. He will frown.
   b. He will relax his facial muscles.
   c. He will start sucking.
   d. He will show no reaction.

14. Which constancy develops last?

   a. brightness
   b. size
   c. shape
   d. colour

15. Intermodal perception has been revealed in infants as young as

   a. newborns.
   b. 2 months old.
   c. 3 months old.
   d. 4 months old.

16. Constancies are _____ that are used by the visual system.

    a. heuristics
    b. rules
    c. bits of information
    d. classifications

17. Hubel & Wiesel called visual cortex cells that integrate information _____ cells.

    a. multiple-input
    b. complex
    c. integration
    d. composite

18. Which of the following is *not* true of ocular dominance columns?

    a. They are of equal widths.
    b. They alternate between left-eye, right-eye.
    c. They are present in the visual cortex of newborns.
    d. They are, literally, columns.

19. Synaptic pruning is the process of _____ synaptic death.

    a. experience-based, selective
    b. experience-based, random
    c. genetically-determined, selective
    d. genetically-determined, random

20. Which of the following statements is accurate regarding the roles of nature and nurture in the development of the visual system?

    a. Nature and nurture act in opposition.
    b. Nature plays a more important role than nurture.
    c. Nature relies on nurture.
    d. none of the above

21. Which of the following was Sidney Bradford able to do after regaining his sight?

    a. resolve the Necker cube
    b. perceive faces
    c. resume his job as a machinist
    d. report the distance between objects

22. Maurer and colleagues found a sleeper effect for

    a. holistic face processing.
    b. depth perception.
    c. colour vision.
    d. object recognition.

23. Contemporary associationists contend that the development of low-level visual processes is a matter of

   a. developing prototypes.
   b. learning about statistical regularities.
   c. conscious learning mechanisms.
   d. none of the above. Contemporary associationists bypass the question of perceptual development.

24. Contemporary associationists are not entirely clear on

   a. whether or not they hold a functional view of perception.
   b. whether perceptual abilities develop.
   c. why a developing individual should rely only on information he has encountered in his lifetime.
   d. the existence of constancies.

25. The take-home message from the tiger example at the end of the chapter is that

   a. One unfortunate encounter with a tiger should be sufficient to allow adaptive behaviour in a subsequent tiger encounter.
   b. The nativist perspective of visual perception is insufficient to account for our behaviour.
   c. Visual processing of tigers is unlike other visual processing.
   d. All that is required to learn from a bad tiger experience and act adaptively in subsequent tiger encounters could not be accomplished from a blank slate perspective.

Study Questions: Answer Key

1. critical periods for the development of the visual system (p. 145)

The Function of Perception: Adaptive Behaviour

1. False—Our perception of the world is not a literal representation of our surroundings. (p. 146)

2. Consider the following in your response:
   - The traditional view is that perception involves passively absorbing the truth about our surroundings.
   - Some propose that the function of perception is to allow us to appreciate the beauty around us.
   - For our purposes, a reasonable answer to this question is that the function of perception is to allow us to behave adaptively in the world (to survive and reproduce). (p. 147)

3. lower; higher (p. 147)

4. Consider the following in your response:
   - Animals have evolved to be able to hear the sounds that are likely to be relevant to the decisions they have to make.
   - For example, discrimination of high-pitched sounds is more important to the survival of a bat than a human. (p. 147)

5. Loomis et al. found that
   - if their research subjects were asked to estimate visually, their estimates were quite inaccurate.
   - if the subjects walked blindfolded to the landmark, their estimates were much more accurate. (p. 148)

6. The function of perception is adaptive behaviour rather than knowledge. (p. 148)

7. If you're tired, you probably shouldn't tackle a steep hill. In this case, our perception helps us make a good decision. (p. 148)

8. Instinct blindness refers to our inability to appreciate the complexity of our mental processes because they seem automatic and inevitable to us. (p. 149)

9. The textbook gives the example of colour vision. Colour perception is, of course, completely effortless for us but it is a tremendously difficult and intricate process (as evidenced by the fact that no computer has ever been able to see colours). There are many, many such examples—think about it! (p. 149)

10. False—There is nothing inherently beautiful about any human face. We find (at least some) human faces beautiful (or at least interesting) because, for humans, faces are a valuable source of social information. Ultimately, our interest in faces is a means of increasing reproductive success. (p. 150)

11. a series of still photographs with no motion (because that's what it really is) (pp. 150–151)

Early Competencies and Interests

1. William James
   - was referring to the barrage of stimuli (visual, auditory, tactile, etc.) that surrounds us.
   - was suggesting that adults have learned to perceive order in the chaos. Keep in mind that the order is *imposed* by us. (p. 151)

2. Orienting devices/Mechanisms (p. 152)

3. Infants are interested in faces because
   - an early preference for faces is adaptive.
   - faces provide social input needed for social development.
   - following gaze direction and attending to the interests of others will lead to learning about important objects. (p. 152)

4. eyes (p. 152)

5. True—This (among other findings) suggests that newborns prefer social stimuli. (p. 152)

6. look in the direction of his father's gaze (i.e. look at the car) (p. 152)

7. In studying the scan path of infants, researchers have found that
   - 1-month-olds are likely to spend more time looking at the outline of the face.
   - 2-month-olds are likely to look at the internal details of the face. (pp. 152–153)

Prenatal Perceptual Development

1. False—The fetus is exposed to many sensory stimuli in the womb. These stimuli provide for a great deal of learning. (p. 153)

2. Vision (p. 153)

3. Vision is developed last because
   - it's dark in there!
   - there isn't a lot of visual stimulation in utero. There is a slight lighter/darker difference between day and night, but that's probably it.
   - a newborn has had very little 'practice' seeing before birth. (p. 153)

4. The fetus can hear
   - the mother's voice
   - other voices
   - ambient sounds
   - the mother's heartbeat and sounds from her digestive system (p. 154)

5. hear their mothers' voices (p. 154)

6. DeCaspar and Fifer found that if a pregnant woman read a story out loud for the last two months of her pregnancy, her newborn preferred to hear the story that was read to him in utero over an unfamiliar story. (p. 154)

7. the fetal heart rate changes when the mother starts to speak (p. 156)

8. 18 (p. 155)

9. People lose the ability to hear high pitches because
   - tiny, pressure-sensitive hair cells in the cochlea (inner ear) deteriorate with age.
   - hair cells are lost, nerve cells are lost, and connections between hair and nerve cells are lost. (p. 155)

10. mosquito alarms (p. 155)

11. We know that a fetus can touch and feel things in utero because
    - it can grasp the umbilical cord.
    - it can suck its thumb. (p. 156)

12. amniotic fluid (p. 156)

13. Consider the following in your response:
    - Inspired by the doctor described in the textbook who sweetened the amniotic fluid to encourage the fetus to drink more of it, you could do the opposite.
    - You could inject a bitter (but harmless) substance into to amniotic fluid.
    - Taste aversion to bitterness would discourage the fetus from drinking the amniotic fluid. (p. 156)

14. Based on the results of the carrot juice study, you would predict that these children would enjoy sardines more than a control group. (p. 157)

15. True—The amniotic fluid will smell like the food the mother has just eaten and the fluid comes into contact with odour receptors. (p. 157)

Postnatal Perceptual Development

1. 600 (p. 157)

2. 20 cm is roughly the distance that the mother's face will be when breast-feeding. (p. 157)

3. fovea (p. 157)

4. Teller acuity (p. 158)

5. Infants do not have adult-like vision because
   - the lens is inflexible so the baby cannot change focus.
   - the fovea of the retina is not fully developed.
   - in the visual part of the brain, cells are not yet myelinated and have not yet specialized to type of visual stimuli that they will respond to. (p. 158)

6. red; green (p. 159)

7. Newborns make limited colour distinctions because
   - there are three types of photoreceptors (cones) and they mature at different rates.
   - the type of photoreceptor that is most sensitive to red and green matures early (by birth). (p. 159)

8. When called to the deep side of the 'visual cliff', infants hesitated and showed fear. This suggested that they perceived depth below them. (pp. 159–160)

9. self-propelled locomotion (p. 160)

10. The kittens that were controlled by other kittens
    - showed abnormal behaviour.
    - failed to reach out a paw when lowered to a horizontal surface.
    - failed to blink when an object was brought right up to their faces. (pp. 160–161)

11. The findings from the kitten experiments suggest that active visual exploration is necessary for the development of the coordination between visual input and behaviour. (p. 161)

12. blink (indicating that they have detected a change in distance) (p. 161)

13. False—In fact, it tends to decrease, indicating interest. (p. 161)

14. True—Depth perception seems to develop very early; it takes longer to learn to equate depth with danger. (p. 161)

15. smiling and encouraging him; show a facial expression of fear (p. 161)

16. False—Newborns have a preference for moving objects. (p. 161)

17. look to the right of where it disappeared (as if expecting to see it as it continues on its trajectory) (p. 161)

18. voices (p. 162)

19. four (p. 162)

20. False—They hear high-pitched sounds better. In fact, infants hear high-pitched sounds better than adults do. (p. 162)

21. The sense of touch develops first
    - around the mouth
    - on the palms of the hands
    - on the soles of the feet (p. 162)

22.
    1. rooting   d) infant turns toward touch on the cheek
    2. sucking   b) infant sucks what is placed in mouth
    3. grasping   a) closes hand to grasp what's there
    4. Babinski   c) in response to stroking sole of foot, toes fan out and foot twists
    (p. 162)

23. Consider the following in your response:
    - One study compared boys who had and had not been anaesthetized during circumcision.
    - At 4 and 6 months, non-anaesthetized boys showed a more intense pain response. (pp. 162–163)

24. sweet; sour; bitter; salty (p. 162)

25. human milk (p. 164)

26. False—Even bottle-fed infants prefer the smell of a lactating woman over the smell of formula. (p. 164)

27. False—They will turn to a breast pad from their own mother on the sixth day but not the second. It seems to take a few days to become familiar with the smell of their own mothers' breast milk. (p. 164)

28.
1.	1 month	f)	look mostly at the outline of faces
2.	2 months	g)	ocular dominance columns have just developed
3.	3 months	e)	tracks a moving object smoothly and accurately
4.	4 months	a)	adult-like colour vision is achieved
5.	6 months	c)	20/40 vision is achieved
6.	9 months	b)	depth perception develops with self-locomotion
7.	5 years	d)	adult-like acuity is achieved (p. 163)

Intermodal Perception

1. Intermodal perception is the integration of percepts acquired via two or more modalities/senses. (p. 164)

2. True—Piaget believed that information from different modalities would be separate for the first few months after birth. (p. 164)

3. True—Associationists would have trouble explaining how a response can transfer from one sense to another. (p. 164)

Constancies

1. Constancies are strategies used by the visual system so that a given object will appear to be the same size, shape, brightness, or colour despite enormous differences in the characteristics of the image on our retina. (p. 165)

2. Consider the following in your response:
    - A dark blue shirt in the store should still look dark blue outside.
    - A mountain in the distance still looks big.
    - There are many, many such examples—think about it! (p. 165)

3. False—That statement *is* mostly true but size constancy is not perfect (as is demonstrated by the paper example described in the textbook). (p. 165)

4. Consider the following in your response:
    - Slater et al. used a habituation paradigm.
    - During the habituation phase, the infant saw a small cube at various distances.
    - After habituation, the infant saw the small cube as well as a larger cube twice as far away.
    - Infants looked longer at the larger cube, showing that they saw it as novel. (p. 166)

5. 7 weeks of age (p. 167)

6. 4 months of age (p. 167)

7. False—Illumination levels and contrasting surfaces greatly impact light wavelength but we usually see the same colour regardless. (p. 167)

8. True—We are not able to achieve colour constancy in artificial light that differs very much from natural terrestrial light. (p. 167)

The Nobel Prize-Winning Work of Hubel and Wiesel: Experience-Expectant Development

1. True—He is from Windsor, Ontario. (p. 168)

2. Some respond to vertical lines; some respond to horizontal lines. (pp. 168–169)

3. Complex cells receive input from a number of simple cells and integrate the information received. (p. 169)

4. An ocular dominance column is a column of neurons in the visual system that responds to input from either the right eye or the left eye. (p. 169)

5. False—Cells in the newborn's visual cortex receive input from both eyes. Ocular dominance columns begin to appear in the first month and are present by two months. (p. 169)

6. cats (p. 169)

7. False—Rather, they form because existing connections are eliminated. (p. 169)

8. We know this because
   - when Hubel and Wiesel deprived kittens of input from one eye, the entire visual system became devoted to processing information from the other eye.
   - The switchover between eyes was irreversible. (p. 169)

9. Synaptic pruning refers to the selective death of synapses based on experience. (p. 169)

10. Consider the following in your response:
    - We must have exposure to visual input in order to learn how to see. That is, visual development requires visual experience.
    - Typically, this works fine because we can (typically) count on being exposed to visual input in the environment. It did not work fine for some of Hubel & Wiesel's cats because they were intentionally deprived of visual information. (p. 170)

11. an infant who sustains an eye injury (p. 171)

Visual Deprivation and Development in Humans

1. Some of Michael May's and Sidney Bradford's visual limitations were
   - lack of depth perception
   - inability to process faces
   - inability to recognize objects (p. 172)

2. True—Presumably, he could do this by transferring the skill he had used to read his watch by touch. (p. 172)

3. fusiform face area (FFA) (p. 172)

4. A natural experiment is a situation in which two or more groups exist through no action of the experimenter, allowing for a comparison between these naturally occurring groups. (p. 172)

5. congenital cataracts (pp. 172–173)

6. Maurer et al. learned that
   - early visual experience is necessary for normal development of face perception.
   - people who had experienced early visual deprivation because of cataracts were significantly worse than a control group at face recognition tasks. (p. 173)

7. A sleeper effect is a developmental effect that is evident only some time after exposure to a particular environmental cue. (p. 173)

8. Holistic face processing describes the way people usually see faces. A face (unlike most other objects) is perceived as a whole, incorporating the feature shapes and the relationships between features. (p. 173)

9. What was most surprising about Maurer's findings is that holistic face processing does not typically develop until around 6 years of age (long after the cataracts were removed). This is an example of a sleeper effect. (p. 173)

10. early visual input is necessary to preserve or establish the optimal neuronal architecture for each task (p. 174)

Associationist Accounts of Visual Development

1. instinct blindness (p. 174)

2. An associationist would propose that size constancy results from adjustments based on experience with predicting whether two objects were the same size or not. (p. 174)

3. was the most useful in the past (p. 174)

4. functional (p. 174)

5. Some phenomena include the following:
   - Critical periods
   - Early competencies
   - Sleeper effects
   - The three above are listed in the textbook but you can certainly come up with more (e.g. early taste and smell preferences) (p. 175)

6. Consider the following in your response:
   - Making the link between a tiger encountered on one day and another on another day presents a complex problem.
   - The baby has to *see* the (camouflaged) tiger, orient to the tiger, see the tiger as an object, recognize the tiger as animate, and survive the first encounter.
   - The baby has to link the past incident to a future moment and must do it under different lighting conditions, distance, and orientation. (p. 175)

Practice Test 1: Answer Key

1. **b** (p. 146)
2. **d** (p. 148)
3. **a** (p. 152)
4. **c** (pp. 152–153)
5. **b** (p. 153)
6. **c** (p. 154)
7. **d** (p. 156)

8. **b** (p. 157)
9. **d** (p. 157)
10. **a** (p. 157)
11. **a** (p. 159)
12. **d** (pp. 159–160)
13. **b** (p. 161)
14. **c** (p. 162)

15. **b** (p. 162)
16. **a** (p. 163)
17. **a** (p. 164)
18. **c** (p. 163)
19. **d** (p. 164)
20. **b** (p. 165)
21. **a** (p. 167)

22. **b** (p. 168)
23. **c** (p. 169)
24. **d** (p. 169)
25. **c** (p. 172)

Practice Test 2: Answer Key

1. **c** (p. 148)
2. **a** (p. 152)
3. **b** (pp. 150–151)
4. **d** (p. 154)
5. **c** (p. 156)
6. **c** (p. 158)
7. **d** (p. 157)

8. **b** (p. 158)
9. **a** (p. 159)
10. **d** (pp. 159–160)
11. **d** (p. 162)
12. **c** (pp. 162–163)
13. **b** (p. 164)
14. **d** (pp. 167–168)

15. **a** (p. 164)
16. **a** (p. 165)
17. **b** (p. 169)
18. **c** (p. 169)
19. **a** (p. 169)
20. **c** (p. 174)
21. **d** (p. 172)

22. **a** (p. 173)
23. **b** (p. 174)
24. **c** (p. 175)
25. **d** (p. 175)

Chapter 6
Concepts, Categories, and Essences

Chapter Summary

We use categories to make predictions about individual things. When asked to 'take a seat', you know enough about the category 'chair' to sit down on *whatever* chair is offered. There are developmental changes in categorization.

What Are Categories and Concepts?

Perceptual stimuli may be classified into discrete sets even when there is no physical discontinuity. For example, we perceive colours categorically even though light wavelength changes gradually.

Categories are mentally-represented groupings of entities that share some kind of psychological similarity. This is not the only definition of a category, but it is the one best suited to our purposes given that we are interested in the development of psychological representations of categories.

'Concept' is a particularly difficult term to operationally define. For our purposes, a *concept* is a psychological grouping together of things (entities, objects, events, characteristics) on the basis of some more or less functional commonality, including an understanding of their interrelationship. Concepts may be invented somewhat artificially but we are particularly interested in natural-kind categories: groupings that infants and children naturally form themselves. Some parallels can be drawn between 'concepts' and 'theories'.

Instinct Blind to Concepts

As with other things that come so easily to us, we are largely instinct blind to the usefulness of the concepts that we all share. We are also instinct blind to the fact that we use only a small subset of logical concepts (only those that confer an evolutionarily advantage).

Universality of Categories and Concepts

In spite of a myriad of environments, children create remarkably similar concepts and categories. There is a great deal of cross-cultural overlap in conceptual distinctions, a sign of functionality in the EEA.

The Classic View of Categories

A *classic category* is one that can be defined in terms of necessary and sufficient features. According to the classic view, categories/concepts can be thought of as unambiguous mental definitions; however, classic definitions for real-world categories are elusive. As well, the classic view assumptions that everything in the category is an equally good example and that there is no ambiguity in category membership are not supported by empirical evidence.

A Prototype and Family Resemblance View

According to the prototype view of categorization, a member of a category is more or less prototypical depending on how many features it shares with other members. There is a large consensus regarding category typicality. The prototype view has more empirical support than the prototype view but it cannot explain everything.

What Would Piaget Say About Children's Categorization?

Piaget's notion of categories fits with the classic view. Piaget employed a free-classification method to test children's understandings of categorization. Using this method, children sort cards according to their own chosen categorical rules. Piaget found that children do not represent categories in a classic way. Those in the preoperational and concrete operational stages were found to be *perceptually-bound*, reliant on visually perceivable factors. Piaget observed that, rather than making adult-like categorizations, children used *thematic associations*, grouping items based on their use together or their prior association in a story. Piaget believed that children had *complexes*—fluid, less well defined groupings—rather than proper concepts. Vygotsky's conclusions regarding children's categorizations were similar to Piaget's.

The Function of Categories and Concepts

Categories are evolved cognitive faculties that allow for adaptive behaviour. Why, specifically, are they adaptive? It has been suggested that they are adaptive as a way to store information more efficiently; however, this explanation doesn't stand up to scrutiny. Despite the existence of categories, people remember the individual items. As well, there is no reason why the human mind would need to be spared storage space. The real value in categorization is the ability to make inferences. This helps us deal with new objects quickly.

Categories (natural categories, especially) are functional. Biological utility has been found to be a stronger factor in categorization than any other statistical regularity. The mind creates categories based partly on the value of items in evolutionary terms.

Early Concept Formation: Function Matters

Categorization is aided by functional reasoning. For example, children are better at categorizing made-up 'wugs' and 'gillies' when functional explanations are provided for their features.

Testing a pre-verbal infant's ability to categorize can be done using a habituation paradigm: dishabituation is expected for an object that is seen as a member of a different category. We know from such experiments that 1-year-old children (and even younger!) have impressive categorization abilities.

Functional fixedness refers to an ability to think of using an object in a way other than its usual purpose. Young children tend not to be as functionally fixed as adults or older children; they seem to have a broader category for function. By extension, their approach to problem solving is somewhat more flexible.

Basic Levels and Hierarchical Categorization

Concepts and categories are organized hierarchically in mind. Relatively broad categories are said to be at the *superordinate level*. Relatively specific categories are said to be at the *subordinate level*.

On the basis of results from *class-inclusion experiments*, Piaget concluded that children do not understand the hierarchical relationship of the categories. When children are presented with ten red flowers and six blue flowers and asked 'Are there more red flowers or more flowers?', they are likely to say that there are more red flowers. There can't possibly be more 'red flowers' than 'flowers' because 'flowers' is higher in the hierarchy and includes 'red flowers'. Children behave as though they do not understand this rule.

Basic-level categories—neither superordinate nor subordinate—are special. They are most easily processed, most easily brought to mind, most easily pictured, and most easily discussed. Basic-level words are also among the first words learned by very young children, although *child*-basic level categories tend to be a bit more general than adult basic-level categories. Basic-level categories are the most amenable to drawing inferences. Children are more open to making inferences from the basic level to the subordinate level than the other way around (as they should be!). For example, if birds have gizzards, it is reasonable to assume that robins have gizzards; if robins have gizzards, it is less reasonable to assume that all birds have gizzards.

Natural Kinds

Natural kinds (naturally occurring categories such as trees, rocks, or cats) allow for rich inferences. They come naturally to us and are easily learned by children.

Concept Development

As children get older, concepts become more refined and categories are better able to accommodate unusual members.

Contrary to what Piaget would have predicted, Gelman & Markman (1986) found that young children make inferences based on category membership rather than perceptual similarity.

Essences and Essentialism

We humans are *essentialists*: we have the sense that an entity's essence is unchangeable. We may not be able to explain *what* the essence is but we know it's there. Essentialist thinking is especially applicable to natural-kinds categories. Between the ages of 4 and 7, the essentialist view of natural kinds becomes more adult-like.

In *transformation experiments*, an object undergoes a series of transformations resulting in the outward appearance of a different object. Children are asked to categorize the transformed object. Children of all ages will (like adults) accept that an artifact has transformed into something else. Older children (like adults) will reject the idea that natural kinds can change category membership. Younger children will accept a natural-kinds change.

Keep in mind that essence is part of human psychology; it is not an objectively valid component of any object, natural kind or otherwise.

Different types of experimental methodology will yield results. Piaget's 'which ones go together?' question seems to have encouraged children to sort on the basis of perceptual similarity. The more naturalistic contemporary inductive *method* reveals inferences and generalizations.

Special Design

Categories are functional and, to a large extent, develop uniformly from person to person and from culture to culture. They contain the hallmarks of specialized design by natural selection.

What Would Associationists Say About Children's Categorization?

Categorizations seem to be made based on mental similarity rather than the objective properties of the object. Associationists' reliance on perceptual similarity makes essentialism very difficult to account for.

Learning Objectives

After reading this chapter, you should be able to:

- Outline the operational definitions of categories and concepts (pp. 183–185)

- Appreciate how much we take for granted in our use of concepts (pp. 185–186)

- Recognize the universality of concepts (pp. 186–188)

- Compare and contrast the classic and prototype views of categories (pp. 188–189)

- Explain Piaget's work on children's categorizations (pp. 190–192)

- Recognize the functional nature of categories (pp. 193–195) and the relevance of function early on in development (pp. 195–197)

- Define the hierarchical nature of categories and learn about the special case of basic-level categories (pp. 197–201)

- Explain how natural-kinds categories differ from nominal categories and artifacts (pp. 201–202)

- Describe how concepts change with age and how categorization is less reliant on perceptual similarity than Piaget proposed (pp. 202–204)

- Define 'essentialism' (pp. 204–209)

- Explain why Piaget and contemporary cognitive psychologists arrived at different conclusions regarding children's categorizations (pp. 207–209)

- Recognize that concepts and categories were naturally selected (p. 209)

- Appreciate how difficult it is for associationists to explain categorization (pp. 209–210)

Suggested Readings

Wittgenstein, L. (2009). *Philosophical Investigations* (4th ed.). Wiley-Blackwell.

One of Wittgenstein's most influential works, this book includes the 'game' thought experiment.

Rosch-Heider, E., & Oliver, D. C. (1972). The structure of the color space in naming and memory for two languages. *Cognitive Psychology, 3*, 337–354.

This article outlines an important finding regarding cross-cultural similarity in perception and categorization despite language differences: The language of the Dani tribe of Papua New Guinea has only two words for colour, but the Dani seem to mentally categorize colour in ways that are similar to the speakers of other languages.

Gelman, S. A., & Wellman, H. M. (1991). Insides and essence: Early understandings of the non-obvious. *Cognition, 38*, 213–244.

A confirmation of children's essentialism: 4-year-olds believe that rabbits will prefer carrots over bananas even if raised by monkeys.

Study Questions

1. Having a broad concept for a new object allows you to make pretty good _____.

What Are Categories and Concepts?

1. Psychology is not the only discipline concerned with categorization. _____ and _____ both have extensive literature on the topic.

2. Define 'perceptual category'.

3. What are some examples of perceptual categories?

4. Define 'category'.

5. How does the above definition of categories differ from traditional definitions?

6. Unlike an ideal category, categories, by our definition, may refer to _____.

7. How are concepts 'a lexicographer's nightmare'?

8. Define 'concept'.

9. How are concepts different than categories?

10. What are the interesting questions that developmental psychologists are likely to ask regarding concepts?

11. Define 'natural-kind category'.

12. How are concepts like theories?

13. Like theories, concepts are the _____ in at least some domains of knowledge.

Instinct Blind to Concepts

1. True or False: Concepts vary a great deal between individuals and between human cultures.

2. In what ways are we instinct blind to concepts?

3. True or False: We do not have a concept for things that weigh less than a dog because it is not a logical category.

Universality of Categories and Concepts

1. Early on, children make a distinction between animals that are _____ and animals that are _____, a distinction that must have been important in the EEA.

2. True or False: The uniformity of category development suggests that some hypotheses are privileged over others.

The Classic View of Categories

1. A classic category can be defined by a list of _____ and _____ features.

2. Category membership, in the classic view, involves no _____.

3. True or False: According to the classic view, everything in the category is an equally good example.

4. True or False: Piaget dealt the first critical blow to the classic view.

5. What are some criticisms of the classic view?

A Prototype and Family Resemblance View

1. Robin is a _____ member of the category 'bird'.

2. The prototype view was pioneered by _____.

3. True or False: Ratings for typicality of category members are very high between individuals.

4. The more _____ a member shares within a category, the more typical it is rated.

5. How are typical members of a category treated differently than non-typical members?

6. The prototype view cannot explain _____.

What Would Piaget Say About Children's Categorization?

1. Describe Piaget's method for testing children's understanding of categorization.

2. The fact that young children were more likely to change criteria in the middle of a sorting task was a sign of _____ according to Piaget.

3. How did Piaget characterize 'mature categorization'?

4. According to Piaget, categorizations of children in the preoperational and concrete operational stages are _____-bound.

5. Michael, a 4-year-old child, is presented with four items: a blue wrench, a blue fork, a red hammer, and a red spoon. If asked to sort them into pairs, how would Piaget predict that Michael would do it?

6. Define 'thematic association'.

7. What is an example of a thematic association that a child might make?

8. According to Piaget, how do children's 'complexes' differ from proper concepts?

9. True or False: Vygotsky and Piaget disagreed about how children categorize.

10. Outline some contemporary evidence for the role of perceptual features in children's categorization.

The Function of Categories and Concepts

1. Some have suggested that we categorize so that our cognitive and memory capacities are not swamped by information. What's wrong with this explanation?

2. We create categories and concepts because they allow us to _____.

3. What inferences can we make when we know that a new entity is an animal?

4. When Krasnow (2008) told participants that an object presented was a fruit, they were fastest at identifying whether _____.

5. When Krasnow (2008) did not tell participants that an object presented was a fruit, they were fastest at identifying whether _____.

6. The take-home message from the Krasnow (2008) study described above is that the mind creates categories according to _____.

Early Concept Formation: Function Matters

1. Children were better at categorizing 'wugs' and 'gillies' when they were given _____.

2. How did McDonough and Mandler (1998) demonstrate that 14-month-old children understand that animals drink?

3. Ryan, an 8-month-old infant, is shown numerous pictures of cars. If Ryan knows the difference between cars and bicycles, then a picture of a bicycle (after all those cars) should cause _____.

4. Sonja searches in vain for a vase to put her flowers in. She doesn't seem to notice that she has many drinking glasses that would work just as well. This is an example of _____.

5. A classic experiment demonstrating the above phenomenon was Duncker's _____.

6. Who is more likely to overlook the drinking-glass-as-vase option: 5-year-old Melissa or 7-year-old Eliza?

7. Why is the above finding counterintuitive?

Basic Levels and Hierarchical Categorization

1. True or False: Superordinate categories are broad and subordinate categories are specific.

2. True or False: A particular object may only be conceptualized at one of the multiple levels of categorization.

3. It's a chilly, fall day. I ask you what you are putting on to go outside. How would you answer at a superordinate level? A basic level? A subordinate level?

4. Design a class-inclusion experiment using blue crayons and yellow crayons.

5. If your subjects were 8-year-old children, what results would you expect from the above experiment and why?

6. Shown ten red flowers and six blue flowers, 8-year-old Cindy states that there are more flowers than red flowers. When asked 'Could you make it so that there will be more red flowers than flowers', she is like to say _____.

7. Conversations usually start with _____-level categories.

8. True or False: To adults, a basic-level category intuitively seems like a high-level category.

9. True or False: Basic-level category words tend to be shorter than superordinate-or subordinate-level category words.

10. Outline some evidence for the special status of basic-level categories among children.

11. What is the difference between basic-level categories and *child-basic level* categories?

12. Organization around basic-level categories develops between _____ and _____.

13. True or False: John, a 3-year-old child, is told that dogs bark. John is likely to infer that Chihuahuas bark.

14. True or False: John, a 3-year-old child, is told that Chihuahuas barks. John is likely to infer that dogs bark.

Natural Kinds

1. True or False: 'Plants' is an example of a 'natural kinds' category.

2. In addition to natural kinds, what other types of categories are there?

3. True or False: 'Squares' is an example of a 'natural kinds' category.

Concept Development

1. Concepts become more _____ as children get older.

2. True or False: As children get older, there are more elaborate distinctions made within categories. Because of this, categories become less able to accommodate unusual category members.

3. How did Gelman & Markman's (1986) experiment with animal categorizations prove Piaget wrong?

4. Follow-ups to Gelman & Markman's (1986) experiment have shown that children as young as _____ use category membership rather than perceptual similarity to make inferences.

5. The fact that children are not reliant on perceptual similarity is a problem for Piaget's theory. It is also a problem for a purely empiricist account. Why?

Essences and Essentialism

1. Define 'essentialism'.

2. True or False: Essentialism proposes that objects have classic definitions.

3. In ten words or less, describe the intuitive essentialist view of what it is to be a dog.

4. True or False: There is a strong link between natural-kinds categories and essentialist beliefs.

5. The idea of essentialism dates back as far as _____ and was discussed by Locke as well as other British philosophers.

6. How was Locke's idea of essences different than the way we see them now?

7. Define 'transformation experiment'.

8. How do the results of transformation experiments differ depending on category type?

9. You have a cat named Rosie. You find a lion costume made for cats and put it on Rosie. You ask 4-year-old Berton if Rosie is now a lion.
   True or False: Berton is likely to agree that Rosie is a lion.

10. You assemble a very human-looking scarecrow out of a broom, clothing, and paint, among other things. You ask 4-year-old Berton if the scarecrow is human.
    True or False: Berton is likely to agree that the scarecrow is human.

11. True or False: DNA holds the essence of a living thing.

12. Match the following conceptual development milestones to the corresponding ages.

    1. Distinguishes cats from dogs   a) 7 years

    2. Appears to have the category 'mammal'   b) 3 months

    3. More likely to draw inferences within
       basic-level categories than across other levels   c) 3 years

    4. Uses functional components to help categorize   d) 3.5 months

    5. Rejects the idea that natural kinds can be
       transformed into a different category   e) 4 years

13. In general, results from contemporary studies differ from early Piagetian research in that they suggest that children have _____ whereas Piagetian research suggested that children rely heavily on _____.

14. In assessing categorization abilities in children, Piaget would ask a question like _____?

15. Contemporary cognitive psychologists use the _____ method or the _____ method.

16. Using the above method, what type of question is a child asked?

17. Piaget assumed that all categories were _____.

18. Why does it matter that Piaget made the above assumption?

Special Design

1. The fact that concepts are _____ suggests that they are an adaptation.

2. 'Comparative' studies compare _____ to _____.

3. In general, what would we expect to find regarding the categories of non-human species?

What Would Associationists Say About Children's Categorization?

1. True or False: Associationists have a prepared explanation for essentialism.

2. The basic quality of a basic-level category is _____. It is not a property of the category.

3. How does Rosch describe basic categories?

4. Categorizing two things as the same requires perceiving a similarity between the two. What constitutes similarity depends on _____.

Practice Test 1

1. Perceptual categories are formed

   a. despite a psychological continuity in the stimuli.
   b. despite a lack of physical discontinuity in the stimuli.
   c. only when there is a physical discontinuity in the stimuli.
   d. only when there is a one-to-one correspondence between objective stimuli and perception.

2. Which of the following statements is *not* true of our definition of a category?

   a. Members of a category are classified together for psychological reasons.
   b. It is different than traditional definitions of a category.
   c. The category grouping may include objects, people, actions, or events.
   d. Categories must refer to something that really exists.

3. Psychological groupings of objects grouped together as they are perceived to be in nature are referred to as _____ categories.

   a. natural
   b. natural-type
   c. natural-kinds
   d. essential

4. Which of the following statements is true regarding culture and categories?

   a. There is absolute uniformity among concepts in all cultures.
   b. There is great uniformity among concepts only in cultures that are similar to one another.
   c. Concepts for social and mental phenomena vary a great deal between cultures.
   d. People from all cultures have a similar understanding of natural things.

5. _____ dealt the first critical blow to the classic view of categories.

    a. Skinner
    b. Rosch
    c. Wittgenstein
    d. Piaget

6. Which of the following is *not* a criticism of the classic view of categories?

    a. Most real-world categories do not seem to have a classic definition.
    b. The classic view does not address features of objects.
    c. The human mind does not view all members of a category as equally good examples.
    d. There is ambiguity in category membership.

7. A prototype

    a. is the most frequently encountered item in a category.
    b. shares many features with members of other categories.
    c. shares few features with other members of the same category.
    d. is what you are likely to mentally picture if asked to think of a member of a particular category.

8. Piaget believed that children in the preoperational and concrete operational stages based their categorization exclusively on

    a. visually perceivable factors.
    b. inductive reasoning.
    c. hierarchies.
    d. functionality.

9. Compared to proper concepts, Piaget's 'complexes' are

    a. less fluid.
    b. rely more on classic definitions.
    c. less well defined.
    d. less common in children than adults.

10. Which of the following is the best answer to the question 'how do categories help us?'?

    a. They enlarge memory capacity.
    b. They allow us to make inferences.
    c. They prevent us from being swamped with information.
    d. They prevent neuronal overload.

11. Krascum & Andrews (1998) found that children who were given _____ were better able to remember 'wug' and 'gillie' categories the day after learning about them.

    a. concept descriptions
    b. colourful illustrations
    c. functional information
    d. none of the above

12. Imagine that you show 4-month-old Fatima many pictures of cats. Then, you show her a picture of a lion. Based on the results of the study by Quinn & Eimas (1996), how would you expect Fatima to react?

    a. She will look more at the lion.
    b. She will habituate to the lion.
    c. She will dishabituate to the cats.
    d. She will look away.

13. Which of the following is *not* true of functional fixedness?

    a. There is a different pattern of functional fixedness for younger compared to older children.
    b. It reflects a kind of mental narrowness.
    c. It exists only in technology-dense cultures.
    d. It is the reason why adults perform poorly on Duncker's candle problem.

14. Which of the following is the best example of a superordinate-level category?

    a. boat
    b. headlight
    c. Harley Davidson motorcycle
    d. vehicle

15. Adults, but not children, usually understand that

    a. the subordinate class is more important than the superordinate class.
    b. the superordinate class is more important than the subordinate class.
    c. there can never be a greater number of members in the superordinate class than in a superordinate class.
    d. there can never be a greater number of members in a subordinate class than in the superordinate class.

16. Which of the following statements is *not* true regarding basic-level categories?

    a. They are *psychologically* basic.
    b. The words used for them tend to be relatively long.
    c. They allow for easy mental groupings.
    d. They usually start conversations.

17. According to Johnson, Scott, & Mervis's (1997) experiment involving facts about birds, children are more likely to make an inference from a _____ object to a member of the _____ category than the reverse.

    a. basic-level; subordinate
    b. subordinate; basic-level
    c. superordinate; subordinate
    d. subordinate; superordinate

18. The textbook listed three types of categories. Which of the following does not belong?

   a. artifacts
   b. nominal
   c. functional
   d. natural kinds

19. Gelman & Markman (1986) taught 4-year-olds new information about animals and then conducted a test of induction. Their results were important because they suggested that

   a. Piaget was right—Children at this age make inferences on the basis of perceptual similarity.
   b. Piaget was wrong—Children at this age were not over-reliant on perceptual similarity.
   c. children at this age made very difference inferences than adults would have.
   d. children at this age were unable to draw inferences.

20. An essence

   a. changes with a disguise.
   b. is something that you should be able to immediately put your finger on.
   c. changes over time.
   d. is something that is shared between members of the same category.

21. In a transformation experiment, a child is asked

   a. to make physical transformations to an object placed in front of her.
   b. to transform her own physical appearance.
   c. whether an item can change category membership through a series of movements.
   d. whether an item can change category membership given the appropriate manipulation of features.

22. The _____ method can reveal what categories children hold and what inferences are warranted within a category.

   a. conjunctive
   b. inference
   c. inductive
   d. deductive

23. It is with regard to special design that categories are not

   a. arbitrary.
   b. precise.
   c. complex.
   d. functional.

24. Which of the following statements best describes why associationists find it difficult to explain essentialism?

    a. The associationist perspective relies heavily on learning principles.
    b. The associationist perspective relies heavily on perceptual similarity.
    c. Essences cannot be associated with objects.
    d. Essentialism is inexplicable.

25. Perception of similarity and difference depends on

    a. our functional relationship with the object in the EEA.
    b. the emotional significance of the object.
    c. objective characteristics of the object.
    d. none of the above

Practice Test 2

1. An example of a perceptual category is

    a. consonant sounds.
    b. colours.
    c. facial expressions.
    d. all of the above

2. Concepts

    a. are lexicalized.
    b. are not as powerful as categories.
    c. have an agreed-upon definition.
    d. apply to objects but not events.

3. Our failure to appreciate the uniformity and the usefulness of our concepts is an example of

    a. essentialism.
    b. associationism.
    c. instinct blindness.
    d. sensory loss.

4. The fact that all children make a distinction between animals that are predators and animals that are prey means that

    a. the distinction between predators and prey is something that all children have direct experience with.
    b. this distinction was functional in the EEA.
    c. there are reliable perceptual differences between predators and prey.
    d. predators and prey is an idiosyncratic concept.

5. The classic view of categories

    a. asserts that a category can be defined by a list of necessary and sufficient features.
    b. does not apply to natural-kinds categories.
    c. refers to an idealized description of concepts.
    d. allows for a certain amount of ambiguity in category membership.

6. According to the prototype view of categorization,

    a. all members of a category can be seen as prototypes.
    b. each member of a category must have a certain number of necessary features.
    c. category membership is unequivocal.
    d. some members of a category are more central to the category than others.

7. Which of the following statements is true regarding typicality ratings?

    a. Typicality ratings vary a great deal between individuals.
    b. People are faster to affirm category membership for less typical items.
    c. Findings regarding typicality ratings can be accounted for by the classic view of categorization.
    d. Number of shared features predicts typicality rating.

8. Piaget used the _____ method in order to test children's understanding of categorization.

    a. free-report
    b. free-classification
    c. open-sorting
    d. unrestricted

9. Thematic associations may lead to groupings based on

    a. prior association in a story.
    b. perceptual similarity.
    c. prototypes.
    d. inferences.

10. Which of the following statements is *not* true regarding Vygotsky and categorization?

    a. Vygotsky believed that there was a qualitative shift from a young child who was perceptually bound to an older child who was conceptual.
    b. Vygotsky found evidence of children's reliance on thematic associations.
    c. Vygotsky's conclusions regarding children's categorization abilities were quite different than Piaget's.
    d. Vygotsky tried to teach children classic categories that he had designed.

11. Max Krasnow proposed that concepts are organized by our minds according to the value of objects. Here, 'value' refers to

    a. amount of information.
    b. biological utility.
    c. predictability.
    d. typicality.

12. McDonough and Mandler (1998), using a toy dog and a cup, showed that 14-months-olds

    a. don't pay any attention to the experimenter's actions.
    b. understand that toys cannot drink.
    c. believe that objects, regardless of category membership, drink.
    d. understand that animals drink and non-animals do not.

13. By _____, children can discriminate between mammals and non-mammals.

    a. 3½ months
    b. 6 months
    c. 1 year
    d. 2 years

14. Research on functional fixedness in 5-, 6-, 7-year-olds, and adults provides support for which of the following counterintuitive statements?

    a. Younger children's categories are better organized than older children's or adult's are.
    b. Younger children are better problem-solvers than older children and adults are.
    c. Children make more inferences than adults do.
    d. Children pay more attention to the function of objects than adults do.

15. Of the following, which is the best example of a subordinate level category?

    a. technological equipment
    b. laptop
    c. MacBook Pro
    d. computer

16. You present 8-year-old Ray with two brown puppies and 11 black puppies. You ask Ray 'Are there more black puppies or more puppies?' What kind of experiment have you done?

    a. group-deduction
    b. group-induction
    c. class-exclusion
    d. class-inclusion

17. In the above experiment, Ray would probably

    a. say that there are more black puppies.
    b. say that there are more puppies.
    c. not be willing to give a response.
    d. none of the above—At 8 years old, Ray's response would be completely unpredictable

18. Which of the following statements is *not* true about children's use of basic-level words/categories?

    a. Basic-level categories develop between infancy and early childhood.
    b. Children's basic-level words are very different than adults'.
    c. Basic-level words are the first words a child learns.
    d. In free-sorting tasks, children are likely to sort based on basic-level categories.

19. Artifacts

    a. are groupings that exist because people have given a name to them.
    b. are treated the same as natural-kind categories.
    c. are things that are made by people.
    d. are categories that are most likely to be universal.

20. As children get older, concepts become more

    a. sub-divided.
    b. general.
    c. natural.
    d. vague.

21. Gelman & Markman (1986) found that 4-year-old children made inferences that were not based on perceptual similarity. This is problematic for

    a. the Piagetian perspective.
    b. a purely empiricist account.
    c. both *a* and *b*
    d. neither *a* nor *b*

22. The results of Keil's (1986) transformation experiment suggest that

    a. young and older children accept the idea of natural kinds changing category membership.
    b. only young children accept the idea of natural kinds changing category membership.
    c. children but not adults accept the idea of artifacts changing category membership.
    d. people, regardless of age, do not accept the idea of changing category membership for any kind of object.

23. A perceived essence is part of

    a. human psychology.
    b. the physical stimulus.
    c. the functionality of the object.
    d. none of the above

24. Piaget's conclusions regarding children's categorization abilities were quite different than those of more contemporary cognitive psychologists. Which of the following statements helps to explain why there is this discrepancy?

    a. Piaget used the inductive method and contemporary researchers do not.
    b. Piaget used the transformation method and contemporary researchers do not.
    c. Piaget's methods were more naturalistic than those used by contemporary researchers.
    d. Piaget examined concepts that differed in nature from those examined by contemporary researchers.

25. When Rosch and her colleagues talk about categories, they are talking about

    a. groupings based on physical properties.
    b. hypothetical groupings.
    c. psychological entities.
    d. all of the above

Study Questions: Answer Key

1. predictions (p. 182)

What Are Categories and Concepts?

1. linguistics; philosophy (p. 183)

2. Perceptual categories are implicit classifications of perceptual stimuli into discrete sets in spite of a lack of physical discontinuity in the stimuli. (p. 183)

3. Some examples of perceptual categories include
   - colour—equal differences in wavelengths may be perceived as either the same colour or a different colour.
   - consonant sounds—we don't hear in-between consonant sounds (e.g. we hear either 'ba' or 'pa', not a mixture of the two).
   - many others—think about it! (p 183)

4. A category is a mentally represented collection of entities (objects, people, actions, or events). (p. 184)

5. In the above definition, we are referring to a *psychological* entity that is classified together for *psychological* reasons. (p. 184)

6. entities that do not really exist (p. 184)

7. Consider the following in your response:
   - A concept is very difficult to define.
   - We have an intuition about what is meant by a 'concept' but it is hard to say exactly what it is. (p. 184)

8. A concept is a psychological grouping together of entities, objects, events, or characteristics on the basis of some more or less functional commonality, including some understanding of their relationship. (p. 185)

9. Consider the following in your response:
   - *Concepts* are lexicalized, meaning that they are associated with a word or short phrase, whereas *categories* may be arbitrary groupings.
   - Entities included in a concept are functionally related. Because of this, concepts can be used to make inferences and predictions. (p. 185)

10. Some questions that developmental psychologists might ask include the following (and many more!):
   - What are the concepts that develop in young children?
   - What is the functional commonality that a child will use to delineate a concept? (p. 185)

11. A natural-kind category is a psychological grouping of the classes of entities that are seen to be natural categories or objects grouped together as they are perceived to be in nature. (p. 185)

12. Concepts are like theories in that
   - both include a distinct set of items.
   - both address phenomena involving members of the set of items.
   - both address a set of causal relationships that apply within, but not outside of, the domain. (p. 185)

13. central organizing force (p. 185)

Instinct Blind to Concepts

1. False—Although it is certainly true that concepts vary somewhat, there is remarkable uniformity. (p. 185)

2. Consider the following in your response:
   - Having concepts that we use everyday without thinking about it makes it hard to imagine not having them.
   - We overlook the fact that our useful concepts are only a small subset of all possible concepts.
   - We tend not to notice the similarity among concepts between individuals. (pp. 185–186)

3. False—It is perfectly logical but it is not functional in the sense of conferring an evolutionary advantage. (p. 186)

Universality of Categories and Concepts

1. predators; prey (p. 187)

2. True—The development of categorization seems to be somewhat constrained. (p. 187)

The Classic View of Categories

1. necessary; sufficient (p. 189)

2. ambiguity (p. 189)

3. True—According to the classic view, dogs are dogs—no kind of dog is 'doggier' than any other. (p. 189)

4. False—Piaget subscribed to the classic view. The first critical blow was dealt by Wittgenstein. (p. 189)

5. Some criticisms of the classic view include the following:
   - Real-world categories don't seem to have a classic definition. People don't represent categories in terms of their necessary and sufficient features.
   - Not all members of a category are seen as equally good examples and items do exist that are ambiguous in terms of category membership. In other words, the tenets of the classic view do not fit with empirical evidence. (p. 189)

A Prototype and Family Resemblance View

1. prototypical (p. 190)

2. Eleanor Rosch (p. 190)

3. True—One study found that agreement was 97 per cent. (p. 190)

4. features (p. 190)

5. Consider the following in your response:
   - People are faster to affirm that a typical member belongs in the category.
   - Given a category name, people are more likely to generate typical members as examples. (p. 190)

6. essentialism (that, for example, a raccoon is a raccoon, even if you make it look like a skunk) (p. 190)

What Would Piaget Say About Children's Categorization?

1. Consider the following in your response:
   - Piaget used the free-classification method.
   - Children sorted items into a pre-specified number of groups without being told how to do the sorting. They were free to make their own rules.
   - The belief is that you can infer the children's categories from the groupings created. (p. 190)

2. immaturity (p. 192)

3. People who are mature in their categorization abilities
   - can identify which items are included and excluded in a category.
   - understand that membership in one category means that the item is not a member of another category at the same level
   - organize categories hierarchically (p. 191)

4. perceptually (p. 191)

5. Consider the following in your response:
   - Piaget observed that children Michael's age are perceptually-bound. That is, they base their categorization exclusively on visually perceivable features.
   - Piaget would predict that Michael would group together the blue things (wrench and fork) and the red things (hammer and spoon).
   - Of course, another (perhaps more reasonable) grouping would be wrench/hammer and fork/spoon but that would require grouping on the basis of function rather than perception. (p. 192)

6. Using thematic associations involves grouping items based on their use together or their prior association in a story rather than on category membership. (p. 192)

7. Some examples of a thematic association include the following (and many more!):
   - Horse and saddle might be grouped together because they are used together.
   - Cat and hat might be grouped together if they child is familiar with *The Cat In The Hat* (p. 192)

8. Compared to a concept, a complex
   - is more fluid
   - is less well defined
   - does not rely on classic definitions (p. 192)

9. False—Vygotsky and Piaget reached similar conclusions. (p. 193)

10. Consider the following in your response:
    - Children are more likely to refer to perceptual attributes when explaining their categorizations.
    - *Which* perceptual features are relied upon changes over time (e.g. colour and shape are used before height and width). (p. 193)

The Function of Categories and Concepts

1. Even though they are categorized, we do remember individual items—so no storage space is saved by categories. There is no reason why the human mind *needs* to save space. We have plenty of neuronal circuitry—enough to handle every event and object. (pp. 193–194)

2. make inferences (p. 194)

3. We can infer that
   - it moves around
   - it seeks food
   - it grows
   - it reproduces
   - it does many other things. The point is that we can make broad, accurate predictions given that one piece of categorical information. (p. 194)

4. the fruit was ripe (p. 195)

5. the fruit was prototypical (p. 195)

6. biological utility (evolutionary value) (p. 195)

Early Concept Formation: Function Matters

1. functional reasons for their features (p. 195)

2. Consider the following in your response:
   - A 14-month-old child was shown a toy dog 'drinking' from a cup.
   - The child was allowed to manipulate the cup, another animal toy, and another non-animal toy.
   - The child gave the other animal toy (but not the non-animal toy) a pretend drink. (p. 196)

3. dishabituation (he should look more at the picture of the bicycle) (p. 196)

4. functional fixedness (p. 197)

5. candle problem (p. 197)

6. 7-year-old Eliza is more likely to overlook the drinking-glass-as-vase option. Younger children have been found to be less functionally fixed. They seem to have broader categories with regard to function. (p. 197)

7. The finding from the question above suggests that problem-solving abilities *decrease* with age. We tend to assume that those abilities increase with age. (p. 197)

Basic Levels and Hierarchical Categorization

1. True—'Super-' is (relatively) broad and 'sub-' is (relatively) specific. (p. 198)

2. False—Superordinate and subordinate can only be judged in relation to other categories. (p. 198)

3. The following answers would be anticipated at the respective levels:
   - Superordinate: 'clothing'
   - Basic: 'jacket'
   - Subordinate: 'fleece pull-over' (p. 199)

4. The following would be an example of a class-inclusion experiment using blue and yellow crayons:
   - Show children five blue crayons and two yellow crayons.
   - Ask the children, 'Are there more blue crayons or more crayons?' (pp. 198–199)

5. Consider the following in your response:
   - The 8-year-olds would be likely to report that there are 'more blue crayons'.
   - At that age, children seem to be mistakenly comparing the number of blue crayons to the number of yellow crayons.
   - They do not seem to understand the impossibility of having more members in the subordinate than the superordinate level category. (p. 199)

6. yes (p. 199)

7. basic (p. 199)

8. False—To adults, basic-level categories are intuitively mid-level categories. (p. 199)

9. True—Consider a couple of examples: 'dog', compared to 'animal' or 'golden retriever'; 'chair', compared to 'furniture' or 'chaise lounge'. (p. 200)

10. Consider the following in your response:
    - Basic-level words are the first words that children learn.
    - In free-sorting tasks, children are more likely to group objects by basic-level categories. (p. 200)

11. The difference between basic-level categories and *child-basic level* categories is
    - child-basic categories are slightly more general.
    - child-basic categories seem to be organized immaturely. Organization of basic-level categories develops between infancy and early childhood. (p. 200)

12. infancy; early childhood (p. 200)

13. True—John will be likely to make an inference from the basic-level object to a member of the subordinate category. (p. 201)

14. False—John will likely be hesitant to make an inference from the subordinate level object to the basic-level category. (p. 201)

Natural Kinds

1. True—Like 'dogs' and 'water', 'plants' is an example of a category that the human mind appears to develop an interest in and a competence with, even without being taught. (p. 201)

2. Other types of categories include
   - 'nominal categories', which exist because humans have named and described them (e.g. 'squares').
   - 'artifacts', which includes things that are made by people. (p. 201)
3. False—'Squares' is better described as a nominal category. (p. 201)

Concept Development

1. refined/precise (p. 202)

2. False—Categories divide to allow for more subtle distinctions but the ability to accommodate unusual category members actually improves. (p. 202)

3. Consider the following in your response:
   - Gelman & Markman showed 4-year-old children pictures of animals.
   - They taught the children some new information about the animals (e.g. 'This fish stays underwater to breathe'.)
   - Children were then shown a picture of a new animal that was very perceptually similar to the original picture but that shared a category label with another.
   - Children were asked which of the newly-learned properties could be applied to the new animal.
   - Contrary to what Piaget would have predicted, children made inferences based on category membership rather than perceptual similarity. (p. 202)

4. 2½ years (p. 202)

5. Consider the following in your response:
   - A pure empiricist would predict that children only have knowledge about things that they have had an opportunity to observe.
   - But observations don't seem to be critical—children have informationally-rich categories in mind that are not perceptually bound. (p. 202)

Essences and Essentialism

1. Essentialism is the view that for any given entity there is an essence—some property that every member of that kind must possess—which gives it its category membership and its category-specific features. (p. 204)

2. False—Essentialism defies classic definitions. According to essentialism, category membership relied on an essence rather than a list of defining features. (p. 204)

3. Can't put a finger on it but know it's there. (p. 204)

4. True—We have an intuitive sense that natural kinds have an essence. (p. 205)

5. Plato and Aristotle (p. 205)

6. Consider the following in your response:
   - Locke proposed that natural kinds objects have an essence.
   - We propose that human psychology *perceives* essences, not that they really exist. (p. 205)

7. A transformation experiment is one in which a child is asked whether an item can change category membership given the appropriate manipulation of features. It is used to test a child's intuitions about essentialism. (p. 205)

8. Results of transformation experiments might differ in the following ways:
   - Children of all ages as well as adults accept transformations of artifacts (e.g. a coffeepot transformed to function as a birdfeeder is now a birdfeeder).
   - Older children and adults reject the idea that natural kinds can be transformed (e.g. a raccoon is a raccoon, regardless of how much you make it look and smell like a skunk).
   - Young children (4-year-olds) are more open to the transformation of natural kinds. (p. 206)

9. False—4-year-olds are somewhat open to the transformation of natural kinds but they require the transformation to be sufficiently convincing—it will take more than a lion costume. (p. 206)

10. False—Children are very reluctant to accept a transformation across the animate–inanimate boundary. (p. 206)

11. False—DNA is really just a large molecule; it is not the key to essence. (p. 207)

12.
   1. Distinguishes cats from dogs — b) 3 months
   2. Appears to have the category 'mammal' — d) 3.5 months
   3. More likely to draw inferences within basic-level categories than across other levels — c) 3 years
   4. Uses functional components to help categorize — e) 4 years
   5. Rejects the idea that natural kinds can be transformed into a different category — a) 7 years (p. 208)

13. rich concepts; perceptual similarity (pp. 207–208)

14. 'Which ones go together?' (p. 208)

15. transformation; inductive (p. 208)

16. Using the inductive method, a researcher asks a child what kinds of inferences can be made from one entity to another. Note that this is quite different from what Piaget asked of the child. (p. 208)

17. classic categories (pp. 208–209)

18. Consider the following in your response:
   - Piaget assumed that a category was a category; he didn't make a distinction between natural-kinds and artificial categories.
   - That matters because, as contemporary cognitive psychologists now know, artificial categories do not support inference and are not easy for children to acquire.
   - This helps to explain differing results for Piagetian research compared to contemporary research. (p. 209)

Special Design

1. functional (p. 209)

2. humans; other animals (p. 209)

3. We would expect other species have different categories than humans; categories that are functional for *them*. (p. 209)

What Would Associationists Say About Children's Categorization?

1. False—Essentialism is very difficult for associationists to explain because the associationist perspective relies heavily on perceptual similarity. (p. 209)

2. in the human mind (p. 210)

3. Rosch describes basic categories as those in which exemplars are the most similar to each other and most dissimilar to exemplars of other categories. (p. 210)

4. our functional relationship with these objects in the EEA (p. 210)

Practice Test 1: Answer Key

1. **b** (p. 183)
2. **d** (p. 184)
3. **c** (p. 185)
4. **d** (p. 185)
5. **c** (p. 189)
6. **b** (p. 189)
7. **d** (p. 189)
8. **a** (pp. 191–192)
9. **c** (p. 192)
10. **b** (pp. 193–194)
11. **c** (p. 195)
12. **a** (p. 196)
13. **c** (p. 197)
14. **d** (p. 198)
15. **d** (p. 198)
16. **b** (p. 199)
17. **a** (p. 201)
18. **c** (p. 201)
19. **b** (p. 202)
20. **d** (p. 204)
21. **d** (pp. 205–206)
22. **c** (p. 208)
23. **a** (p. 209)
24. **b** (p. 209)
25. **a** (p. 210)

Practice Test 2: Answer Key

1. **d** (p. 183)
2. **a** (p. 184)
3. **c** (p. 186)
4. **b** (p. 187)
5. **a** (p. 188)
6. **d** (p. 189)
7. **d** (p. 190)
8. **b** (p. 190)
9. **a** (p. 192)
10. **c** (p. 193)
11. **b** (p. 194)
12. **d** (p. 196)
13. **a** (p. 196)
14. **b** (p. 197)
15. **c** (p. 198)
16. **d** (pp. 198–199)
17. **a** (p. 199)
18. **b** (p. 199)
19. **c** (p. 202)
20. **a** (p. 202)
21. **c** (p. 202)
22. **b** (p. 206)
23. **a** (p. 207)
24. **d** (p. 208)
25. **c** (p. 210)

Chapter 7
Core Knowledge Part I: Physics, Space, Biology, and Number

Chapter Summary

The Acquisition of Knowledge

The quest to explain knowledge acquisition has spanned centuries and has often been framed as a nature versus nurture debate. Knowledge is best thought of not as 'stuff' that resides in the brain, but as a pattern of neuronal organization. The organization of neurons is the result of developmental processes influenced by both genetics and environment.

Framing the Question of Knowledge Acquisition

Computer scientists who have attempted to create human-like abilities in machines have discovered that 'blank slates' don't learn very well; some initial structure is necessary. Animals have that structure in the form of *constraints on learning*: biased heuristics that are built into the system and are used in acquiring information.

What constraints are humans endowed with? In examining the constraints, keep in mind that the infant will inherit his parents' genes as well as their environment. As well, remember the developmental processes evolved in the EEA. An understanding of core knowledge cannot be gained without consideration of the informational priorities in *that* environment.

Core Knowledge

Core knowledge refers to privileged domains of knowledge that children learn easily by virtue of developing cognitive preparedness that is specific to those domains. These domains evolved because they offered a fitness advantage. A *domain* can be thought of as a knowledge system that includes information about the relevant entities, as well as rules that describe how the entities behave. Domains are specialized, with powerful learning mechanisms that work only within the realm of the domain.

Piaget did not believe that children had specialized processing in different domains. When contemporary developmental psychologists demonstrate sophisticated core knowledge in children, it is a refutation of Piaget's views. The domain-specific learning proposed by core knowledge theorists is also somewhat at odds with the associationist view, which contends that only a few general learning mechanisms are necessary for knowledge acquisition.

Areas of Core Knowledge

Core knowledge is reliably developing, domain-specific, and relevant to survival in the EEA. *Intuitive physics* is one specific domain of core knowledge. Very early on (long before Piaget's estimates), infants have a sophisticated understanding of their own laws of physics.

Piaget asserted that infants younger than 8 months of age fail to realize that an object exists even when it is out of sight. That is, he proposed that object permanence takes 8 months to develop. It turns out that Piaget's methodology relied too heavily on behaviours. Using more sensitive techniques, we now know that infants younger than 8 months have permanent mental representations of objects that include useful details.

In addition to object permanence, infants younger than 8 months have expectations regarding *continuity* (moving objects must continually occupy a place), *contact* (to influence another object, contact must be made), and *cohesion* (objects must remain a unified whole). By 3 months, infants understand that unsupported objects fall down. By 6 months, they understand that the bottom of an object needs to be supported sufficiently to prevent falling. In short, young infants have an impressive understanding of gravity. These early understandings are consistent with the core-knowledge view and difficult to square with the associationist view.

Young infants develop an early understanding of *occlusion events* (where an object becomes invisible as it moves behind a nearer objects), *containment events* (where an object moves into a container, possibly becoming invisible), and *covering events* (where an object becomes invisible as it is hid by a cover). Early on, infants apply rules and use informative variables for each event category independently. Relative height, for example, is used as a factor in occlusion events at 3½ months but not until 7½ months for containment events. This very narrow application of intuitive physics argues against the idea of domain-general observational learning mechanisms. It is also noteworthy that infants' impressive knowledge of physics applies only to objects and not to non-object substances such as liquids. Accounting for that discrepancy would be difficult if you only believed in observational learning mechanisms because infants presumably have as much experience watching non-objects as objects.

Piaget's claims regarding intuitive physics in infants during the sensorimotor period are summarized as follows:

- Substages 1 and 2 (birth to 4 months)
  - infant can fixate and track a moving object
  - no evidence of object permanence

- Substage 3 (4 to 8 months)
  - infant shows anticipatory eye movements
  - will reach for a partially (but not fully) occluded object

- Substage 4 (8 to 12 months)
  - infant will grasp and retrieve hidden objects
  - commits the A-not-B error
    - if a toy is repeatedly hidden in one location and then (while the infant is watching) hidden in another, the infant will look in the first location

- Substage 5 (12 to 18 months)
  - infant can resolve the A-not-B problem, but only if the displacement was visible

- Substage 6 (18 to 24 months)
  - all of the above difficulties are resolved

Infants show early development of an understanding of space. They use spatial location to define an object; they have strategies for navigating in space; and they are able to use geometry of a room as a spatial cue. As early as 6 months, infants can use landmarks to locate objects. At 2 years, toddlers show some degree of *dead reckoning*, the ability to continuously keep track of one's location relative to the starting point and get back to it.

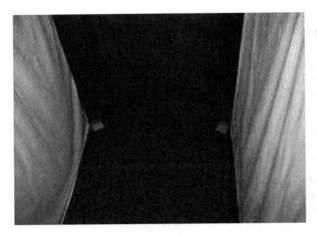

In the spatial navigation experiments described here, toddlers are disoriented before they search for an object. First they are shown the location of an object, then they are spun around with their eyes covered, then they are allowed to search for the hidden object. Using this method, researchers can make inferences about what cues young children use in navigation.

Babies will use the geometry of a room as a spatial cue but will not, and apparently cannot, use other cues such as colour. If a toy is hidden under a box in one of the corners of the room, the geometry of the room will be a clue, so the baby will correctly look to the right of the shorter wall, for example, but will never reliably use the only blue wall in the room as a cue (Hermer-Vazquez, Spelke, & Katsnelson, 1999).

In early and middle childhood, there is evidence of an impressive and non-tutored understanding of biology. Children seem to develop an understanding that plants and animals are different than other objects and they have some understanding of basic biological processes. It is difficult to assess children's understanding of biology because they are not usually able to describe what they know; however, several techniques have been developed. The method of induction assesses inferences made by the child about biological entities and the relationships among them. The transformation technique tests what sort of transformations children will accept. Finally, children can simply be asked about their understanding of biological processes.

Young children understand basic principles of inheritance. They understand that children will resemble their biological, rather than their adoptive, parents for physical traits. Children appreciate that living things, but not non-living things, grow. Although their understanding of growth is immature in some ways, they do understand that re-growth is expected after a living thing is damaged, that growth requires food for animals and water for plants, and that growth of living things is beyond intentional control. Children seem to have an understanding of death before the age of 4.

According to the core-knowledge perspective, an intuitive knowledge of biology was naturally selected in the EEA. An understanding of food sources and bodily processes was adaptive. There seem to be commonalities across cultures in children's understandings of biology that reflect a universal cognitive architecture. Children's understandings of biology are less reliant on visual perception and more sophisticated in general than Piaget would have predicted.

Regardless of formal education, all children acquire a basic understanding of numbers and basic arithmetic at about the same age. As evidenced by dishabituation, 5-month-old infants can appreciate the equality or difference of small sets of objects. An appreciation of *ordinality* follows *numerosity*—infants can be taught to indicate 'greater than' or 'less than'. Infants as young as 5 months can even perform simple arithmetic as shown by surprise when the math is wrong. Young infants are quite numerically precise with very small numbers and approximately accurate for larger orders of magnitude. They seem to have distinct core systems for large and small sets. Children start counting not long after they learn to talk. By 2½ or 3, they appear to have a set of counting rules:

- *The one-to-one principle*: Each item gets a unique number label.
- *The stable-order principle*: Number labels should be spoken in the same order every time.
- *The cardinal principle*: The last number label assigned is the total.
- *The abstraction principle*: *Anything* can be counted.
- *The order-irrelevant principle*: Counting order doesn't matter; the total should be the same regardless of order.

A Cross-Species Comparison

The nature of domains of knowledge is can be illuminated by comparing them across species. Animals such as rats and rhesus monkeys show evidence of a core number system that is in some ways similar to humans'. Humans seem to be much better prepared to develop the concept of ordinality than other animals or birds.

Different species of land animals face many common problems. As such, we would expect similar cognitive solutions and, in fact, there is evidence that many land animals show cognitive development for understanding objects that is similar to human infants.

All species have navigational strategies but which cues are used for navigation varies a great deal between species. Species are equipped with specific, well-designed learning mechanisms.

Learning Objectives

After reading this chapter, you should be able to:

- Conceptualize what knowledge *is* and, by extension, how it is acquired (pp. 216–218)

- Understand that learning requires constraints on learning (pp. 218–221)

- Examine the nature of domains of core knowledge (pp. 221–223)

- Appreciate infants' impressive intuitive understanding of physics (pp. 224–233)

- Summarize Piaget's claims regarding the development of intuitive physics (pp. 233–234)

- Appreciate infants' impressive intuitive understanding of space (pp. 235–238)

- Explain how we test children's understanding of biology (pp. 238–239)

- Appreciate young children's impressive intuitive understanding of biological processes including inheritance, growth, and death (pp. 239–243)

- Appreciate infants' impressive intuitive understanding of numbers (pp. 245–248)

- Compare human domains of knowledge to those of other species (pp. 248–250)

Suggested Readings

Baillargeon, R. (1987). Object permanence in 3½- and 4½-month-old infants. *Developmental Psychology, 23*, 655–664.

> This article is an experiment demonstrating the existence of object permanence in infants as young as 3½ months—long before Piaget would have predicted.

Atran, S., & Medin, D. (2008). *The Native Mind and the Cultural Construction of Nature.* Cambridge, MA: MIT Press.

> This book is a summary of and commentary on work done by Scott Atran and colleagues in assessing how people think about the natural world with particular focus on the similarities and differences between cultures.

Wynn, K., Bloom, P., & Chiang, W-C. (2002). Enumeration of collective entities by 5-month-old infants. *Cognition, 83,* B55–B62.

> This is a well-known study of infants' numerical knowledge. 5-months-olds are able to do basic arithmetic!

Study Questions

The Acquisition of Knowledge

1. _____ is the ancient Greek branch of philosophy concerned with questions about knowledge acquisition.

2. True or False: Early rationalists believed that some knowledge is provided *a priori*.

3. The question of acquisition of knowledge has usually been framed in terms of a _____ debate.

4. It is sometimes assumed that knowledge acts like physical 'stuff'. What is another way of thinking about it?

Framing the Question of Knowledge Acquisition

1. True or False: Work in artificial intelligence has revealed that knowledge acquisition is more efficient when there is no built-in structure.

2. Define 'constraints on learning'.

3. True or False: Any behaviour that is paired with a reinforcement will be learned and repeated.

4. Back up your answer to the previous question with an example.

5. Pigs and raccoons can be taught to carry a token to exchange for food. But what happens if the distance the token has to be carried is too long?

6. The more constrained knowledge acquisition is, the _____ the learning.

Core Knowledge

1. Define 'core knowledge'.

2. What do core-knowledge theorists mean when they say that knowledge is domain specific?

3. Define 'domain (of knowledge)'.

4. According to the core-knowledge perspective, human cognition is a collection of _____.

5. A limitation of a domain is that it does not offer help in _____.

6. How do domain-specific learning mechanisms differ from general knowledge acquisition?

7. Developmental psychologists with a core-knowledge perspective often design experiments with the goal of probing _____'s claims.

8. An experiment that refutes _____ or _____ is seen by many to pass the litmus test of an interesting contribution to the field.

9. Kevin favours domain-general explanations of learning. Everett believes in domain-specific preparedness for knowledge acquisition. In a nature–nurture debate between Kevin and Everett, who would be likely to take which side?

10. True or False: The idea that learning takes place through domain-specific mechanisms and the idea that learning takes place though general-learning mechanisms (like classical and operant conditioning) are mutually exclusive.

Areas of Core Knowledge

1. Define 'intuitive physics'.

2. True or False: Infant laws of physics are the same as adult laws of physics.

3. Object permanence refers to an understanding that _____.

4. Piaget claimed that object permanence was absent in infants younger than _____.

5. What observation led Piaget to believe that young infants do not have object permanence?

6. What would have happened if Piaget had made his observation with the lights turned off?

7. Describe a piece of evidence in support of the idea that infants younger than 8 months have knowledge about the size of an unseen object.

8. Piaget's biggest methodological shortcoming was that he restricted his observations to infants' _____.

9. Researchers since Piaget have instead observed infants' _____.

10. According to Elizabeth Spelke, in addition to object permanence, infants have expectations regarding what three things about physical objects?

11. True or False: Spelke's experiment involving two rods extending above and below a rectangle moving together back and forth demonstrated that 4-month-olds, unlike adults, perceived two separate bars.

12. What type of paradigm was used the above experiment?

13. Tim, a 6-month-old infant, is shown a block moving from a stationary state after it was hit by a moving block. Later on, Tim is shown a block moving from a stationary state just before it was hit by a moving block. Which event would Tim look longer at?

14. How would Tim's response change if he were watching people rather than blocks?

15. Leslie and Keeble's contact experiment showed that 27-month-olds understand launch events. If a pause occurs at the point of contact between block, then _____.

16. What does 'object cohesion' mean?

17. When an object comes apart rather than staying connected, 3-month-old infants _____.

18. Outline Baillargeon and colleagues' proposed developmental progression of understandings of the kind of support an object needs not to fall down due to gravity?

19. True or False: Unlike infants, it is easy to determine what adults know.

20. At 3 months of age, infants accept that contact with the side of another object is enough to keep an object from falling. How could that be explained from the associationist perspective?

21. Define 'occlusion event'.

22. Define 'containment event'.

23. Define 'covering event'.

24. True or False: Infants apply rules and use informative variables for each event category independently.

25. As early as _____ months of age, babies are responsive to violations in occlusion, containment, and covering events.

26. True or False: By 7½ months, transparency of the container is a deemed a factor to consider in occlusion events.

27. Height is seen as an informative variable in _____ events at 3½ months. It is not until 7½ months that height is seen as an informative variable in _____ events.

28. Describe evidence in support of the use of height as an informative variable for one type of event at 3½ months and for another type of event at 7½ months.

29. When is height seen as an informative variable for covering events? How do we know that?

30. True or False: Infants' concepts in the area of intuitive physics are applied quite broadly.

31. Infants have an impressive knowledge of physics early on. However, there are some specific physical concepts that infants are lacking. What are some examples?

32. True or False: Infants know as much about the physics of liquids as they do about the physics of objects.

33. Fill in the age range for each of Piaget's sensorimotor sub-stages.
    a) Sub-stages 1 and 2   _____ to _____
    b) Sub-stage 3   _____ to _____
    c) Sub-stage 4   _____ to _____
    d) Sub-stage 5   _____ to _____
    e) Sub-stage 6   _____ to _____

34. Match the following Piagetian substages to the corresponding behavioural observations.

   1. Sub-stages 1 and 2   a) commits the A-not-B error

   2. Sub-stage 3   b) can deal with 'visible displacement' but not 'invisible displacement'

   3. Sub-stage 4   c) can search systematically through a series of possible hiding places for a hidden object

   4. Sub-stage 5   d) immediately loses interest in an object that disappears from view

   5. Sub-stage 6   e) will reach for an object that is partially occluded but not one that is totally covered

35. True or False: There is no clear evidence that an infant younger than 4 months of age holds a representation of an object that has disappeared from view.

36. It is hard to blame Piaget for concluding that infants younger than 8 months do not have object permanence because at sub-stage 3, they do some bizarre things. Like what?

37. Igor, a 10-month-old infant, watches as a toy is hidden under a washcloth again and again. Next, he watches as it is hidden under a different washcloth. He is then given a chance to search for the toy. What error is he likely to make and what is that error called?

38. True or False: No one is sure why the A-not-B error happens.

39. What does it mean to say that in sub-stage 5, infants understand 'visible displacement' but not 'invisible displacement'?

40. Describe the experimental results that allow us to conclude that 5-month-olds define objects based on spatial location.

41. In strategic encoding of spatial information, humans (and other animals) encode the location of an object with respect to _____ or with respect to _____.

42. True or False: Infants tend to be egocentric in their use of spatial knowledge.

43. Adults can use colour as a spatial clue but toddlers cannot. Describe the experimental results that allow us to draw that conclusion.

44. As early as 6 months of age, infants can use landmarks to locate objects. However, two things must be true of the landmark. What are the two things?

45. Define 'dead reckoning'.

46. At 2 years of age, children show some degree of dead reckoning. Describe the experimental results that allow us to draw that conclusion.

47. True or False: Toddlers are better able to use spatial cognition to find a correct location when they move to the location themselves (rather than being carried).

48. Why is it of limited value to *ask* a young child what he knows about biology?

49. Name three techniques for learning about children's understanding of biology?

50. To make an induction is to generalize from _____ to _____.

51. Spinger and Keil have found that young children believe that a child will resemble a parent with respect to _____ traits but not with respect to _____ traits.

52. Julia is adopted. Her biological mother has blue eyes and her adoptive mother has brown eyes. Hearing this, a 5-year-old would predict that Julia has _____ eyes.

53. A 7-year-old would predict that Julia has _____ eyes.

54. Between a 4-year-old and a 7-year-old, who is more of a nativist and who is more of an empiricist?

55. Preschoolers appreciate that _____ grow and _____ do not.

56. How is the understanding of growth in young children different than in adults?

57. Matthew is 5 years old. He is shown three photos: one of a tree, one of a puppy, and one of a pencil. Matthew is asked to choose photos of what the tree, puppy, and pencil will look like in 2 years. For which (if any) is he likely to choose a larger image?

58. True or False: Four-year-olds expect that both living things and artifacts show re-growth after damage.

59. What other knowledge do young children have regarding growth in living things?

60. True or False: 4-year-old children are unable to make a distinction between sleeping animals and dead animals.

61. Why would intuitive knowledge of biology be adaptive in the EEA?

62. Children possess impressive amounts of intuitive biological knowledge. Infants do not. Why would this make sense developmentally and evolutionarily?

63. True or False: At the age of 4 or 5, children living in low-technology conditions (similar to the EEA) apply essentialist thinking to species but children in contemporary, industrialized cultures do not.

64. A researcher named Atran has found that North American children and Yukatek Mayan children (who live a close-to-Aboriginal lifestyle) use the same _____ to make inferences between animals.

65. Sarah, a preschooler, is shown pictures of a bat with wings outstretched, a hummingbird with wings outstretched, and a flamingo. She is asked which two go together. What would Piaget have predicted as her response?

66. Which of the pictures described above do preschoolers actually group together?

67. True or False: Children in every known culture acquire a basic understanding of numbers and arithmetic at about the same age.

68. At the age of _____, infants can discriminate between sets of up to three entities.

69. After the development of numerosity comes the development of _____.

70. How did Karen Wynn use a violation of expectation paradigm to show that infants can perform basic arithmetic?

71. Match the following skills with the age at which each is acquired.

1. 4 months   a)   appreciates that height is important in a covering event

2. 5 months   b)   expects continuity if a partly occluded object moves behind a screen

3. 7½ months   c)   appreciates that height is important in a containment event

4. 8 months   d)   will manually search for a previously seen object in a dark room

5. 1 year   e)   shows object permanent, according to Piaget

72. What are infants' two systems of numbers?

73. True or False: Rick, a 12-month-old baby, watches as an experimenter puts three cookies in one container and four cookies in another. Rick is offered a choice of two containers. He is more likely to choose the container with four cookies.

74. Children have a set of rules that they follow for counting. What are they?

75. There is evidence that children are beginning to learn the above rules at the age of _____.

A Cross-Species Comparison

1. Like humans, _____ and _____ show evidence of a large-numbers-approximate core number system.

2. _____ also show evidence of a small-numbers-precise core number system.

3. True or False: Like humans, other mammals, as well as some birds, acquire a concept of ordinality without formal training.

4. Ants show dead reckoning but do not show a use of _____ for navigation.

5. Species-specific navigational strategies cannot be explained by universal general-purpose learning mechanisms. Rather, each species is equipped with _____.

Practice Test 1

1. Knowledge is best thought of as

    a. something lost from the person who imparted it.
    b. patterns of organization.
    c. 'stuff' in the brain.
    d. determined by 'nurture'.

2. Constraints on learning

    a. are avoided when programming machines to learn.
    b. interfere with species-typical behaviours.
    c. increase the speed of learning.
    d. are present in some animals but not humans.

3. Core domains of knowledge

    a. have been shaped by natural selection.
    b. differ cross-culturally.
    c. are built by general learning mechanisms.
    d. offer help in making inferences outside the domain.

4. The results of Piaget's 'out of sight' experiment would have been different if he had

    a. made the object more attractive to the infant.
    b. made the object larger.
    c. watched the infant's body positioning.
    d. turned out the lights.

5. Six-month-old infants know that

    a. movement always requires contact with something else.
    b. movement of people does not require contact with something else.
    c. contact is unrelated to movement.
    d. contact with something else matters for moving but not stationary objects.

6. Which of the following statements describes a 3-month-old infant's understanding of gravity?

    a. Contact with the side of a stable object is enough to prevent falling.
    b. The bottom of an object must be supported to prevent falling.
    c. Support is not necessary to prevent falling.
    d. An understanding of gravity must be preceded by an understanding of object permanence.

7. Early on, infants use informative variables in event categories

    a. only for covering events.
    b. in ways that are very similar to how adults use them.
    c. for everything except containment events.
    d. independently.

8. Infants' concepts in the area of intuitive physics are applied

    a. very narrowly.
    b. consistently when the same props are used.
    c. to people but not objects.
    d. uniformly across all domains.

9. Which of the following statements is *not* true regarding humans' knowledge of non-objects?

    a. Adults can keep track of moving objects better than moving non-objects.
    b. Infants have knowledge about objects and not non-objects because their experience is limited to objects.
    c. When sand is poured behind a screen and then the screen is removed to reveal no sand, 8-month-olds are not surprised.
    d. Infants tend to apply rules to objects but not non-objects.

10. Piaget's sub-stage 3 spans from _____ months of age.

    a. 2 to 3
    b. 2 to 6
    c. 4 to 6
    d. 4 to 8

11. Tatiana, who is 14 months old, watches as her mother repeatedly hides a toy under a blanket placed to Tatiana's left. Her mother then hides the toy under a blanket placed to Tatiana's right. What do you think Tatiana will do?

    a. She will reach for the toy under the blanket to her right.
    b. She will reach for the toy under the blanket to her left.
    c. She will act as though she believes the toy has disappeared.
    d. She will reach for the toy under the blanket to her left and then check under the blanket to her right.

12. An experiment described in the textbook that involved hiding toys in the corner of a rectangular room showed that for adults, but not for infants, _____ can be used as a spatial cue.

   a. size
   b. room geometry
   c. auditory cues
   d. colour

13. The ability to continuously keep track of one's location relative to a starting point is referred to as

   a. location maintenance.
   b. absolute reckoning.
   c. dead reckoning.
   d. position maintenance.

14. Which of the following is *not* a useful technique for learning about children's understandings of biology?

   a. Ask them what they know.
   b. The inference technique.
   c. The transformation technique.
   d. The method of induction.

15. Morgan is 7 years old. For which of the following characteristics would she say a child should resemble his adoptive parents more than his biological parents?

   a. height
   b. eye colour
   c. intelligence
   d. none of the above

16. Stavros is 4 years old. He probably does not understand that

   a. re-growth will occur in a living thing that has been damaged.
   b. growth may involve qualitative changes.
   c. growth is beyond intentional control.
   d. plants need water to grow.

17. Which of the following statements is true with regard to children's intuitive understanding of death?

   a. The understanding is different in children growing up in a contemporary industrialized culture compared to children growing up in conditions similar to the EEA.
   b. The understanding seems to develop before the age of 2.
   c. At 4 years of age, children can discriminate between animals that are asleep and animals that are dead.
   d. none of the above

18. Piaget believed that preschoolers are pre-causal. If he was right, then they shouldn't be able to

   a. distinguish between growing because you've been fed and growing because you want to grow.
   b. understand that living things get bigger.
   c. see a similarity between a hummingbird and a bat.
   d. understand that living things die.

19. Which of the following statements is *not* true regarding number understanding?

   a. Mathematical understanding appears to be an evolved, domain-specific cognitive process.
   b. A basic understanding of numbers is acquired at about the same age in children of all cultures.
   c. Formal education is necessary for a basic understanding of arithmetic.
   d. It is intuitive.

20. Which of the following statements is true about numerosity?

   a. Very young infants will not dishabituate when the number of objects in a display changes.
   b. Very young infants cannot match numbers across modalities.
   c. Numerosity in young infants exists for objects but not events.
   d. Researchers disagree about whether very young infants have true representations of numbers.

21. The textbook describes an experiment in which infants were taught to touch a screen in response to visual arrays. The results of this experiment suggested that infants had

   a. the ability to perform arithmetic.
   b. a non-numeric representation of amount.
   c. a sense of ordinality.
   d. an approximate sense of large numbers.

22. Infants have two systems of numbers:

   a. a precise system for small numbers and an approximate system for large numbers.
   b. an approximate system for small numbers and a precise system for large numbers.
   c. a precise system for visually-represented numbers and an approximate system for aurally-presented numbers.
   d. a precise system for aurally-represented numbers and an approximate system for visually-presented numbers.

23. According to a habituation study cited in the textbook, 6-month-olds cannot discriminate between

   a. 8 and 16 items.
   b. 16 and 32 items.
   c. 8 and 12 items.
   d. none of the above

24. The idea that each item in an array should get a unique number label is called

    a. the one-to-one principle.
    b. the abstraction principle.
    c. the order-irrelevant principle.
    d. the matching principle.

25. Which of the following statements is *not* true regarding navigational skills?

    a. Navigational cues are species-specific.
    b. Within species, navigational strategies are universal.
    c. All species use landmarks in navigation.
    d. Navigational skills cannot be explained by general-purpose learning mechanisms.

Practice Test 2

1. Specialized learning mechanisms that are endowed in an individual may be referred to as

    a. core knowledge.
    b. innate domains.
    c. privileged domains.
    d. any of the above

2. Infants have an intuitive knowledge of the laws of physics that

    a. is the same as adults' knowledge of the laws of physics.
    b. exceeds Piaget's estimate.
    c. requires extensive experience with objects.
    d. is slow to develop.

3. Piaget believed that infants do not acquire object permanence until they are _____ old.

    a. 3 months
    b. 6 months
    c. 8 months
    d. 1 year

4. The main reason that Piaget underestimated infants' object knowledge was that

    a. his methodology was not sensitive to infants' true object knowledge.
    b. he spent very little time actually observing infants.
    c. he used the violation of expectation paradigm exclusively.
    d. he was not interested in infants' object knowledge.

5. Spelke's experiment with a moving rod behind an occluder demonstrated that 4-month-old infants have an understanding of

   a. cohesion.
   b. contact.
   c. continuity.
   d. consistency.

6. In Leslie & Keeble's contact experiment, 27-month-old children did not perceive a launch when

   a. there was no point of contact.
   b. a smaller block made contact with a larger block.
   c. the event was shown very quickly.
   d. there was a delay between contact and movement.

7. We know that 3-month-old infants expect an object to maintain cohesion because they will express surprise when

   a. two objects touch each other.
   b. part of an object remains when another part is lifted.
   c. objects move by themselves.
   d. one object causes damage to another.

8. In general, the results from experiments testing infants' knowledge of gravity

   a. are best explained from an associationist point of view.
   b. are consistent with a core-knowledge view.
   c. neither *a* nor *b*
   d. both *a* and *b*

9. In occlusion events, an object

   a. is placed into a container.
   b. suddenly disappears.
   c. becomes invisible as it moves behind a nearer object.
   d. becomes hidden by a cover.

10. At 3½ months old, infants recognize height as an important variable in _____ events. It is not recognized in _____ events until 7½ months.

    a. occlusion; containment
    b. containment; occlusion
    c. occlusion; covering
    d. covering; occlusion

11. Infants are lacking in their knowledge of

    a. the effects of gravity on objects in motion.
    b. momentum.
    c. inertia.
    d. all of the above

12. When an object disappears from his view, 1-month-old Jerry is likely to

    a. express surprise.
    b. continue looking at the spot where it disappeared.
    c. lose interest immediately.
    d. any of the above—1-month-old infants are unpredictable.

13. Infants in Piaget's sub-stage 4 are likely to make the _____ error.

    a. A-and-B
    b. A-not-B
    c. A-if-B
    d. A-without-B

14. Infants in Piaget's sub-stage 5 have one limitation to an adult-like understanding of objects: a lack of understanding of

    a. moving displacement.
    b. non-moving displacement.
    c. invisible displacement.
    d. visible displacement.

15. There is evidence that 5-month-old infants use _____ to define an object.

    a. appearance
    b. spatial location
    c. colour
    d. shape

16. Which of the following statements is *not* true regarding the development of spatial cognition?

    a. Self-locomotion is important.
    b. At 6 months, infants are able to use any available landmark to locate an object.
    c. 2-year-old children are not perfectly able to keep track of their location relative to a starting point but they are better than chance.
    d. It is hard to explain using associationist learning.

17. Making an induction involves

    a. generalizing from a category to an instance.
    b. generalizing across categories.
    c. discriminating between instances.
    d. inferring from an instance to a category

18. Preschoolers reject the idea

    a. of quantitative change.
    b. that living things grow larger.
    c. that plants grow larger.
    d. that very small animals grow.

19. Cross-cultural research on intuitive biology shows that

    a. an understanding of non-human species is a matter of borrowing ideas about humans.
    b. children from different cultures use different taxonomies to make inferences between animals.
    c. perceptual similarities override species-level groupings in making biological inferences.
    d. all children apply essentialist thinking to species by the age of 4 or 5 years.

20. Infants as young as _____ can discriminate between sets of up to three entities.

    a. 1 week
    b. 1 month
    c. 2 months
    d. 1 year

21. The textbook describes an experiment involving two Minnie Mouse dolls placed behind a screen. The results of this experiment suggested that

    a. young infants' expectations are driven by perceptual similarity.
    b. young infants seem to be able to add 1 + 1.
    c. young infants are not surprised by unexpected number changes.
    d. young infants can subtract.

22. At 10 months of age, infants are capable of discriminating between items of a ratio of

    a. 1:2.
    b. 2:3.
    c. 3:4.
    d. both *a* and *b*

23. The cardinal principle of counting is that

    a. anything can be counted.
    b. number labels should be spoken in the same order every time.
    c. total number remains the same regardless of counting order.
    d. whatever number label you give to the last item is the total.

24. At 3 years old, children apply counting principles with a consistency of about _____ per cent.

    a. 10
    b. 30
    c. 50
    d. 90

25. Like humans, _____ appear to have a core number system representing a small number of individual items.

   a. rats
   b. ants
   c. bats
   d. rhesus monkeys

Study Questions: Answer Key

The Acquisition of Knowledge

1. Epistemology (p. 216)

2. True—Early rationalists believed that at least some knowledge exists without having to be taught. (p. 217)

3. nature vs. nurture (p. 217)

4. Consider the following in your response:
   • Knowledge acquisition can be thought of in terms of information processing.
   • Acquisition of knowledge, as with a computer file transfer, doesn't take anything from anywhere. Rather, it changes the organization of information in the recipient. (pp. 217–218)

Framing the Question of Knowledge Acquisition

1. False—The acquisition of knowledge actually requires some kind of preparedness. (p. 218)

2. Constraints on learning are biased heuristics or privileged hypotheses that an animal uses when acquiring information about the world. (p. 219)

3. False—Animals are not blank slates; operant conditioning works for some behaviours and not others. (p. 219)

4. Consider the following examples:
   • Male stickleback fish can be conditioned to bite a glass rod, but not to swim through a hoop, with the 'reward' of seeing another male stickleback fish.
   • Male stickleback fish can be conditioned to swim through a hoop, but not to bite a glass rod, with the 'reward' of seeing a female stickleback fish. (p. 219)

5. Consider the following in your response:
   • Pigs may stop and try 'rooting'.
   • Raccoons may start washing their tokens.
   • Both are species-typical behaviours that are associated with food. Both demonstrate that animals are not blank slates. (p. 219)

6. faster (p. 219)

Core Knowledge

1. Core knowledge consists of privileged domains of knowledge that children learn easily by virtue of developing cognitive preparedness that is specific to those domains. These domains reflect a fitness advantage in our evolutionary history. (p. 222)

2. In saying that knowledge is domain specific, core-knowledge theorists mean
   - that many aspects of adult and child psychology are processed by specialized psychological processes.
   - that these processes have been shaped by natural selection and focus on areas of knowledge that were adaptive in the EEA. (p. 222)

3. A domain is a knowledge system that includes information about what entities are included in the domain as well as rules that describe how the entities in the domain behave. (p. 222)

4. domain-specific systems of knowledge (p. 222)

5. making inferences *outside* of the domain (p. 222)

6. Domain-specific mechanisms are
   - more specific (obviously).
   - more powerful.
   - important tools for children developing in the EEA. (p. 222)

7. Piaget (p. 223)

8. Piaget's stages; Piaget's rejection of the idea of sophisticated knowledge in very young children (p. 223)

9. Answer:
   - Those who favour domain-general explanations are skeptical of a large role of constraints on learning (constraints that were shaped by natural selection) so Kevin would likely be on the nurture side.
   - Those who favour domain-specific explanations expect little to develop if there are no built-in mechanisms so Everett would likely be on the nature side. (p. 223)

10. False—Behaviours can unquestionably be taught using classical or operant conditioning. It's just that some behaviours are much more easily taught in some domains. (p. 223)

Areas of Core Knowledge

1. Intuitive physics refers to knowledge relevant to physics and objects that develops early in human infants. (p. 224)

2. False—They are not necessarily the same. (p. 224)

3. an object exists even when it is out of sight (p. 224)

4. 8 months (p. 224)

5. Consider the following in your response:
   - Piaget observed that infants younger than 8 months will not look for an object that has suddenly been removed from view.
   - He assumed that this meant they had no mental representation of the object. (p. 224)

6. With the room dark, a 5-month-old infant may reach out and manually search for an object, exploring the last place it was seen. Contrary to Piaget's claim, they do seem to know that an object they can't see still exists. (p. 225)

7. If a 6-month-old infant hears the sound of a familiar large object, he will reach for it with two hands; if he hears the sounds of a familiar small object, he will reach for it with one hand. (p. 225)

8. spontaneous *behaviours* (p. 225)

9. looking times (p. 225)

10. Infants have expectations regarding the following:
    - Continuity
    - Contact
    - Cohesion (p. 225)

11. False—Like adults, 4-month-old infants represented one solid bar. That is, they represented the bar as continuous. (p. 226)

12. Consider the following in your response:
    - A habituation paradigm was used.
    - After habituating to the stimulus, the rectangle occluder was removed. Infants who were shown two separate rods dishabituated (looked longer).
    - This suggests that the image of two separate rods is different than their perception of the stimulus they had habituated to. (p. 226)

13. Tim would probably look longer at the second event because it would violate his expectation that an object must be in contact with another in order to have an influence on its movement. (pp. 226–227)

14. Tim's looking time would probably not be greater for the second event because infants accept that, unlike blocks, people can affect each other's behaviour without contact. (p. 227)

15. no launch is perceived (pp. 227–228)

16. An object has cohesion if it stays together in one piece when it is moved. (p. 228)

17. look longer (indicating surprise) (p. 228)

18. The developmental progression of the understanding of gravity is as follows:
    - 3 months: Infants understand that an object needs some contact with a solid support in order not to fall.
    - 5 months: Infants understand that contact has to be made with the top of the support structure (not the side) or the object will fall.
    - 6 months: Infants understand that most of the bottom of the object must be supported or it will fall. (p. 229)

19. False—It is not as simple as asking adults what they know. Adults can be instinct blind and they may not be able to access their own decision-making processes. (p. 230)

20. It couldn't be explained from an associationist perspective. Associationists believe that experience determines behaviour and the infant has never seen an object supported by side contact. (p. 230)

21. An occlusion event is one in which an object becomes invisible as it moves behind a nearer, occluding object. (p. 231)

22. A containment event is one in which an object moves into a container, possibly becoming invisible. (p. 231)

23. A covering event is one in which an object becomes invisible as it is hidden by a cover. (p. 231)

24. True—The realization that height, for example, is important for occlusion events does not necessarily imply a realization that height is important for containment events. (p. 231)

25. 2½ (p. 231)

26. True—7½-month-old infants understand that objects should remain visible if they go behind an occluder that is transparent. (p. 231)

27. occlusion; containment (pp. 231–232)

28. Consider the following in your response:
    - 3½-month-old infants do not expect a tall object that goes behind a short occluder to disappear entirely.
    - Infants younger than 7½ months do not express surprise when a cylinder that is taller than a tube is hidden by the tube. (pp. 231–232)

29. Height is not used as an informative variable for covering events until 12 months. Infants younger than 12 months do not show surprise if a shorter tube is lowered onto a taller cylinder. (p. 232)

30. False—As detailed in the answers to the above three questions, such concepts are applied very narrowly. (p. 233)

31. Infants are lacking ideas about
    - inertia
    - momentum
    - effects of gravity on objects in motion (p. 233)

32. False—Although they have presumably had plenty of opportunity to observe the characteristics of liquids, their knowledge about physics seems to apply only to objects. (p. 233)

33. a) Sub-stages 1 and 2   birth to 4 months
    b) Sub-stage 3   4 to 8 months
    c) Sub-stage 4   8 to 12 months
    d) Sub-stage 5   12 to 18 months
    e) Sub-stage 6   18 to 24 months (p. 234)

34. 1. Sub-stages 1 and 2   d) immediately loses interest in an object that disappears from view
    2. Sub-stage 3   e) will reach for an object that is partially occluded but not one that is totally covered
    3. Sub-stage 4   a) commits the A-not-B error
    4. Sub-stage 5   b) can deal with 'visible displacement' but not 'invisible displacement'
    5. Sub-stage 6   c) can search systematically through a series of possible hiding places for a hidden object (p. 234)

35. True—When an object disappears from view, an infant younger than 4 months loses interest immediately. If he continues to look toward the spot where the object disappeared, it is only for a moment. (p. 234)

36. Consider the following in your response:
    - If an object is occluded while the infant is reaching for it, he will drop his hand as if the object has been forgotten.
    - Even if it is already in her grasp, an infant will not lift an object toward herself if it has become occluded. (p. 234)

37. Igor is likely to search for the toy under the first washcloth. This is called the A-not-B error. (p. 234)

38. True—It is a persistent puzzle in cognitive development. (p. 234)

39. If an infant in sub-stage 5 sees you move an object to a particular location (visible displacement), she will look for it there. If you secretly move the object to a different location, she will persist in looking for it where she last saw it. She is incapable of expanding her search to other locations. (p. 234)

40. Consider the following experiment in your response:
    - An experimenter digs a hole in a sandbox and buries an object with the 5-month-old watching.
    - Ten seconds later, the experimenter digs in the same location and retrieves the object.
    - The experimenter repeats this four times.
    - The fifth time, the experimenter digs up the item from a different location.
    - The infant expresses surprise by looking longer. The infant will not express surprise if a completely different object is dug out of the different location. (p. 235)

41. themselves; other landmarks (p. 235)

42. True—Presented with two attractive toys, young infants will reach for the object that is closer to them. (p. 235)

43. Consider the following experiment in your response:
    - An experimenter hides a toy in one of four corners of a rectangular room. People are disoriented and then allowed to search for the object.
    - When all the walls are the same colour, both adults and toddlers are more likely to search in the correct corner or the opposite corner than the other two corners. This suggests that they are using room geometry to inform their search.
    - When one of the walls is painted a different colour than the other three, adults use the colour information to solve the problem—they always choose to look for the object in the correct corner. One differently-coloured wall doesn't help infants at all. (pp. 235–237)

44. The landmark must be
    - obvious.
    - located close to the hidden object. (p. 237)

45. Dead reckoning is the ability to continuously keep track of one's location relative to the starting point and thus return directly to it. (p. 237)

46. Consider the following experiment in your response:
    - 2-year-olds are shown an attractive toy that is then hidden in sand.
    - They are led in a different direction, following an indirect route, in a room without landmarks.
    - Their ability to return to the toy is better than chance. (p. 237)

47. True—Self-locomotion matters. (p. 238)

48. They are not usually able to describe the things they know. (p. 238)

49. Three techniques for learning about children's understanding of biology are
    - method of induction
    - transformation technique
    - just ask them (pp. 238–239)

50. an entire class; a single instance (p. 238)

51. biological; social (p. 239)

52. brown (p. 240)

53. blue (p. 240)

54. Consider the following in your response:
    - You could argue that the 4-year-old is more of an empiricist. Younger children often base answers on nurture: an animal raised by a goat is a goat.
    - You could argue that the 7-year-old is more of a nativist. Older children often base answers on nature: a kangaroo raised by goats doesn't lose any 'kangaroo-ness'. (p. 240)

55. living things; non-living things/artifacts (p. 240)

56. Compared to adults, young children
   - reject the idea of qualitative change (e.g. changing from a caterpillar to a butterfly).
   - reject the idea that very small animals (e.g. worms) grow. (p. 240)

57. Consider the following in your response:
   - For both the tree and the puppy, he will probably choose a larger image.
   - For the pencil, he will probably choose a same-size image.
   - This demonstrates an appreciation that living things grow and artifacts do not. (p. 240)

58. False—At 4 years of age, children expect damaged living things to re-grow but not artifacts. (p. 240)

59. Regarding living things, children understand that
   - food (for animals) and water (for plants) is necessary for growth.
   - growth is beyond intentional control. (p. 240)

60. False—At 4 years of age, children can distinguish between sleeping animals and dead animals. (p. 241)

61. Intuitive knowledge of biology was adaptive in the EEA because
   - plants and animals were our ancestors' food sources. Knowledge of food sources would have been adaptive.
   - this knowledge would have helped in understanding and controlling bodily processes, which would have been adaptive. (pp. 241–242)

62. Infants don't yet need biological knowledge—parents/caregivers manage their biological needs. (p. 242)

63. False—Children across cultures apply essentialist thinking to species. (p. 242)

64. taxonomies (p. 242)

65. Piaget would have predicted that she would group the bat and the hummingbird together because they are more perceptually similar. (p. 244)

66. They actually group the birds together, separate from the bat. (p. 244)

67. True—Basic understanding of numbers and arithmetic emerges at roughly the same age, regardless of formal education. (p. 245)

68. (less than) 1 week (p. 245)

69. ordinality (p. 245)

70. Consider the following experiment in your response:
   - 5-month-old infants were shown a single object.
   - A screen rose in front of the object, occluding it.
   - A hand carried a second identical object behind the screen and exited empty-handed.
   - When the screen dropped and there was only one object, infants showed surprise (more looking time).
   - This suggests that they did the math and were surprised when it didn't add up. (p. 246)

71.
   1. 4 months   b) expects continuity if a partly occluded object moves behind a screen
   2. 5 months   d) will manually search for a previously-seen object in a dark room
   3. 7½ months   c) appreciates that height is important in a containment event
   4. 8 months   e) shows object permanent, according to Piaget
   5. 1 year   a) appreciates that height is important in a covering event (p. 244)

72. Infants' systems of numbers are as follows:
   - The first system represents large numbers. They are represented very approximately.
   - The second system represents very small numbers (1, 2, and possibly 3). They are represented very precisely. (p. 246)

73. False—He would not be more likely to choose the one with 4 cookies. He *would* be more likely to choose 3 over 2 and 2 over 1 but 3 vs. 4 seems to be over the limit for what a 12-month-old can keep track of. (p. 246)

74. Answer:
   - The one-to-one principle: Each item gets a unique number label
   - The stable-order principle: Number labels should be spoken in the same order every time
   - The cardinal principle: The last number label assigned is the total
   - The abstraction principle: *Anything* can be counted
   - The order-irrelevant principle: Counting order doesn't matter; the total should be the same regardless of order (p. 248)

75. 2½ years (p. 250)

A Cross-Species Comparison

1. rats; rhesus monkeys (p. 249)

2. Rhesus monkeys (p. 249)

3. False—Other mammals and some birds can be taught ordinality but it requires hundreds of trials and sometimes years of training. (p. 249)

4. landmarks (p. 250)

5. specific, well-designed learning mechanisms (p. 250)

Practice Test 1: Answer Key

1. **b** (p. 216)	8. **a** (p. 233)	15. **c** (p. 240)	22. **a** (p. 246)
2. **c** (p. 219)	9. **b** (p. 233)	16. **b** (p. 240)	23. **c** (p. 245)
3. **a** (p. 222)	10. **d** (p. 234)	17. **c** (pp. 241–242)	24. **a** (p. 248)
4. **d** (p. 225)	11. **a** (p. 234)	18. **a** (pp. 244–245)	25. **c** (p. 250)
5. **b** (p. 227)	12. **d** (p. 235)	19. **c** (p. 245)	
6. **a** (p. 229)	13. **c** (p. 237)	20. **d** (p. 245)	
7. **d** (p. 231)	14. **b** (p. 238)	21. **c** (pp. 245–246)	

Practice Test 2: Answer Key

1. **d** (p. 222)	8. **b** (p. 229)	15. **b** (p. 235)	22. **d** (p. 246)
2. **b** (p. 224)	9. **c** (p. 231)	16. **b** (p. 237)	23. **d** (p. 248)
3. **c** (p. 224)	10. **a** (p. 231)	17. **a** (p. 238)	24. **b** (p. 248)
4. **a** (p. 225)	11. **d** (p. 233)	18. **d** (p. 240)	25. **d** (p. 249)
5. **c** (p. 226)	12. **c** (p. 234)	19. **d** (p. 242)	
6. **d** (pp. 227–228)	13. **b** (p. 234)	20. **a** (p. 245)	
7. **b** (p. 228)	14. **c** (p. 234)	21. **b** (p. 246)	

Chapter 8

Core Knowledge Part II:
Face Perception, Animacy Perception, and Theory of Mind

Chapter Summary

As an *obligate social species*, humans must be with others in order to survive. Interacting with others was adaptive in the EEA and therefore we have a strong social imperative.

Social Contact as a Need: Harry Harlow's Social Experiments

Harry Harlow looked at the effects of social isolation on rhesus monkeys. Partial isolation resulted in abnormal behaviours (e.g. self-mutilation, pacing). The effects of total isolation were extreme, far-reaching, and resistant to rehabilitation.

Why the Big Brain?

Human brains are very large and costly (evolutionarily, developmentally, and metabolically). What led to the evolution of our enormous brains? One possibility is that it is a result of *ecological pressures*: A large brain is necessary for capitalizing on available food sources. Another possibility is that a large brain is necessary for navigating social challenges; this is called the *social brain hypothesis*. This hypothesis is supported by the fact that humans are most adept at interacting with large groups of people (about 150 to 200, a much larger group than any other primate). Further, as would be predicted by the social brain hypothesis, the size of species' neocortex correlates with group size (and not with ecological demands). Brain size is also predicted by social complexity.

The Big Brain and Long Childhood

Humans are slow to 'grow up'. A long childhood appears to be necessary to acquire social knowledge expertise.

What Would Piaget Say about Social Cognitive Development?

Piaget believed that children in the preoperational stage were *egocentric*; that is, they understood the world from their own point of view only. Piaget used the idea of egocentrism to explain why young children failed the classic three mountain task. They were unable to appreciate that another person has knowledge and visual access that is different than theirs. Children's speech contains traces of egocentrism, the assumption that everyone else knows what they know.

Other signs of cognitive immaturity, according to Piaget, are *animism* (attributing mental states to inanimate objects) and *realism* (attributing physical characteristics to mental entities).

What Would Associationists Say?

A strict empiricist would say that personality is determined by learning from the environment. In the empiricist tradition, social learning theory emphasizes learning from observation and imitation.

Social Domains of Core Knowledge

Young children, adult chimpanzees, and adult orangutans perform at a similar level on physical cognitive tests. However, young children far out-perform the other two groups on social cognitive tests. Humans have a great deal of social expertise with each cognitive skill dependent on specialized, reliably developing cognitive machinery.

Social Cognitive Development in Infancy

Young infants need adults to manage their needs. Social cognitive skills are designed to elicit help from others.

Young children are not quite as egocentric as Piaget proposed. Flavell has proposed that 2- and 3-year-old children have a Level 1 understanding of perspective; they understand that, in order to see something, a person must have open eyes and a clear line of sight to the object. Level 2 understanding exists for 4- and 5-year-old children; they realize that another person might see an object differently than they do.

As early as 5 or 6 weeks after birth, infants imitate adults' facial behaviours, creating an interactive relationship. Babies can also recognize (and take pleasure in) others imitating them.

By 9 months of age, babies show aspects of *joint attention* (sharing an object of attention with another person), demonstrating an awareness of mental processes in others. As well, early on, children use *social referencing* to formulate a response in an ambiguous situation.

Pretend Play

Most of children's awake time is spent playing. Play does not require any explicit instruction. Piaget distinguished between *sensorimotor play*, involving object manipulation, and *pretend play*, involving imagined actions, objects, or characters. Pretend play, according to Piaget, provides practice for events in the social world. It can also be seen as evidence for a developing theory of mind. Pretend play emerges by the age of 18 months and becomes more sophisticated over the preschool years. Though it is, literally, child's play, pretend play is a complex cognitive accomplishment.

Face Perception

Face perception in humans is unique from other visual perception. An area in the brain called the *fusiform face area* is specialized for face processing. We tend to be most interested in looking at faces.

Face processing is disrupted when a face is inverted. The disruption from inversion is larger for faces than other visual stimuli, suggesting that faces are processed differently. Another hallmark of face perception is *holistic processing*: faces are processed as a whole, not as a combination of parts.

From 2 months of age, infants prefer to look at faces (with the features in the proper configuration) over non-faces. In fact, face preference is evident much earlier than that: 9-minute-old infants were shown to turn their heads and eyes more to follow face than non-face images. Face preference follows a *U-shaped curve*, appearing early on, temporarily disappearing, and then re-appearing. It is likely that very early preference is mediated by one psychological process and later preference is mediated by another.

Face perception becomes more specialized with age. Six-month-olds are better than 9-months-olds at discriminating between non-human (monkey) faces, presumably because 9-month-olds have a greater degree of *perceptual narrowing*.

Animacy and Intentionality Perception

A fundamental building block to social cognition is *animacy perception*: an understanding of which entities have psychological goings-on. At 1 year old, babies have different expectations of the behaviour of animate versus inanimate objects.

At 3 months of age, infants prefer a social display of animacy over a non-social display. As early as 1 year, infants expect rational behaviour from animate objects. They also seem to attribute dispositional states to agents and use those dispositions to predict the behaviour of the agent and others around it.

Toddlers understand the intentions of another person, even if the intention fails. They can infer mental states, given behaviour. They are able to parse other people's actions into separate acts, each with a perceived goal.

Theory of Mind

Humans are able to understand other people's mental states; that is, humans have *theory of mind*. At 12 months, infants have a basic theory of mind, an understanding of mental constructs that helps in interpreting and predicting the behaviour of others.

The appearance–reality distinction was a focus of early studies on the understanding of mental states. It is not until the age of 11 or 12 that children are proficient at understanding and discussing the fact that something can look different than how it really is. Tests of the appearance–reality distinction may underestimate theory of mind competence.

False-belief tasks are another measure of theory of mind. In these tasks, the child must appreciate a character's false belief in order to predict or explain her behaviour. Three-year-olds (but not 5-year-olds) routinely fail a false belief task. For example, if shown that a Smarties box actually contains pencils, a 3-year-old will predict that a friend (who has never seen inside the box) will know that it contains pencils.

New and innovative research methods have demonstrated the development of theory of mind in children much younger than 3 years. At 15 months, babies show evidence of an appreciation of an actor's belief when choosing locations to look for a toy.

Autism: What If There Were No Theory of Mind?

Autism is a developmental disorder that involves a deficit in social cognition, a delay in communication development, and an adherence to routine or repetitive behaviours. Baron-Cohen proposed that a theory of mind deficit is the defining feature of autism. Evidence supports this proposal, and researchers have found that children with autism spectrum disorders (ASD) are relatively unable to identify animate objects, have deficits in joint attention, and have difficulty with false-belief tasks.

Face processing in children with ASD seems to be accomplished using atypical strategies. Face recognition and the identification of emotional facial expressions are challenging. Children with ASD do not show the typical preference for looking at the eyes of the face. This is significant because the eyes provide a great deal of information about emotions (complex emotions in particular).

Children with ASD show a different social development trajectory than other children. They do not orient normally to social stimuli, devoting relatively little attention to eyes, eye gaze, emotional facial expressions, and so on. They do not, therefore, gather the social information that is necessary for typical development.

An investigation of autism is useful practically (for diagnosis and treatment) and theoretically (for testing hypotheses about typical development of social cognition).

Learning Objectives

After reading this chapter, you should be able to:

- Appreciate humans' *need* to be around others (pp. 256–257)

- Discuss the devastation caused by social isolation in an obligate social species (Harlow's rhesus monkeys) (pp. 258–260)

- Understand why humans have such large brains and such a long childhood (pp. 260–264)

- Summarize Piaget's stance (pp. 265–266) and the associationists' stance (pp. 266–267) on social cognitive development

- Compare the physical and social cognitive abilities of young humans to those of chimpanzees and orangutans (pp. 267–268)

- Discuss early cognitive skills in humans, including imitation, joint attention, and social referencing (pp. 268–271)

- Understand the purpose and complexity of pretend play (pp. 271–273)

- Appreciate the special case of face perception (pp. 274–278)

- Summarize how much infants and toddlers know about animacy (distinguishing animate from inanimate objects) and the intentionality of other people's actions (pp. 278–282)

- Trace the development of theory of mind (pp. 283–287)

- Examine what we can learn about theory of mind and social cognition from the case of autism (pp. 287–291)

Suggested Readings

Emery, N., Clayton, N., & Frith, C. (2008). *Social Intelligence: From Brain to Culture*. Oxford, UK: Oxford University Press.

This book is an examination of the development and evolution of social intelligence in different species.

Meltzoff, A. N., & Moore, M. K. (1994). Imitation, memory, and the representation of persons. *Infant Behavior & Development, 17*, 83–99.

Six-week-old infants were found to imitate facial expressions (immediately and 24 hours later).

Gladwell, M. (2005). *Blink: The Power of Thinking Without Thinking*. New York: Little, Brown and Company.

This book summarizes psychological issues, and is written for a wide audience. Much of the book is tangential to the current topics but there is a fascinating discussion of autism and the interpretation of facial expressions.

Study Questions

1. The hallucination of _____ is one of the most common in circumstances of social isolation.

2. Define 'obligate social species'.

3. True or False: Humans *need* other humans.

4. Explain how social skills would have been naturally selected in humans living in the EEA.

5. True or False: Sociability is less important for infants and young children than it is for adults.

6. Starting at the age of _____, newborns smile interactively with caregivers.

Social Contact as a Need: Harry Harlow's Social Experiments

1. Experimenting with *human* social isolation would be unethical. Harry Harlow used _____ instead.

2. What was the difference between the partial and total isolation conditions in Harlow's experiments?

3. What were the results of partial isolation?

4. What were the results of total isolation?

5. What happened when the former isolates became mothers?

6. True or False: Once reunited with other monkeys, the former isolates were quickly rehabilitated.

7. What was the most successful therapy for the former isolates?

Why the Big Brain?

1. How are brains 'costly'?

2. What does it mean to say that a big brain may be the result of ecological pressures?

3. What does it mean to say that a big brain is the result of social demands?

4. True or False: High intelligence in humans is the consequence of social integration.

5. How does human group size compare to other primates?

6. True or False: The neocortex is the 'oldest' part of the brain.

7. Among primates, the size of a species' neocortex correlates with _____.

8. Among primates, the size of a species' neocortex does *not* correlate with _____.

9. In addition to the size of the group, the _____ and _____ of social relationships predicts brain size.

10. What specific measures of social complexity have been found to predict brain size?

11. Humans congregate in groups, but so do sheep. What's the difference?

The Big Brain and Long Childhood

1. True or False: Neocortex size correlates with the length of the reproductive lifespan.

2. Why do humans take so long to 'grow up'?

What Would Piaget Say about Social Cognitive Development?

1. Define 'egocentrism'.

2. What is the three mountain task?

3. How does a child who is younger than 9 or 10 years of age respond to the three mountain task?

4. Describe an example of egocentrism in children's speech?

5. Define 'animism'.

6. Define 'realism'.

What Would Associationists Say?

1. Bandura's _____ theory is the most prominent contemporary empiricist theory that addresses social development.

2. True or False: Bandura's theory emphasizes the effects of rewards and punishments on learning.

Social Domains of Core Knowledge

1. True or False: At 2½ years of age, children out-perform adult chimpanzees on physical cognitive tests (e.g. memory for object locations, quantity discrimination).

2. What types of tests are young humans better at?

Social Cognitive Development in Infancy

1. Why do newborns cry?

2. True or False: At 18 months old, babies know that, in order to see something, there must be a direct line of vision between the eyes and the object.

3. Describe Flavell's Level 1 understanding of perspective.

4. Describe Flavell's Level 2 understanding of perspective?

5. At the age of 5 or 6 weeks, infants will imitate adults' _____.

6. Why are developmental psychologists quite sure that the behaviour described above is a *social* behaviour?

7. Fourteen-month-old Walter is seated in front of 2 adults, one of whom is imitating the other's behaviours and one of whom is not. How will Walter react?

8. Define 'joint attention'.

9. What are some indicators of joint attention in 9-month-old infants?

10. Joint attention behaviours are thought to be evidence of a developing _____.

11. Young Omar is introduced to his older cousin for the first time. He looks back and forth between his cousin and his father, assessing his father's reaction to this new person. Omar is demonstrating _____.

Pretend Play

1. Children spend most of their awake time engaged in _____.

2. Define 'sensorimotor play'.

3. Define 'pretend play'.

4. Pretend play can be seen as evidence of the child's developing _____.

5. Outline the developmental timeline of pretend play.

Face Perception

1. The area of the brain that is dedicated to face perception is the _____.

2. Define the 'inversion effect'.

3. The inversion 'cost' (in terms of percent accuracy) for faces is _____; for non-faces, it is _____.

4. Define 'holistic processing'.

5. How does the composite face task provide evidence for holistic face processing?

6. How do we know that faces are special to 2-month-old infants?

7. True or False: Minutes-old newborns demonstrate face preference.

8. How does face preference follow a U-shaped curve?

9. In what other ways (other than face preference) do infants orient to social information?

10. Define 'perceptual narrowing'.

11. True or False: At 6 months of age, infants are good at discriminating between two human faces but not two monkey faces.

12. True or False: By 9 months, infants are good at discriminating between two human faces but not two monkey faces.

Animacy and Intentionality Perception

1. If the first step in understanding the social world is to figure out *what* in the world has intentions, agency, or mental states, then _____ perception may be a fundamental developmental building block.

2. One-year-old Evan watches as a dog walks across a stage. He then watches as a book moves across the stage of its own accord. How would you predict that Evan would react?

3. Define Baron-Cohen's 'intentionality detector'.

4. Preschoolers distinguish animate from inanimate objects based on an object's ability to _____.

5. Rochat and colleagues found that 3-month-old infants spent more time looking at a computer screen that depicted two balls apparently chasing each other than a screen that depicted random movement of two balls. How would you interpret this result?

6. Gergely and colleagues conducted a habituation experiment with 1-year-olds. Did the infants dishabituate to *different* movement of the object or to '*irrational*' movement of the object?

7. Julie is 20 months old. She watches as her mother tosses a small pillow toward the couch. The pillow misses the couch and lands on the floor in front of Julie. How would you predict that Julie will react?

8. True or False: If Julie watches a robotic arm throw the pillow and miss the couch, her reaction would be the same as above.

9. Infants who watch a human arm repeatedly reach for an object in the same location will assume that the action is directed toward the _____, not the _____.

Theory of Mind

1. Define 'theory of mind'.

2. What does it mean to say that young children have a 'naïve psychology'?

3. What are the three constructs at the centre of naïve psychology?

4. It is not until a child is roughly _____ years of age before she understands that there can be a difference between what something appears to be and what is really is.

5. Even at the age when they have started to understand the appearance–reality distinction, children still find it difficult to _____.

6. True or False: Measuring a child's understanding of mental states using the appearance–reality distinction probably overestimates theory of mind competence.

7. What is the Smarties false-belief task?

8. How does a typical 3-year-old child respond in the Smarties false-belief task?

9. In what ways will a typical 5-year-old respond differently?

10. In the Sally-Anne task, children with a well-developed theory of mind will answer '_____' when asked 'Where will Sally look for her ball first?'

11. In the green box/yellow box experiment, infants expected the actor's actions to be guided by the actor's _____.

12. Experiments that have shown that infants as young as 13 months expect actions to follow beliefs (the preferred food experiment, for example) have used _____ as a dependent variable.

13. Do non-humans have theory of mind?

Autism: What If There Were No Theory of Mind?

1. Define 'autism'.

2. Baron-Cohen proposed that a deficit in _____ was the defining feature of autism.

3. ASD stands for _____.

4. True or False: The single most reliably measurable deficit in children with ASD is a deficit in joint attention.

5. Results from the false-photo test suggest that children with ASD who fail the false-belief task do so because of trouble understanding mental states, not trouble understanding _____.

6. How do children with ASD differ from other children in terms of face perception?

7. Match the following ages with the corresponding social skills milestones.

   1. 6 weeks   a) perceives goals
   2. 9 months   b) engages in parallel play
   3. 18 months   c) displays joint attention
   4. 2 years   d) has a sense of ownership
   5. 3 years   e) smiles in response to others

8. True or False: When studies have matched ASD and non- ASD children on verbal IQ, ASD children do not tend to show impairments in recognition of emotions.

9. Which types of emotions are particularly difficult for those with ASD to recognize?

10. People with ASD do not preferentially attend to the _____ of the face (the part of the face that is particularly important for interpreting emotions).

11. How do people with ASD recognize emotional expressions?

12. The social-orienting view of autism suggests that the cause of social cognitive deficits is an early failure to _____.

13. What are some practical reasons for studying autism?

14. What are some theoretical reasons for studying autism?

Practice Test 1

1. At what age do infants start to smile interactively with caregivers?

    a. 1 week
    b. 6 weeks
    c. 3 months
    d. 6 months

2. The fact that humans have co-evolved adaptations that are appropriate to solve adaptive problems on multiple sides of a relationship reflects our status as

    a. a coercive social species.
    b. an obligate social species.
    c. an induced social species.
    d. an observant social species

3. Harlow found that self-mutilation, catatonia, emotional disturbances, and even death were all potential outcomes when monkeys

    a. were not given adequate access to food and water.
    b. were subjected to neglect and abuse from their mother.
    c. were not kept clean.
    d. were raised in partial or total isolation.

4. Which of the following is *not* true regarding our enormous human brain?

    a. It is the reason we are born prematurely.
    b. It is prioritized when bodily resources are scarce.
    c. It was naturally selected despite the fact that the cost was not out-weighed by the benefits.
    d. It is large compared to other animals, even when body size is corrected for.

5. Which of the following statements is *not* true regarding imaginary companions?

    a. Children who have imaginary companions are more shy than those who do not.
    b. Children who have imaginary companions are more likely to be firstborn or 'only' children.
    c. Children and their imaginary companions are usually about the same age.
    d. Imaginary companions are not necessarily imaginary friends.

6. The social brain hypothesis is supported by the fact that

    a. humans are most adept at interacting with about 50 people.
    b. humans face greater environmental obstacles than other primates.
    c. social problems decline as group size increases.
    d. humans congregate in groups far larger than other ape groups.

7. Neocortex size compared across species does *not* correlate with

    a. rates of tactical deception use.
    b. size of home range.
    c. clique size.
    d. number of day-to-day companions.

8. In addition to brain size, another evolutionary result of humans' complex social lives is a prolonged _____ period.

    a. juvenile
    b. lactation
    c. reproductive
    d. gestational

9. Piaget proposed that the social cognitive limitation at the preoperational stage is

    a. a lack of social referencing
    b. an inability to perceive emotions.
    c. egocentrism.
    d. a lack of object permanence.

10. Piaget's notion of 'animism' refers to

    a. being unable to consider views other than your own.
    b. a preference for animals over objects.
    c. the attribution of physical characteristics to mental entities.
    d. the attribution of mental states to inanimate objects.

11. Social learning theory emphasizes

    a. classical conditioning.
    b. observation and imitation.
    c. rewards and punishments.
    d. individual personalities.

12. According to Flavell, a Level 1 understanding of perspective means that you

    a. are completely egocentric.
    b. understand that another person sees an object differently than you.
    c. know whether or not another person can see an object.
    d. do not understand that a clear line of sight is necessary to see an object.

13. Joint attention is thought to be evidence of a developing

    a. social referencing skill.
    b. understanding of perspective.
    c. mastery of sensorimotor play.
    d. theory of mind.

14. Pretend play does *not*

    a. become more sophisticated with age.
    b. emerge before 1 year of age.
    c. indicate a developing theory of mind.
    d. reflect a significant cognitive accomplishment.

15. The area of the brain that is dedicated to face perception is the _____ face area.

    a. fusiform
    b. hippocampal
    c. functional
    d. formative

16. Holistic processing of faces refers to the fact that we

    a. see faces as a sum of their component parts.
    b. tend to notice only the top half of a face.
    c. see faces as a gestalt.
    d. perform well on a composite face task.

17. Who prefers to look at faces over non-faces?

    a. 9-minute-old infants
    b. 1-month-old infants
    c. 2-month-old infants
    d. both *a* and *c*

18. The process of perceptual mechanisms becoming more specialized is called

    a. perceptual focusing.
    b. perceptual restriction.
    c. perceptual narrowing.
    d. perceptual contouring.

19. The results of Rochat's experiment displaying moving balls to infants suggest that 3-month-old infants

    a. prefer a social display over a non-social display.
    b. prefer movement to non-movement.
    c. prefer inanimate to animate objects.
    d. see all types of movement as equivalent.

20. Mark, who is 5 years old, is shown a box of crayons. The box is opened to reveal that it is empty. Mark is asked what his friend Liang, who is waiting outside the room, will think is in the box. What is Mark likely to say?

    a. 'Liang will think it is empty.'
    b. 'Liang will think there are crayons in the box.'
    c. 'Liang will not have any idea what is in the box.'
    d. 'Who's Liang?'

21. New and innovative methods have used _____ to reveal theory of mind reasoning in very young children.

    a. looking times
    b. stated beliefs
    c. the appearance–reality distinction
    d. none of the above

22. ASD stands for

    a. Autistic Symptoms of Disorder
    b. Autism Scale of Deficits
    c. Autism Specialization Deficits
    d. Autism Spectrum Disorder

23. Autism is *not* characterized by

    a. deficits in logical thought.
    b. an adherence to repetitive behaviours.
    c. a deficit in social cognition.
    d. a communication delay.

24. At the age of _____, children start to show some sense of ownership and will defend their own possessions.

    a. 1 year
    b. 2 years
    c. 3 years
    d. 4 years

25. When ASD and non- ASD children are matched on _____, deficits in emotion perception are not found.

    a. age
    b. problem-solving ability
    c. verbal IQ
    d. non-verbal IQ

Practice Test 2

1. The social imperative is greatest for

   a. infants.
   b. young children.
   c. adolescents.
   d. older adults.

2. Harlow's attempts to rehabilitate monkeys who had been isolated were most successful when the former isolate

   a. became a parent.
   b. was prevented from having offspring.
   c. was paired with a normally reared monkey that was younger than it.
   d. was paired with a normally reared monkey that was older than it.

3. Kenny believes that the large human brain is the result of ecological pressures. That is, he believes that humans evolved a large brain because they had to

   a. hunt for food.
   b. navigate a large home range.
   c. have a large memory for foraging.
   d. all of the above

4. Human group size is roughly

   a. 25 to 30.
   b. 50 to 100
   c. 150 to 200
   d. 200 to 300

5. One difference between the social groups of humans and the social groups of a herding animal is that humans _____ and herding animals do not.

   a. develop hierarchies
   b. know each other as individuals
   c. congregate to protect themselves from predators
   d. establish alliances

6. A lengthy childhood seems to have evolved in humans as a way to learn a sufficient amount about

   a. food gathering.
   b. tool use.
   c. cultural technology.
   d. social information.

7. Six-year-old Adam is looking at a landscape with three mountains. His view of the landscape is 'View 1'. Adam's friend is sitting across the table. Adam's friend's view of the landscape is 'View 2'. Adam is shown photos of View 1 and View 2 and is asked what his friend sees. Adam will

    a. say View 1.
    b. say View 2.
    c. protest that it is neither View 1 nor View 2.
    d. be equally likely to say View 1 or View 2

8. Bandura found that children were more likely to hit a doll if

    a. they had been rewarded for doing it.
    b. they had an aggressive personality.
    c. they had played with the doll before.
    d. they had just seen an adult do it.

9. Compared to adult chimpanzees and orangutans, 2½-year-old children performed better on a test of

    a. memory for object location.
    b. eye gaze following.
    c. object permanence.
    d. all of the above

10. By the age of 5 or 6 weeks, infants imitate adults'

    a. hand gestures.
    b. vocal expressions.
    c. tongue protrusions.
    d. head turns.

11. When young Finnegan looks at his older brother when deciding whether or not to join in a game, he is demonstrating

    a. social referencing.
    b. theory of mind.
    c. social cuing.
    d. authority priming.

12. The difference between sensorimotor play and pretend play is that pretend play

    a. occurs earlier than sensorimotor play.
    b. involves creating imaginative representations.
    c. involves object manipulation.
    d. is primarily a means for mastering action sequences.

13. Which of the following is a hallmark of face processing?

    a. the mirror effect
    b. component processing
    c. the symmetry effect
    d. the inversion effect

14. The results of Goren, Sarty, and Wu's (1975) experiment on newborn face perception were ignored for many years because

    a. they were invalid.
    b. they were unpublished.
    c. they did not fit with what people believed to be true.
    d. people were not interested in newborn face perception until recently.

15. The U-shaped curve for face preference probably requires _____ to explain it.

    a. two different psychological processes
    b. three different psychological processes
    c. perceptual narrowing
    d. schematic processing

16. Six-month olds are

    a. better at discriminating between two human faces than two monkey faces.
    b. better at discriminating between two monkey faces than two human faces.
    c. equally good at discriminating between human faces and monkey faces.
    d. better than 9-month-olds at discriminating between two human faces.

17. The mechanism proposed by Baron-Cohen that interprets movements in terms of volitional mental states is called

    a. a goal detector
    b. a movement predictor.
    c. a predictability mechanism.
    d. an intentionality detector.

18. Gergely and colleagues experiment with black balls jumping over a barrier demonstrated that, by 12 months of age, infants expect _____ behaviour from intentional objects.

    a. random
    b. rational
    c. illogical
    d. intelligent

19. Which of the following statements is true about young children's understanding of the intentions of others?

    a. They do not understand another person's intentions unless the actor's goal was fulfilled.
    b. They are likely to imitate another person's behaviour without a comparison between the other person's abilities and their own abilities.
    c. They are able to parse other people's actions.
    d. The completion of a task must be modeled for them to successfully complete it.

20. At 6 or 7 years of age, children

    a. are baffled by the appearance–reality distinction.
    b. find it difficult to describe the difference between appearance and reality.
    c. truly 'get' the appearance–reality distinction.
    d. are resistant to a demonstration of the difference between appearance and reality.

21. Which of the following animals has theory of mind abilities that rival humans'?

    a. chimpanzees
    b. dogs
    c. orangutans
    d. none of the above

22. The fact that children with ASD perform well on _____ tests but not _____ tests suggests that they have trouble understanding mental states, not the logical structure of the problem.

    a. false-photo; false-belief
    b. false-belief; false-photo
    c. false-statement ; false-belief
    d. false-belief; false-statement

23. It seems that there are ASD-specific impairments in the recognition of

    a. anger
    b. fear
    c. surprise
    d. all of the above

24. People with ASD have been found to be relatively unable to use information from _____ to correctly identify complex emotions.

    a. vocal pitch
    b. body posturing
    c. the eyes
    d. the mouth

25. Which of the following is *not* a practical reason for studying autism?

    a. It will allow us to test hypotheses about typical development.
    b. It will be helpful in creating effective treatments for autism.
    c. It will aid clinicians in assisting parents of children with autism.
    d. It will help us identify autism earlier.

Study Questions: Answer Key

1. another person/people (p. 255)

2. Obligate social species are those that *must* be with others in order to survive and who are co-evolved in order to interact with others. (p. 256)

3. True—As an obligate social species, humans require interaction with others. (p. 256)

4. Consider the following in your response:
   - Social skills are required for establishing friendships, monitoring allegiances, monitoring insults and exploitation, avoiding offense, and fulfilling obligations.
   - A failure of these social skills could result in ostracism.
   - Ostracism would have been deadly in the EEA, making the individual vulnerable to predation, starvation, or exposure.
   - Therefore, only those individuals with the skills to get along with others survived. (p. 257)

5. False—Sociability is actually *more* important for infants and young children because they are dependent (*completely* dependent in the case of infants) on others for care. (p. 257)

6. 6 weeks (p. 257)

Social Contact as a Need: Harry Harlow's Social Experiments

1. rhesus monkeys (p. 258)

2. The difference between partial and total isolated conditions was
   - partial isolate monkeys lived in wire cages where they could hear, smell, and see other monkeys but were never in physical contact with them.
   - monkeys in total isolation lived in isolation chambers and had no experience at all of other monkeys. (pp. 258–259)

3. The results of partial isolation were
   - self-mutilation
   - catatonia
   - stereotyped pacing or circling (p. 258)

4. Monkeys in total isolation
   - experienced 'emotional disturbances'
   - no longer played or explored
   - rarely moved
   - stopped eating and died, as was the case for one monkey. (p. 259)

5. Former isolates were incapable of effective parenting behaviour. They were either neglectful or abusive to their infants. (p. 259)

6. False—Rehabilitation was not very successful for the monkeys that had been in total isolation. (pp. 259–260)

7. Former isolate monkeys
   - some showed limited improvement with surrogate mothers.
   - showed most improvement when paired with normally-reared monkeys that were younger than they were; this was the *most* successful therapy. (p. 260)

Why the Big Brain?

1. Brains are 'costly' because
   - they are complex and, therefore, they take a long time to evolve in a species and a long time to develop in individuals.
   - they are metabolically costly in that they use a lot of energy and receive priority over other tissues when resources are scarce. (p. 260)

2. Humans may have needed a large mental map (to navigate the environment), major cognitive skills to be able to use resources (to forage and hunt), and a large memory capacity (to remember how and where to obtain resources). In other words, getting sustenance from the environment is hard and it requires a big brain. (p. 260)

3. Humans may have had a great information-processing demand in order to form alliances, negotiate, scheme, convince, etc. In other words, living in large groups is hard and it requires a big brain (p. 260)

4. False—It is probable that social integration and intelligence evolved *together*. (p. 260)

5. Consider the following in your response:
   - Humans tend to be most adept at interacting with about 150–200 people (a large number of individuals to keep track of, socially).
   - This is a much larger group size than any other primate—even great apes rarely live in groups of more than 50. (p. 262)

6. False—The neocortex is the 'newest' part of the brain (evolutionarily) and it is associated with relatively high-level cognitive processing. (p. 261)

7. the size of the group that they live in (p. 261)

8. any measure of ecological demands (e.g. size of the home range) (p. 261)

9. nature; longevity (p. 262)

10. Measures of social complexity that predict brain size include the following:
    - Deception rates
    - Grooming clique size
    - Coalition size
    - Amount of time spent in social activity during the day
    - The extent to which pairs of individuals develop a committed relationship (p. 262)

11. The main difference between human groups and sheep groups is that
    - sheep congregate to reduce the risk of predation.
    - membership in the group of sheep is not stable and belonging to a particular group is not valuable.
    - sheep, unlike humans, do not have rich social relationships. (p. 262)

The Big Brain and Long Childhood

1. False—Neocortex size correlates with the length of the juvenile period. (p. 264)

2. A lengthy period of adolesence seems to have evolved as a way to acquire social knowledge expertise. (p. 264)

What Would Piaget Say about Social Cognitive Development?

1. Egocentrism is Piaget's term for a child's inability to appreciate other points of view besides his/her own. (p. 265)

2. The three mountain task involves the following:
   - The child faces a model landscape of three mountains.
   - A doll sits at a different vantage point.
   - The child is asked whether the doll could see certain objects.
   - Correctly answering the question requires taking another's perspective. (p. 265)

3. Consider the following in your response:
   - Children younger than 9 or 10 years of age are poor at appreciating the viewpoint of another.
   - When asked what the doll could see, children at that age typically select the photo that depicts their own vantage point. (p. 265)

4. When describing events, children will often give inadequate information to the listener—they will assume that the listener knows what they know. If you have the chance to observe a young child, you may notice other evidence of egocentrism. For example, a young child talking on the telephone might nod her head for 'yes', not realizing that the other person can't see her non-verbal response. (p. 266)

5. Animism is the attribution of mental states to inanimate objects. (p. 266)

6. Realism is the attribution of physical and mechanical characteristics to mental entities. (p. 266)

What Would Associationists Say?

1. social learning (p. 267)

2. False—Bandura's theory emphasizes observation and imitation. (p. 267)

Social Domains of Core Knowledge

1. False—Performance was equal for 2½-year-old children and chimpanzees (and orangutans) for those types of tests. (pp. 267–268)

2. Young humans out-perform chimpanzees (and orangutans) on social cognitive tests. Among other things,
   - they better understand someone's cue regarding food location.
   - they are better able to communicate to receive food.
   - they are more able to consider another's attentional state.
   - they are better at following eye gaze. (pp. 267–268)

Social Cognitive Development in Infancy

1. Newborns cry because
   - compared to other species, human infants are born very immature. They are very dependent on others to meet their needs.
   - crying is one tool that a newborn has to attract the attention of adults and to manipulate adults' behaviour. (p. 269)

2. True—Infants at that age, when asked to show an adult something, will try to establish a direct line of vision (moving the adult's hands away from her eyes, if necessary). (p. 268)

3. Level 1 understanding is present at the age of 2 and 3. At this level
   - children know whether or not you can see something, but they do not know that you may be looking at it differently than they are.
   - children know that, to see something, a person's eyes must be open and there must be a clear line of sight to the object. (pp. 268–269)

4. Level 2 understanding is present by the age of 4 or 5. At this level, children know that another person might see an object but see it differently. (p. 269)

5. facial behaviours (e.g. mouth opening, tongue protrusion) (p. 269)

6. Infants do not imitate non-animate objects (e.g. robotic faces). Therefore, imitation of facial behaviours seems to be a social behaviour. (pp. 269–270)

7. Walter will be likely to look more at the imitator and smile more at the imitator. (p. 270)

8. Joint attention refers to an individual's ability to tell when he shares an object of attention with another person. (p. 270)

9. A 9-month-old infant will
   - follow his mother's line of sight (look at what she is looking at).
   - follow his mother's pointed finger (look at what she is pointing at). (p. 270)

10. theory of mind (p. 270)

11. social referencing (p. 270)

Pretend Play

1. play (p. 271)

2. Sensorimotor play involves object manipulation as a means for the practice and mastery of action schemas. (p. 271)

3. Pretend play involves the use of actions or objects to represent real life or imagined actions, objects, or characters. (p. 272)

4. theory of mind (p. 272)

5. Pretend play
   - emerges at around 18 months.
   - becomes more elaborate and sophisticated over the preschool years. (p. 273)

Face Perception

1. fusiform face area (FFA) (p. 274)

2. The inversion effect refers to the disruption in face processing that is observed when a face is inverted. (p. 274)

3. 25; 10 (p. 274)

4. Holistic processing involves the integration of visual information from the whole of the perceived visual region of interest (the whole face), in contrast to the perception and representation of component parts. (p. 274)

5. Consider the following in your response:
   - In the composite face task, participants must report whether the upper half of a face is the same in two images that show the upper halves of faces aligned with different bottom halves.
   - People find it very difficult to recognize when the two are the same. The bottom half doesn't seem to be a component that they can separate from the top and ignore. People can't help but see the *whole* face. (p. 274)

6. Given a choice between images of faces and images of non-faces, 2-month-old infants prefer to look at faces. (p. 275)

7. True—At only 9 minutes old, a newborn will turn his eyes and head to look at a schematic face than a scrambled or blank stimulus. (p. 276)

8. Consider the following in your response:
   - Face preference is demonstrated by newborns.
   - It then goes away and then re-emerges at approximately 2 months.
   - Early face preference and later face preference may be mediated by different psychological processes. (p. 276)

9. Consider the following in your response:
   - Related to face preference, infants look at objects that have contours, that are relatively large, that move, that have high light–dark contrast, and that are either brightly coloured or light in colour. Faces meet these criteria. Therefore, infants usually orient to faces.
   - Infants prefer human speech over other sounds.
   - Infants are attentive to human voices.
   - Infants are adept at parsing speech sounds. (p. 277)

10. Perceptual narrowing is a developmental process in which perceptual mechanisms become more specialized such that infants lose ability to discriminate between categories that are irrelevant. (p. 278)

11. False—At 6 months old, infants *are* good at discriminating between two human faces but they are *also* good at discriminating between two monkey faces. (p. 278)

12. True—By 9 months, there is a perceptual narrowing in face processing. Infants have specialized; there is now good discrimination between human, but not monkey, faces. (p. 278)

Animacy and Intentionality Perception

1. animacy (p. 278)

2. Consider the following in your response:
   - Evan would probably demonstrate surprise at the book's movement by looking more at it than the dog.
   - We would conclude from this that he distinguishes between animate and inanimate objects and has different expectations for each. (p. 278)

3. The intentionality detector is a mechanism that interprets the movement of an object in terms of volitional mental states. That is, the movement of an object informs our knowledge of its goals. (p. 279)

4. move by itself (p. 280)

5. Based on the results of this experiment, you could conclude that
    - the 3-month-olds prefer a display that depicted a more social display (with the balls interacting).
    - the infants may have perceived the chasing balls as alive in some way, based on their movements. (p. 280)

6. The 1-year-olds dishabituated to irrational movement. They did not dishabituate to different movement if it was seen to match original intent. It seems that 1-year-olds expect animate objects to behave rationally. (pp. 280–281)

7. It is quite possible that Julie will (assuming she is physically able) pick up the pillow and place it on the couch. This demonstrates that Julie understands her mother's intention, even though the intention failed. (pp. 281–282)

8. False—In the case of a machine, a young child will not infer intentionality and will not complete the task. (p. 282)

9. object; location (p. 282)

Theory of Mind

1. Theory of mind refers to our ability to understand another person's mental states. (p. 283)

2. To say that young children have a 'naïve psychology' means they have a common-sense level of understanding of other people and themselves. (p. 283)

3. The three constructs at the centre of naïve psychology are
    - desires
    - beliefs
    - actions (p. 283)

4. 6 or 7 (p. 284)

5. discuss and describe what the difference is (p. 284)

6. False—It probably underestimates theory of mind competence. (p. 284)

7. The Smarties false-belief task involves the following:
    - A child is shown a box of Smarties.
    - The experimenter asks what the child believes is in the box (children always reply 'Smarties').
    - The box is opened to reveal pencils.
    - The experimenter then asks what a friend waiting outside the room would think is in the box. (p. 284)

8. A typical 3-year-old will say that the friend will know there are pencils in the box. They believe that the friend will know what they know—they do not appreciate that the friend will have a false belief. (p. 284)

9. A typical 5-year-old will say that the friend will think there are Smarties in the box. This demonstrates an understanding of the friend's mental states—they know that the friend will have a false belief. (p. 284)

10. the basket (p. 285)

11. belief (whether the belief was true or not) (p. 285)

12. looking time (p. 285)

13. Consider the following in your response:
    - A dog that is forbidden to take food will attempt to take the food less often when that person is looking. Therefore, dogs seem to understand what a person is paying attention to.
    - Chimpanzees are more likely to request food from an experimenter who knows where the food is. Therefore, chimps seem to understand some mental states.
    - However, non-humans probably do not have the full range of human theory of mind abilities. (p. 287)

Autism: What If There Were No Theory of Mind?

1. Autism is a developmental disorder that is defined and characterized by a deficit in social cognition, a delay in the development of communication, and an adherence to routine or repetitive behaviours. (p. 287)

2. theory of mind development (p. 287)

3. autism spectrum disorders (p. 287)

4. True—This deficit can be seen in children with ASD as early as 18 (or possibly even 12) months. (p. 287)

5. the logical structure of the problem (p. 288)

6. Children with ASD
    - have trouble with face recognition and the identification of emotional facial expressions.
    - may be able to perceive basic emotions much like other people do, but they may be using atypical strategies.
    - may have specific impairments in the recognition of some emotional expressions (anger, disgust, surprise, and fear). (p. 288)

7.
   1. 6 weeks   e) smiles in response to others
   2. 9 months   c) displays joint attention
   3. 18 months   a) perceives goals
   4. 2 years   d) has a sense of ownership
   5. 3 years   b) engages in parallel play (p. 289)

8. True—But they *do* show impairments when the groups are matched on non-verbal IQ. (p. 289)

9. It is particularly difficult for people with ASD to recognize complex social emotions that require identifying with the mental state of others (e.g. arrogance, flirtatiousness). (p. 289)

10. eyes (p. 289)

11. People with ASD
    - may develop compensatory strategies.
    - may examine individual features of the face and use rule-based strategies for emotion recognition. (p. 290)

12. orient normally to social stimuli (p. 290)

13. Research into autism will have clinical applications, allowing us to identify it earlier and create effective treatments for those who are affected by it (pp. 290–291)

14. Research into autism can help test some hypotheses about typical development. Children with ASD have specific deficits as well as preserved areas of cognitive development. This allows for an examination of developmental precursors to later-developing cognitive skills. (p. 291)

Practice Test 1: Answer Key

1. **b** (p. 257)	8. **a** (p. 263)	15. **a** (p. 274)	22. **d** (p. 287)
2. **b** (p. 256)	9. **c** (p. 265)	16. **c** (p. 274)	23. **a** (p. 287)
3. **d** (pp. 258–259)	10. **d** (p. 266)	17. **d** (p. 276)	24. **b** (p. 289)
4. **c** (p. 260)	11. **b** (p. 267)	18. **c** (p. 278)	25. **c** (p. 289)
5. **a** (p. 259)	12. **c** (p. 268)	19. **a** (p. 280)	
6. **d** (p. 261)	13. **d** (p. 270)	20. **b** (p. 284)	
7. **b** (p. 261)	14. **b** (p. 273)	21. **a** (p. 285)	

Practice Test 2: Answer Key

1. **a** (p. 257)	8. **d** (p. 266)	15. **a** (pp. 276–277)	22. **a** (p. 288)
2. **c** (p. 260)	9. **b** (p. 268)	16. **c** (p. 278)	23. **d** (p. 288)
3. **d** (p. 260)	10. **c** (p. 269)	17. **d** (p. 279)	24. **c** (pp. 289–290)
4. **c** (p. 261)	11. **a** (p. 270)	18. **b** (pp. 280–281)	25. **a** (pp. 290–291)
5. **b** (p. 262)	12. **b** (pp. 271–272)	19. **c** (p. 282)	
6. **d** (p. 264)	13. **d** (p. 274)	20. **b** (p. 284)	
7. **a** (p. 265)	14. **c** (p. 276)	21. **d** (p. 287)	

Chapter 9
Language Development

Chapter Summary

Language Is Part of Our Psychology

Language is a universal human trait. It is a fundamental part of who we are as a species. Humans are born with specialized psychological mechanisms that are attuned to human speech and designed to learn language.

Language as a Case Study in Evolutionary Psychology

Language is clearly learned. Just as clearly, there are nature-determined mechanisms that are involved in language acquisition. Nature and nurture work together.

Noam Chomsky and the Language Acquisition Device

The behaviourist B. F. Skinner believed that language was acquired via simple operant principles. Noam Chomsky argued that, given the complex rules, fast pace of acquisition, and lack of explicit instruction, such principles were inadequate for language learning. He proposed that children have an innate *language acquisition device*. The language device helps children learn how to derive *deep structure* (meaning) from surface structure. Chomsky also put forward the idea of a *universal grammar*, a set of principles and adjustable parameters that is common to all human languages.

The Brain Basis of Human Language

For most right-handed people, language processing occurs primarily in the left hemisphere of the brain. At the lower edge of the motor cortex is Broca's area. Damage to this area will not significantly impair comprehension but will result in halting speech that lacks grammatical organization. People with damage to Wernicke's area, near the auditory cortex, will speak fluently but nonsensically.

Infant Speech Perception

Humans are born prepared to perceive speech sounds. Early on, infants can discriminate between a huge number of speech sounds from all languages. Around the age of 10 months, they lose the ability to discriminate between speech sounds in foreign languages and can only discriminate those that are used in their native languages.

Even when speech sound stimuli differ continuously, infants (and adults) perceived them categorically. Sounds in the auditory stream are collapsed into categories automatically.

Proto-Babbling and Babbling

'Cooing', the production of vowel sounds, begins at around 2 months. 'Babbling', which involves adding consonants, starts at about 4 or 5 months. Infants babble as a way of exploring the sounds they can make.

Eventually the babbling comes to sound more and more like adult speech sounds. All infants start babbling at roughly the same age. This is true even for deaf infants, who will babble with their hands.

Word Learning

At about 1 year of age, infants produce their first words. By the age of 2, children have typically built up a sizable vocabulary and begin to put words together into two-word utterances. Although word learning comes easily, it is not simple.

With just a single exposure, young children are able to connect words to their meanings through a phenomenon called *fast mapping*. Acquisition of word meaning follows several rules: the *whole-object assumption* (that new words apply to whole objects), the *taxonomic assumption* (that words are grouped conceptually), and the *mutual exclusivity assumption* (that new words apply to new objects or new properties). Children are also able to use adults' focus or attention, emotional reactions, and intentionality as pragmatic cues to word learning.

What Would Associationists Say About Language Acquisition?

According to associationists, language is learned like any other developing behaviour: through conditioning and imitation. These processes, though, are insufficient to account for how quickly and efficiently children learn language. As well, they cannot account for idiosyncratic utterances that children produce but have never heard before.

Adults' Roles in Children's Language Learning

Adults do not give children much explicit language instruction. This is partly because they themselves do not know the rules and partly because such instruction is unnecessary.

Adults do engage in *infant-directed speech* when talking to an infant. Infant-directed speech is high-pitched, exaggerated in intonation, and slow. It is grammatically pure without being grammatically simple. It focuses on the here-and-now, with an emphasis on concrete objects.

In children's speech, parents are likely to correct factual, but not grammatical, errors.

Critical Periods for Language Learning

Because of the high cost of both brain material and a language acquisition device, there is a critical period for language learning. The critical period comes early in life and, as such, learning second languages later in life is difficult. Cases of feral children suggest that a lack of early language exposure during the critical period has devastating, permanent effects on language use. Damage to areas of the brain that are important for language also has devastating, permanent effects unless the individual is young enough to have considerable plasticity.

The left hemisphere seems to be used for second-language acquisition if the learning takes place before the age of 3. When people learn a second language between the ages of 4 and 6, there is more right-hemisphere activation for language tasks. When second-language learning takes place at 11 to 13 years, left- and right-hemisphere activation for language tasks is roughly equal.

Learning Grammar

Even when children are producing only single words, they can decode the meaning that is encoded in the grammar of sentences. Between the ages of 2 and 3, they begin to use grammatical markers. They may occasionally over-apply grammatical rules, making over-regularization errors.

Children Generate Language

When two or more adult language communities merge, a *pidgin language* may be created that borrows words from the contributing languages. Pidgin languages are choppy and non-standardized. They have inconsistent word ordering and an absence of grammatical organization. Children who acquire the pidgin language as their native language turn it into something else. From it, they create a creole that is grammatical and sophisticated. A creole is every bit as much of a language as any other established language.

Creole-ization has been documented somewhat recently in Hawaii and in a sign language invented by deaf children in Nicaragua.

Language Is Species-Specific

Human language is far more complex than the communication of other animals. Although some non-humans communicate, they do not have a generative grammar, meaning that they cannot combine words to produce unlimited ideas. Communication in non-humans does not take place in brain areas that are analogous to human language areas.

Efforts have been made to teach human language to non-human primates. Even when attempts have employed sign language (to bypass limitations in the vocal apparatus), success has been limited. Chimpanzees, for example, can build a modest vocabulary but they will not spontaneously use language to comment on things or participate in conversations. At best, they will use repetitive utterances to make requests.

One price paid by humans for our ability to produce spoken language is a vocal tract anatomy that leaves us vulnerable to choking.

Can a Gene Cause the Development of Grammar?

Roughly half of the members of the English KE family have a dominant genetic mutation on Chromosome 7 that is associated with a characteristic set of language deficits. While there is no 'grammar gene', this case does demonstrate that the complex psychological machinery of language acquisition can be messed up by a single deleterious mutation.

Learning Objectives

After reading this chapter, you should be able to:

- Appreciate the place of language as a cornerstone of humanity (pp. 298–301)
- Understand Noam Chomsky's contribution to the field of language acquisition (pp. 301–302)
- Discuss the brain areas that are significant for language processing (pp. 302–304)
- Understand the impressive speech sound perception of young infants (pp. 304–309)
- Examine early language production abilities (pp. 309–310)
- Appreciate how infants build a vocabulary (pp. 310–314)
- Outline how associationists have accounted for language acquisition (p. 314)
- Examine the role of adults in children's language learning (pp. 314–316)
- Summarize how the critical periods place limits on language learning (pp. 316–320)

- Discuss grammar acquisition (pp. 320–321)

- Appreciate the remarkable ability of children to invent languages (pp. 321–326)

- Differentiate between human and non-human communication (pp. 326–330)

- Explain how a genetic mutation can interfere with the complex psychological machinery that underlies complex grammar (pp. 330–331).

Suggested Readings

Chomsky, N. (2006). *Language and Mind*. New York: Cambridge University Press.

Now in its third edition, Chomsky's collection of essays makes a revolutionary contribution to linguistic theory.

Fromkin, V., Krashen, S., Curtiss, S., Rigler, D., and Rigler, M. (1974). The development of language in Genie: A case of language acquisition beyond the "Critical Period". *Brain and Language, 1*, 81–107.

The case study of 'Genie'.

Bickerton, D. (1983). Creole languages. *Scientific American, 249*, 116–122.

This article is an invaluable discussion of what we can learn about the nature of innate grammar from creole languages.

Study Questions

1. Peter Marler described young sparrows as having an instinct to _____.

2. Why was Marler's claim revolutionary?

3. True or False: Vervet monkeys could be said to have a vocabulary.

4. Vervet communication is impressive but it is significant that their communication never involves _____.

Language Is Part of Our Psychology

1. Why is language believed to be 'part of our psychology'?

Language as a Case Study in Evolutionary Psychology

1. True or False: Theorists are divided on whether language acquisition is the result of nature or nurture.

2. The fact that dogs and cats (and other non-humans) do not acquire language underlines the fact that _____ and _____ cannot explain all learning.

Noam Chomsky and the Language Acquisition Device

1. Noam Chomsky is known as the Father of _____.

2. What led Chomsky to propose that general-purpose learning mechanisms were inadequate for language acquisition?

3. Define 'language acquisition device'.

4. A friend of yours says that children learn language by imitating how others speak. How would you respond to this?

5. 'Eats shoots and leaves' and 'Eats, shoots, and leaves' are very similar in terms of _____ structure and very different in terms of _____ structure.

6. Define 'universal grammar'.

7. Because of a universal grammar, _____ is all that is necessary for young children to acquire language.

8. Define 'home signs'.

9. How might home signs be evidence of a universal grammar in development?

The Brain Basis of Human Language

1. For most right-handed people, language processing occurs primarily in the _____ hemisphere.

2. True or False: Specialization of one hemisphere for language processing decreases with age.

3. Broca's area is located near the _____ cortex and Wernicke's area is located near the _____ cortex.

4. What happens when people suffer damage to Broca's area?

5. What happens when people suffer damage to Wernicke's area?

Infant Speech Perception

1. Human infants have 'programmes', designed by natural selection, to decode the _____.

2. Outline some evidence that infants come into the world prepared to perceive speech sounds.

3. Different languages use different subsets of _____.

4. True or False: Very young infants are not as good as adults at discriminating between sounds.

5. The conditioned head-turn procedure uses the principles of _____ to test infant sound discrimination abilities.

6. True or False: Speech sound discrimination abilities decline suddenly.

7. According to Werker & Tees' (1984) findings on speech sound discriminations over the first year of life, when do infants lose speech sound discrimination abilities for languages other than their native language?

8. Define 'categorical perception'.

9. How do the speech sounds /ba/ and /pa/ differ?

10. The cut-off VOT between unambiguously-perceived 'ba' and unambiguously-perceived 'pa' is _____ ms.

11. True or False: In infants who are a few months old, the physical property of voice onset time is all that matters for perception of speech sounds.

12. The fact that we are incapable of comparing the physical difference between two /ba/ sounds with the physical difference between a /ba/ and a /pa/ sound reflects our _____.

13. True or False: Newborns tend to have preferences between foreign languages.

Proto-Babbling and Babbling

1. What is the difference between cooing and babbling?

2. True or False: Hearing infants babble; deaf infants do not.

3. By the end of their first year, infants are producing the _____ patterns and _____ patterns of their own language.

Word Learning

1. The 'normal' developmental time course for saying a first word is anywhere from _____ months to _____ months.

2. In terms of language development, what comes after the first words?

3. True or False: A typical 6-year-old child has a vocabulary of about 10,000 words.

4. If you point to a guitar and say 'guitar', a young child *could* assume that 'guitar' refers to things that have strings, things that make noise, things that are in the room, or any number of other possibilities. This is what Quine referred to as the _____.

5. The fact that young children have word learning assumptions that help to avoid the confusion alluded to above, demonstrates that _____.

6. True or False: Children must have a vocabulary of about 500 words before they start putting words together.

7. 'Want cookie' is an example of _____ speech.

8. True or False: Between the ages of 2 and 6, children learn about a word a day.

9. The ability to connect a word with a concept after as few as one encounter with the word is referred to as _____.

10. Define the 'whole-object assumption'.

11. Define the 'taxonomic assumption'.

12. Define the 'mutual exclusivity assumption'.

13. What are some higher-level, 'pragmatic' cues that are known to be available to young children for word learning?

What Would Associationists Say About Language Acquisition?

1. True or False: B. F. Skinner believed that children have specialized machinery for language learning.

2. In addition to operant conditioning, behaviourists have proposed that _____ is part of the language acquisition process.

3. General-learning mechanisms are not powerful enough to explain language acquisition. What (specifically) are they not able to explain?

Adults' Roles in Children's Language Learning

1. True or False: Adults must engage in a great deal of active language teaching in order for children to become adequate language users.

2. True or False: Most adults are able to describe the complex grammatical rules that they use to form sentences.

3. True or False: A child can learn to speak his native language just by watching television.

4. What are some hallmarks of infant-directed speech?

5. True or False: Infant-direct speech is grammatically simple.

6. True or False: Infant-directed speech is a human universal.

7. When a group of Shuar (South American hunter-horticulturalists who could not understand English words) was presented with recordings of North American mothers speaking, what were they able to understand?

8. Infant-directed speech tends to emphasize words for _____, making it easier for children to acquire labels.

9. What kinds of corrections do parents tend to make to their children's speech?

Critical Periods for Language Learning

1. A critical period is a finite period during development during which the developing organism can
   _____.

2. Why do critical periods exist?

3. Imagine you have a 4-year-old daughter. You are planning to move to China with her. Until now, she has only ever spoken English but you want her to be fluent in Chinese. When should you move?

4. Cases of feral children who are deprived of language input do not provide good scientific evidence of the effect of early language exposure on language production because _____.

5. 'Genie', rescued from isolation at age 13, never successfully acquired a _____.

6. True or False: Isabelle, who was rescued from isolation at the age of 6½ learned to speak grammatical complex and correct English.

7. True or False: A child who sustains damage to the left hemisphere will not learn language.

8. What patterns of left–right hemisphere brain activation do you see for language tasks in people who learned a second language before the age of 3? Between the ages of 4 and 6? Not until 11 to 13?

9. What conclusions can we make from the above findings?

10. True or False: Learning more than one language at once impedes learning in general.

11. What are some cognitive advantages to bilingualism?

Learning Grammar

1. True or False: Language learning involves comprehension, production, and perception. Of these, production comes last.

2. True or False: A 2-year-old child is likely to interpret the sentence 'The dog chased John' as the same thing as 'John chased the dog'.

3. Match the following ages with the corresponding language development milestones.

   1. birth   a) perceives speech sounds categorically
   2. 1 month   b) uses voice to attract attention
   3. 3 months   c) prefers the mother's language to a foreign language
   4. 6 months   d) understands several words
   5. 9 months   e) starts babbling
   6. 1 year   f) starts cooing

4. Match the following ages with the corresponding language development milestones.

   1. 15 months   a) echoes adult speech
   2. 18 months   b) can refer to past, present, and future
   3. 2 years   c) can communicate needs using vocalization
   4. 3 years   d) vocabulary reaches about 50 words
   5. 4 years   e) speaks in sentences
   6. 5 years   f) consistently uses prepositions

5. Define 'over-regularization'.

6. In language learning, practice and feedback are necessary for _____ but not _____.

7. How would associationists explain over-regularization errors?

Children Generate Language

1. True or False: Parents are more important to language learning than peers.

2. When are pidgin languages created?

3. How are pidgin languages different from established languages?

4. What happens when children are born into a community that speaks a pidgin language primarily?

5. A somewhat recent example of pidgin and creole language creation happened in _____.

6. The only component of language that creole-inventing children take from their parents is _____.

7. True or False: Sign language is a proper language, with its own grammatical rules.

8. A pidgin, and then a creole language, *sign language* was created in _____.

9. True or False: Blind people do not use hand gestures.

10. An experiment described in the textbook analyzed gestures made during descriptions of a movie. The descriptions were given by deaf people who began communicating with sign language when they were younger and by deaf people who began communicating with sign language when they were older. What was the difference?

Language Is Species-Specific

1. How does the structure of the brain provide a clue that the communication of other primates is psychologically different from human language?

2. Part of the reason that Viki the chimpanzee did not learn to speak was what could be called a 'hardware' problem. Viki did not have the proper _____.

3. The influence of findings with language training in apes has, in some cases (including that of Koko the gorilla), been limited by _____.

4. Researchers have concluded that the smartest chimps probably have a vocabulary of _____ words.

5. What do chimps *not* do, language-wise?

6. The downside of humans' language-ready vocal tract anatomy is _____.

7. True or False: Human newborns have a vocal tract that is similar to non-human primates.

Can a Gene Cause the Development of Grammar?

1. Many members of the KE family in England have a characteristic set of language deficits. Those family members also have a _____.

2. True or False: There is a 'grammar gene'.

Practice Test 1

1. Vervet monkeys

    a. use gestures, but not sounds, to communicate.
    b. combine alarm calls to generate new ideas.
    c. have nothing that could be called a vocabulary.
    d. have functional communication

2. Language development illustrates what has been called the

    a. nurture drive.
    b. instinct to learn.
    c. constraining instinct.
    d. natural intuition.

3. The sentences 'The boy was pushed by the girl.' and 'The boy pushed the girl.' have

    a. similar deep structures and dissimilar surface structures.
    b. dissimilar deep structures and similar surface structures.
    c. similar deep structures and similar surface structures.
    d. dissimilar deep structures and dissimilar surface structures.

4. For _____, language processing occurs primarily in the left hemisphere.

    a. 70 per cent of people who are right-handed
    b. 90 per cent of people who are right-handed
    c. 70 per cent of people who are left-handed
    d. 90 per cent of people who are left-handed

5. _____ aphasia results in telegraphic speech.

    a. Temporal
    b. Wernicke's
    c. Auditory
    d. Broca's

6. The conditioned head-turn procedure

    a. is visually-reinforced.
    b. is auditorially-reinforced.
    c. involves habituation.
    d. involves classical conditioning.

7. Infants become significantly worse at speech sound discriminations at the age of about

   a. 4 months.
   b. 6 months.
   c. 8 months.
   d. 10 months.

8. At the age of about 2 months, infants start

   a. distinguishing between speech sounds.
   b. learning the meaning of several words.
   c. cooing.
   d. babbling.

9. The 'problem of reference' is solved by

   a. a number of rules for acquiring words.
   b. creating conjunctive categories.
   c. asking for clarification.
   d. perceptual abilities.

10. Only when vocabulary reaches about 200 words, do children start to

    a. perceive subtle differences in speech sounds.
    b. solve the problem of reference.
    c. babble.
    d. put two words together.

11. Fast mapping requires _____ encounter(s) for word learning to occur.

    a. 0
    b. 1
    c. several
    d. many

12. The _____ assumption tells children how to generalize their new words.

    a. categorization
    b. mutual exclusivity
    c. taxonomic
    d. whole-object

13. Which of the following is a 'pragmatic cue' that children use for word learning?

    a. adults' intentionality
    b. adults' emotional reactions
    c. adults' focus of attention
    d. all of the above

14. Infant-direct speech does *not* involve

    a. fast speech.
    b. high pitch.
    c. exaggerated intonation.
    d. exaggerated facial expressions.

15. Words for _____ are emphasized in infant-directed speech.

    a. the past
    b. ideas
    c. nouns
    d. emotions

16. Learning a native language

    a. is easy.
    b. requires a certain level of intelligence.
    c. takes place in every individual.
    d. all of the above

17. Adults are not particularly adept at learning a second language. This stems from the fact that

    a. adults are not good at learning.
    b. there are no extensive training programs for second languages.
    c. an individual in the EEA would rarely, if ever, have encountered a person who spoke an unintelligible language.
    d. they have not worked to maintain their language acquisition device.

18. Which of the following statements is *not* true regarding bilingualism?

    a. The cognitive advantages of bilingualism can serve as a buffer against cognitive decline in old age.
    b. Learning two languages at once causes significant interference that results in a lag in language milestones.
    c. Bilingual children have greater executive control than monolingual children.
    d. There are economic and cultural advantages to bilingualism.

19. In language learning, which comes last?

    a. comprehension
    b. production
    c. exposure
    d. perception

20. Pidgin languages

    a. are standardized.
    b. have consistent word orderings.
    c. carry grammatical information
    d. borrow vocabulary from other languages.

21. Nicaraguan Sign Language (NSL)

    a. is a pidgin language.
    b. was created by linguists.
    c. employs grammatical conventions.
    d. involves lip-reading.

22. Which of the following statements is true about human language, compared to non-human communication?

    a. Only human language has a generative grammar.
    b. Only human language has a vocabulary.
    c. Only human language effectively conveys messages.
    d. all of the above

23. Which of the following was *not* a non-human primate that received language training?

    a. Koko, a gorilla
    b. Kanzi, a bonobo
    c. Nim Chimpsky, a chimpanzee
    d. Isabelle, an orangutan

24. One downside to the fact that we humans are, quite literally, built for language is that

    a. we 'wear out' our brains at a relatively young age.
    b. our movement must be bipedal.
    c. we are relatively likely to choke.
    d. we waste lung power.

25. What can we conclude from the KE family?

    a. There is a 'grammar gene'.
    b. A deleterious mutation can cause problems for language abilities.
    c. If one family member has a language deficit, the other family members must too.
    d. Nature trumps nurture.

Practice Test 2

1. Which of the following statements is *not* true of human language?

    a. In terms of sophistication, there is no difference between language in modern culture and the language of a pre-industrialized culture.
    b. Language would have been available to the developing child in the EEA.
    c. All known groups of humans (present and past) have spoken a language.
    d. Spoken language is an innovation.

2. Chomsky was the first to argue that _____ were inadequate for the acquisition of language.

    a. instincts
    b. genetically-determined characteristics
    c. general-purpose learning principles
    d. brain processes

3. 'Home signs' can be taken as evidence for

    a. deep structure.
    b. a universal grammar.
    c. hemispheric dominance in language processing.
    d. a critical period of language acquisition.

4. Which of the following statements is true of individuals with Wernicke's aphasia?

    a. They have damage to a brain area at the lower edge of the motor cortex.
    b. Their comprehension abilities are largely intact.
    c. Their speech is lacking in grammatical morphemes.
    d. They have very fluent speech.

5. Perceiving qualitative differences among stimuli that differs continuously is called

    a. categorical perception.
    b. incremental perception.
    c. continuous perception.
    d. conceptual perception.

6. The _____ for saying 'ba' is 15ms.

    a. enunciation segment
    b. vocal onset time
    c. pronunciation time
    d. vocal start

7. Compared to a foreign language, a days-old infant does *not*

    a. prefer the inflection of his native language.
    b. prefer the melody of his native language.
    c. prefer backwards-played sounds in his native language.
    d. suck at a faster rate when listening to his mother's language.

8. Which of the following statements is true regarding babbling?

    a. There is a great deal of variability in terms of when an infants starts to babble.
    b. Babblings consists mostly of vowel sounds.
    c. Babbling involves very little repetition.
    d. Deaf infants babble.

9. A typical 6-year-old child has a vocabulary of about _____ words.

    a. 5,000
    b. 10,000
    c. 20,000
    d. 30,000

10. Which of the following is an example of 'telegraphic speech'?

    a. 'ca-er'
    b. 'cracker'
    c. 'want cracker'
    d. 'me want cracker'

11. According to the mutual exclusivity assumption,

    a. new words are assumed to apply to new objects.
    b. words are grouped conceptually rather than thematically.
    c. words refer to objects rather than features.
    d. none of the above

12. Robbie tells 18-month-old Cindy that he wants to find a 'stofwus'. He then looks at a new object and smiles broadly. Cindy is likely to

    a. assume that Robbie's name is Stofwus.
    b. assume that the new object is a stofwus.
    c. incorporate the new object into a separate taxonomical category.
    d. be confused.

13. Associationists would say that all of the following are vehicles of language acquisition *except*

    a. imitation.
    b. specialized learning devices.
    c. operant conditioning.
    d. general learning principles.

14. The grammatical rules of our spoken language are

    a. explicitly taught to young children.
    b. explicable by adult language users.
    c. more sophisticated than the rules we learn in school.
    d. known only to a few dozen psycholinguists.

15. Infant-directed speech involves

    a. abstract topics.
    b. grammatically-simple utterances.
    c. current topics.
    d. numerous grammatical errors.

16. Parents tend to correct _____ in their children's speech.

    a. factual inaccuracies
    b. grammatical errors
    c. mistakes in word order
    d. nothing

17. _____ is roughly the cut-off for learning to speak a second language as well as a native speaker.

    a. 10 months
    b. 2 years
    c. 7 years
    d. 13 years

18. The pattern of language disabilities in 'wild children' should not be taken as good scientific evidence of the effect of early language exposure on language production because

    a. no wild children have been carefully studied.
    b. wild children have been deprived of more than just language.
    c. wild children usually have extensive exposure to some type of language.
    d. wild children are usually completely rehabilitated in a very short period of time.

19. Who would show the most right-hemisphere activation for a language task?

    a. Jim, who learned Spanish as a second language at the age of 6 months.
    b. Svetlana, who learned Spanish as a second language at the age of 2 years.
    c. Sanjay, who learned Spanish as a second language at the age of 5 years.
    d. Brenda, who learned Spanish as a second language at the age of 12 years.

20. In terms of language learning milestones, which of the following comes last?

    a. consistently uses prepositions
    b. uses past tense verbs
    c. speaks 50+ words
    d. produces word order that is appropriate for the native language

21. Which of the following is an example of over-regularization?

    a. 'You have two feet'.
    b. 'want cookie'
    c. 'go you there'
    d. 'Where are the mouses?'

22. Creole languages are *not*

    a. invented by children.
    b. as sophisticated as more established languages.
    c. created very often.
    d. developed from pidgin languages.

23. Non-human primates' communication is controlled by which brain area(s)?

    a. the cortex
    b. the limbic system and the brainstem
    c. the temporal lobe
    d. Broca's area

24. Chimps with extensive language training

    a. build a modest vocabulary.
    b. comment on things.
    c. use language spontaneously.
    d. take turns, conversationally.

25. Some members of the KE family have

    a. a recessive genetic mutation on Chromosome 23.
    b. a dominant genetic mutation on Chromosome 23.
    c. a recessive genetic mutation on Chromosome 7.
    d. a dominant genetic mutation on Chromosome 7.

Study Questions: Answer Key

1. learn (p. 297)

2. Marler's claim was ground-breaking in the 1960s and 1970s because instinct and learning had, until then, been regarded as mutually exclusive. (p. 297)

3. True—Vervets have three acoustically-different alarm calls (one for snake, one for leopard, and one for eagle). (p. 297)

4. combining calls to general new ideas (p. 297)

Language Is Part of Our Psychology

1. Language is 'part of our psychology' for the following reasons:
   - All people, unless they are severely disabled, learn language.
   - A group of children raised without a native language will invent one.
   - All languages are equally complex and sophisticated.
   - As far as we know, every human culture has, and has always had, language.
   - Language seems to be a core part of who we are as a species. (pp. 298–299)

Language as a Case Study in Evolutionary Psychology

1. False—It is very clearly the result of both. (pp. 299–300)

2. operant conditioning; classical conditioning (pp. 300–301)

Noam Chomsky and the Language Acquisition Device

1. Modern Linguistics (p. 301)

2. The following evidence led Chomsky to his proposal:
   - Human language involves complex, abstract rules for word and sentence formation.
   - Children learn the rules very quickly, before other cognitive abilities.
   - Although we follow language rules, most of us are unaware of what the rules are.
   - Adults do not teach children the rules. (p. 301)

3. Language acquisition device refers to the learning mechanisms that young children have that allow them to analyze the language they hear and to acquire and produce their own native language. (p. 302)

4. You would probably tell your friend that imitation is insufficient for language learning because
   - adults do not provide good language models for children.
   - children produce novel sentences that they have never heard before. (p. 302)

5. surface; deep (p. 302)

6. The universal grammar is the set of principles and adjustable parameters that are common to all known and presumably undiscovered human languages. (p. 302)

7. mere exposure (p. 302)

8. Home signs are a system of communication that is developed by deaf children of hearing parents in cases where the children are not regularly exposed to adult sign language. (p. 302)

9. Consider the following in your response:
   - Home signs are distinct from manual gestures that hearing children and adults use to accompany spoken language.
   - It has also been found that home signs include subjects, objects, and actions and are kept in a particular order.
   - This is the case even though home signs are specific to an individual and not shared by a group. (p. 302)

The Brain Basis of Human Language

1. left (p. 303)

2. False—Specialization increases with age. (p. 303)

3. motor; auditory (p. 303)

4. When people suffer damage to Broca's area,
   - they can produce only 'telegraphic speech'—single-word, halting, laboriously-produced word strings—with little grammatical organization.
   - language comprehension remains largely intact. (p. 303)

5. When people suffer damage to Wernicke's area,
   - they are unable to understand other people's speech.
   - their own speech is fluent and largely grammatical, but nonsensical. (p. 304)

Infant Speech Perception

1. speech stream (p. 304)

2. Consider the following in your response:
   - Newborns are most sensitive to sounds in the frequency range of the human speaking voice.
   - Newborns prefer to listen to human speech over pure tones. (p. 304)

3. speech sounds (p. 304)

4. False—Young infants are actually better than adults at sound discrimination. (p. 304)

5. operant conditioning (p. 305)

6. True—The ability to discriminate between non-native speech sounds disappears quickly. (p. 306)

7. The ability is largely reduced somewhere around 10 months of age. 10- to 12-month-old infants are significantly worse in making discriminations than 8- to 10-month-old infants. (p. 306)

8. Categorical perception means that stimuli that differ continuously are perceived categorically, as qualitatively different. (p. 306)

9. Consider the following in your response:
   - The speech sounds /ba/ and /pa/ are produced nearly identically.
   - They differ only in *voice onset time* (*VOT*), the time that passes between when a stop-consonant is released and when the vocal folds begin to vibrate (when voicing begins).
   - The VOT for 'b' is about 15ms; the VOT for 'pa' is about 100ms. (p. 306)

10. 25 (p. 307)

11. False—1- to 4-month-old infants will dishabituate to sounds from a different speech category. They will not dishabituate to equally physically different sounds that are not from a different speech category. (p. 308)

12. instinct blindness (to language processing) (p. 308)

13. False—Newborns do prefer to listen to their native languages over non-native languages but they don't have preferences among non-native languages. (p. 309)

Proto-Babbling and Babbling

1. Consider the following in your answer:
   - Cooing refers to noises that sound like vowels; babbling involves adding consonant sounds.
   - Cooing starts at around 2 months; babbling starts at around 4 or 5 months. (p. 309)

2. False—Deaf infants babble with their hands. (p. 309)

3. consonant-vowel; intonation (pp. 309–310)

Word Learning

1. 8; 18 (p. 310)

2. After the first words, toddlers start to combine words, creating two-word phrases. (p. 310)

3. True—They also have the ability to put words together into elaborate, mostly grammatical sentences. (p. 310)

4. problem of reference (p. 310)

5. infants come into the world prepared with powerful, well-designed machinery and rules for acquiring words (p. 311)

6. False—Putting words together comes when vocabulary is about 200 words (around the age of 2). (p. 311)

7. telegraphic (p. 311)

8. False—They actually learn about a half a dozen words per day. (p. 311)

9. fast mapping (p. 311)

10. In the whole-object assumption, children narrow the set of possible meanings that might be associated with a novel word by assuming that novel words will refer to whole objects. (p. 311)

11. In the taxonomic assumption, children assume that novel words will refer to object that are grouped conceptually or categorically rather than thematically. (p. 312)

12. In the mutual exclusivity assumption, children assume that novel words applied to a new object will refer to a novel property rather than to the whole object or a known property. It is assumed that a novel word does not duplicate a known word but means something else. (p. 313)

13. Consider the following in your response:
    - Young children can perceive and use adults'
        - focus of attention
        - emotional reactions
        - intentionality
    - If an adult uses a novel word while looking back and forth between the infant and the object in a playful, animate manner, the child is likely to interpret the new words as an invitation to play rather than a label for the object. (pp. 313–314)

What Would Associationists Say About Language Acquisition?

1. False—Skinner believed that language is learned via operant conditioning, like any other developing behaviour. (p. 314)

2. imitation (p. 314)

3. General-learning mechanisms can't explain
    - the rapidity and efficiency of language learning.
    - children's generation of novel utterances. (p. 314)

Adults' Roles in Children's Language Learning

1. False—Adults do not have to do much active teaching at all. (p. 314)

2. False—The complex grammatical rules of spoken language are not explicitly known and explicable by most adults. (pp. 314–315)

3. False—Some sort of interaction is necessary. (p. 315)

4. Compared to adult-directed speech, infant-directed speech
   - involves a higher pitch
   - involves extreme, exaggerated intonation
   - is slower
   - is typically accompanied by exaggerated facial expressions
   - is more grammatically pure
   - focuses on concrete and current topics rather than abstract, hypothetical, or future topics (p. 315)

5. False—It is grammatically pure, but not grammatically simple. (p. 315)

6. False—Infant-directed speech is used in all cultures in which adults talk to infants, but there are cultures in which adults never speak to children until the child is conversational. (p. 315)

7. The Shuar could
   - understand the intention of the utterance (prohibitive, approval, comfort, or attention).
   - distinguish between infant-directed and adult-directed speech (and were faster and more accurate at identifying intention in infant-directed speech). (p. 316)

8. concrete objects (p. 316)

9. Parents tend to correct utterances that are factually incorrect, but they do not tend to correct utterances that are grammatically incorrect. (p. 316)

Critical Periods for Language Learning

1. learn something (p. 316)

2. Critical periods exist because
   - a language acquisition device is costly. It requires brain activity which is very costly metabolically.
   - it is more efficient to use the device during a specified time and then spend the brain activity on other things. This means that we are not very well-equipped to learn new languages later in life but people in the EEA rarely had the opportunity to do that anyway.
   - childhood is the only time period when the benefits justify the costs. (p. 316)

3. Consider the following in your response:
   - The sooner the better!
   - If you want your daughter's Chinese to be accent-free and grammatically-perfect, you should move by the time she is 7.
   - If you relocate between the ages of 8 and 15, her Chinese will still be quite good. (p. 317)

4. those children were abused, neglected, and deprived of more than just language (p. 318)

5. fully grammatical language (p. 318)

6. True—She spoke proper English by the time she was 8 years old. (p. 318)

7. False—Plasticity in the brain of a child will allow for language learning. An adult with damage to the left hemisphere will often show permanent language deficits. (p. 318)

8. Answer:
   - Those who learned before the age of 3 will use the left hemisphere almost exclusively for grammatical processing.
   - Those who learned between 4 and 6 will show significantly more right-hemisphere use for grammatical tasks.
   - Those who learned at 11 to 13 show almost equal left- and right-hemisphere activation for grammatical tasks. (p. 319)

9. Based on the above findings, it seems that
   - people who are exposed to a second language *during* the critical period are able to make use of specialized language acquisition processes that are located in the left hemisphere of the brain.
   - those exposed to a second language *after* the critical period must rely on alternative processes for language acquisition. The alternative processes are not biased to the left hemisphere. (pp. 319–320)

10. False—Researchers currently favour a multi-system view of bilingual language learning whereby children learn each language using dedicated cognitive systems and interference between the languages is minimized. (p. 320)

11. Consider the following in your response:
    - Bilingual children have been found to have greater executive control than monolingual children.
    - They are better able to control their own attention, disregard irrelevant stimuli, and focus their own cognitive processes.
    - It seems that this cognitive advantage remains throughout adulthood and provides a buffer against cognitive declines in old age. (p. 320)

Learning Grammar

1. True—Production lags behind perception and comprehension. (p. 320)

2. False—2-year-olds seem to be able to decode the meaning encoded in the grammar of sentences. (p. 321)

3.
   1. birth — c) prefers the mother's language to a foreign language
   2. 1 month — a) perceives speech sounds categorically
   3. 3 months — f) starts cooing
   4. 6 months — e) starts babbling
   5. 9 months — b) uses voice to attract attention
   6. 1 year — d) understands several words (p. 322)

4.
   1. 15 months — c) can communicate needs using vocalization
   2. 18 months — a) echoes adult speech
   3. 2 years — d) vocabulary reaches about 50 words
   4. 3 years — e) speaks in sentences
   5. 4 years — f) consistently uses prepositions
   6. 5 years — b) can refer to past, present, and future (p. 322)

5. Over-regularization involves over-applying grammatical tools. For example, since '–ed' is typically added to the end of words to indicate the past tense, a child might say 'I goed' instead of 'I went'. (p. 321)

6. production of speech sounds; grammatical understanding (p. 321)

7. Associationists couldn't really explain over-regularization errors. Those errors are evidence of language generation rather than learning by association—they involve producing utterances that children would never have heard from adults. (p. 321)

Children Generate Language

1. False—Without parents, children can learn spoken language just fine from their peers. In fact, children are much more influenced by peers than parents when acquiring accents, local vocabulary, and speech mannerisms. (p. 321)

2. Pidgin languages are created in situations when two (or more) language communities come into contact for the first time. (pp. 321–322)

3. Compared to established languages, pidgin languages
   - are choppy and non-standardized.
   - have a word order that may vary from speaker to speaker.
   - lack grammatical inflections.
   - borrow vocabulary from each of the adult language communities. (p. 323)

4. When children are born into a community that speaks a pidgin language, the children turn the pidgin language into a creole language. A creole language is a bona fide language—it includes complex grammatical structures equal to any established language. (p. 323)

5. Hawaii in the late 1800s (p. 323)

6. vocabulary (*not* auxiliaries, prepositions, case markers, relative pronouns, words orders, or grammatical markers) (p. 323)

7. True—The signs do not just represent English. In fact, American Sign Language is not even related to English. (p. 324)

8. Nicaragua in the 1970s (p. 324)

9. False—People use hand gestures even if both the speaker and the listener are blind. (p. 325)

10. The early signers included segmented and sequenced signs in their descriptions. In contrast to the older signers, they used language and followed grammatical rules. They were not simply using their hands to emphasize what they were saying. (p. 325)

Language Is Species-Specific

1. Consider the following in your response:
   - The calls and vocalizations of non-human primates are not controlled by brain areas that are analogous to those that control language in humans.
   - Calls and vocalizations of non-human primates are controlled by older brain structures, specifically those associated with emotions (e.g. the limbic system and the brain stem). (p. 328)

2. vocal apparatus (p. 328)

3. the trainers' failure to publish results and apparent unwillingness to share raw data (p. 328)

4. about 25 (p. 329)

5. Chimps do not
   - comment on things.
   - take conversational turns.
   - use language spontaneously (with very rare exceptions, and when they do, it is almost always to make a request).
   - construct long and intricate sentences.
   - learn language without extensive and explicit training attempts (p. 329)

6. a vulnerability to choking (p. 330)

7. True—The language-ready vocal tract develops after the first several months of life. In fact, it gradually becomes more adult-like until puberty, meaning that a developing child must continuously relearn speech sound articulation. (p. 330)

Can a Gene Cause the Development of Grammar?

1. mutation on Chromosome 7 (p. 331)

2. False—While there is a strong association between having a genetic mutation on Chromosome 7 and having difficulty in the development of grammar, all developmental resources work together in typical language development. (p. 331)

Practice Test 1: Answer Key

1. **d** (p. 297)	8. **c** (p. 309)	15. **c** (p. 316)	22. **a** (p. 327)
2. **b** (p. 299)	9. **a** (p. 310)	16. **a** (p. 317)	23. **d** (p. 328)
3. **b** (p. 302)	10. **d** (p. 311)	17. **c** (p. 317)	24. **c** (p. 330)
4. **b** (p. 303)	11. **b** (p. 311)	18. **b** (p. 320)	25. **b** (p. 331)
5. **d** (p. 303)	12. **c** (p. 312)	19. **b** (p. 320)	
6. **a** (p. 305)	13. **d** (p. 313)	20. **d** (p. 323)	
7. **d** (p. 306)	14. **a** (p. 315)	21. **c** (p. 324)	

Practice Test 2: Answer Key

1. **d** (pp. 298–299)	8. **d** (p. 309)	15. **c** (p. 315)	22. **c** (p. 323)
2. **c** (p. 301)	9. **b** (p. 310)	16. **a** (p. 316)	23. **b** (p. 328)
3. **b** (p. 302)	10. **c** (p. 311)	17. **c** (p. 317)	24. **a** (p. 329)
4. **d** (p. 304)	11. **a** (p. 313)	18. **b** (p. 318)	25. **d** (p. 331)
5. **a** (p. 306)	12. **b** (p. 314)	19. **d** (p. 319)	
6. **b** (p. 306)	13. **b** (p. 314)	20. **a** (p. 322)	
7. **c** (pp. 308–309)	14. **d** (pp. 314–315)	21. **d** (p. 321)	

Chapter 10
Social Contexts for Development

Chapter Summary

Learning about One's Own Context

Learning mechanisms are adaptive in that they allow for taking advantage of regularities in the environment. Learning also allows for the opportunity to assess circumstances before choosing strategies. *Social facultative adaptations* are designed to respond to specific cues in the social environment, enabling humans to pursue advantageous social strategies.

Psychological Adaptations for Culture

Although non-humans can learn from each other, they cannot be said to have cultures. Only humans have the cognitive machinery to permit and support the evolution and transmission of culture. Humans alone are able to build artifacts by adding innovations to innovations.

As illustrated by the Hadza and !Kung hunter–gatherers, local ecology affects cultural practices. The !Kung, who live in a harsher climate than the Hadza, employ very different parenting practices. They tend to be less attentive and more strict with their children and children are expected to work more and at an earlier age. Investment in children is greater for !Kung men than Hadza men. !Kung women have longer birth intervals. Such differences in behaviours are consistent with the optimization of reproductive success, which varies depending on ecological conditions.

Life History Theory

Life history theory is meant to account for and predict the timing of major life events across development. There is a trade-off between allocating resources for growth and reproduction. Individuals must choose whether to mate and reproduce earlier in life or defer reproduction until life circumstances are more conducive to child-rearing. The strategy that is employed depends on environment. The level of *paternal investment* in the individual's society is one consideration in the choice of either strategy. Men and women can maximize their reproductive success by choosing to behave differently depending on circumstance.

Empirically, males and females have been found to vary in personality characteristics (e.g. dominance, competitiveness), sexual activity, and pubertal timing depending on paternal investment. To explain these findings, researchers have suggested that there are evolved psychological mechanisms that act during a critical period to assess the environment in terms of how easily and predictably available resources are. This assessment may guide the child into one reproductive life strategy or another.

Attachment

Harlow compared the effects of maternal nutritional contribution and maternal contact comfort in rhesus monkeys. Regardless of the source of nutrition, infant monkeys chose to spend most of their time with a terry-cloth surrogate mother over a wire surrogate mother.

Harlow's findings are consistent with Bowlby's attachment theory, which proposes that attachment is not a result of the need for food; rather, it serves the evolutionarily-favoured functions of keeping the infant safe and allowing for exploration.

Mary Ainsworth's strange situation task is a way of assessing types of infant attachment. The reactions of an infant to a series of separations and reunions with the caregiver and a stranger are observed. The infant can then be classified into one of four attachment types: secure, resistant, avoidant, and disorganized.

A more versatile alternative to the strange situation task is the Attachment Q-sort, which can be used in an in-home observational situation.

Emotional Development More Generally

Stranger anxiety and separation anxiety provide the earliest evidence of fear in infants (at around 6 to 8 months of age). Positive emotions are demonstrated earlier, with the first social smiles occurring as early as 6 weeks of age. Very early on, infants show general distress by face grimaces and crying. Distress, pain, and anger seem to be expressed and perhaps experienced indistinctly. Because parental response does not need to differ between those emotions, similar expressions for all three is adequately functional.

Parents, Alloparents, Siblings, and Peers

Parental investment increases an offspring's change of surviving and reproducing at the cost of the parent's ability to invest in other offspring. Strategic allocation of parental investment is tremendously important in terms of natural selection and varies depending on environment.

Inclusive fitness is a measure of an individual's evolutionary fitness that incorporates the number of viable offspring as well as the number of viable relatives, discounted by relatedness. *Parent–offspring conflict* arises due to the fact that parents and offspring have different fitness interests.

Hamilton's rule predicts altruistic behaviour using the following equation: $rB > C$. An actor will altruistically help a family member if the cost (C) to the actor is less than the benefit (B) to the family member, discounted by genetic relatedness (r).

Differences in Parenting Make Little Difference

Excluding cases of abuse and neglect, it seems that parenting makes little difference in a child's development, including the development of personality traits, political values, and language. Evolution has led to a resilience to differences in environment as long as the differences are within a broad, species-typical range. Scarr described parenting behaviours that fall within this range as *good-enough parenting*.

Socialization—the process that leads to the acquisition of culture (beliefs, values, language, skills)—may be less dependent on parenting than has been traditionally thought. Instead, peer groups may be the driving force.

Peer Influence

Harris' group socialization theory proposes that peers and siblings, especially acting in groups, segregated by age, sex, abilities, and interests, have a measurable effect on a child's personality development. Members of these groups adopt the group's attitudes and norms of behaviours. Elements of adult culture are selected and rejected and novel elements are invented. Traditions may be passed on for centuries from older children to younger children.

Alloparents are all of the people who contribute to a child's upbringing other than the child's parents. Extended family members and family friends may provide supportive contributions.

Grandparents may make significant contributions to a child's upbringing, thus advancing their own genetic interests after child-bearing years.

Step-Parents

Step-parents, as they share no genetic relatedness to the child, would not be expected to invest in stepchildren to the extent that a biological parent would. Indeed, in general, they do not invest as much as biological parents, as evidenced by weaker feelings for the children and less time spent with them, among other things. Children who live with a step-parent are many times more likely to be abused and murdered. Daly and Wilson have proposed that this is not because step-parents have any adaptations designed for harming stepchildren (as do some non-humans) but because they do not have the nurturing adaptations that a biological parent has.

Mothers and maternal relatives of a newborn are likely to allege that the baby looks like the father. This may reflect a drive to let the father know that he is not a cuckold. As well, men (and not women) have been found to show bias toward a photograph of a child that was altered to look like them. It seems that men may have evolved psychological processes to protect them against cuckoldry.

Birth order may affect an individual's personality. Sulloway proposed that, since first-born children are more likely to inherit the parent's home and status, they may identify most strongly with the parents and authority figures in general. Because later-born children must seek their fortunes elsewhere, Sulloway argued that they are more likely to be risk-takers. The effects of birth order illustrate the power of non-shared environment on an individual's development. Birth order may lead to an increased difference between family members, with siblings more different than strangers.

Learning Objectives

After reading this chapter, you should be able to:

- Appreciate social facultative adaptations, those that are designed to allow us to navigate the social environment (pp. 338–340)

- Summarize how fitness strategies contribute to culture (pp. 340–343)

- Examine the principles of life history theory (pp. 343–351)

- Understand attachment from an evolutionary perspective (pp. 351–356)

- Explain how infants can be categorized into different attachment types using the strange situation task (pp. 354–356)

- Track the development of different types of emotions across the first year of life (pp. 356–358)

- Examine strategies of parental investment from both the parent's and the child's perspectives (pp. 358–362)

- Appreciate how little parenting matters for socialization (pp. 362–363)

- Examine the significant role of peers in social development (pp. 364–366)

- Analyze the contributions of alloparents and grandparents to a child's development (pp. 366–367)

- Compare how step-parents differ from biological parents in their attitudes (and behaviours) toward children (pp. 367–369)

- Appreciate why physical resemblance to an infant matters to a father (pp. 369–370)

- Examine the role of birth order in developing personality (pp. 370–373)

Suggested Readings

Marlowe, F. (2010). *The Hadza: Hunter–Gatherers of Tanzania.* Berkeley, CA: University of California Press.

Marlowe examines the culture of one of the last remaining hunter–gatherer societies.

Harlow, H. F., & Zimmerman, R. R. (1959). Affectional responses in the infant monkey. *Science, 130,* 421–432.

This classic paper examines monkeys' preference for surrogate mothers who offer soft body contact.

Harris, J. R. (2009). *The Nurture Assumption: Why Children Turn Out the Way They Do, Revised and Updated.* Free Press.

Harris details the evidence for the greater influence of peer groups than parents on development.

Study Questions

Learning about One's Own Context

1. What 'engineering problems' might learning solve?

2. Define 'social facultative adaptation'.

Psychological Adaptations for Culture

1. What are some examples of social learning in non-humans?

2. True or False: Culture is unique to humans.

3. Human tools and non-human tools are different in that human tools are _____.

4. How does environment differ for the Hadza and !Kung groups?

5. The birth interval is shorter for Hadza women than for !Kung women. What does that imply?

6. How do the Hadza and !Kung people differ with respect to their responsiveness to their children?

7. Compared to !Kung men, Hadza men are more likely to _____, _____, and _____.

8. Jones and Hawkes believe that the above differences between the Hadza and the !Kung can be explained by differences in immediate ecological circumstances rather than culture. Explain their rationale.

Life History Theory

1. Life history theory is meant to account for and predict _____.

2. An individual must allocate a finite supply of resources, time, and energy across the competing goals of _____, _____, and _____.

3. What are two broad reproductive strategies?

4. The better of the above strategies depends on _____.

5. True or False: Paternal investment is obligatory in all human cultures.

6. Define 'Hamilton's rule'.

7. In a society in which paternal investment is the norm, in which men can and do invest in their offspring, and in which men marry and remain with their families, a woman's best reproductive strategy is to _____.

8. True or False: Women in a high-paternal-investment society are best not to have an extramarital affair.

9. In a society in which paternal investment is *not* the norm, in which men do not invest in their offspring, and in which men do not make long-term commitments to their sexual partners, a woman's best reproductive strategy is to _____.

10. The greatest damage (evolutionarily speaking) to a man who chooses the family-man strategy is to be _____.

11. In evolutionary terms, why is such a danger to be cuckolded?

12. In a society in which there is _____, a man may have greater reproductive success by being a playboy instead of a committed father.

13. There seems to be a _____ in developing children for learning what kind of society they are growing up in.

14. Match 'Father Absent' or 'Father Present' with the following descriptions of *women*.

    1. Father Absent   a) better liar

                                                  b) more securely attached

                                                  c) more sexual partners

                                                  d) later puberty

                                                  e) lower androgen levels

2. Father Present
     f) low-investing society

     g) more dominant

     h) smiles more frequently

     i) sexually active earlier

     j) high-investing society

15. Match 'Father Absent' or 'Father Present' to the following descriptions of *men*.

 1. Father Absent   a) high-investing society

           b) more stable romantic relationships

 2. Father Present   c) more manipulative

           d) more competitive

           e) low-investing society

16. Elizabeth Cashdan showed that women and men who expected that paternal investment was scarce showed a more _____.

17. Puberty in humans marks the beginning of the end of _____ for an individual and the beginning of the _____.

18. True or False: The earlier in a girl's life her father leaves, the later her puberty.

19. What are three early factors that inform a developing child about the social and ecological circumstances in which she is growing up?

20. These early factors, in turn, influence a girl's subsequent social development as well as her _____, _____, _____, and _____.

21. What are some specific family stressors during childhood that can lead to earlier puberty, earlier sexual relationships, and more sex partners?

22. True or False: Mortality rates affect reproductive strategies.

23. As local mortality rates increased across neighbourhoods in a large Chicago-area sample, so did the probability of _____.

24. Young women in Gloucestershire who had their first babies in their teens were more likely to report _____ than women who had their first babies after their teenage years.

Attachment

1. Harlow's experiments with baby rhesus monkeys and surrogate mothers allowed comparison of the effects of _____ of the mother and _____ of the mother in terms of social development.

2. True or False: Harlow's monkeys preferred to spend time with whichever surrogate mother provided nutrition.

3. What other signs of attachment did the monkeys show to the terry-cloth mother (other than preferring to spend time with it)?

4. What happened to monkeys who were provided with only a wire mother?

5. Harlow's findings were a challenge to the _____ view because they showed that food was not the ultimate reward that led children to love their parents.

6. Harlow's findings suggest that the driving force behind attachment is _____, not nutrition.

7. Define 'attachment'.

8. John Bowlby was the first to write about developmental psychology from a(n) _____ perspective.

9. What sparked Bowlby to develop his theory on attachment?

10. True or False: The imprinting mechanism that is seen in some bird species is designed to imprint on the baby's mother.

11. Bowbly followed the tradition of ethologists, thinking in _____ terms and in a(n) _____ context.

12. According to Bowlby's theory, attachment serves what two functions?

13. What does it mean to say that an infant uses her caregiver as a 'secure base'?

14. Mary Ainsworth was a student of _____.

15. What two factors did Ainsworth believe were key in assessing the quality of a child's attachment?

16. For the strange situation task, match the following episode numbers with the corresponding descriptions of the episodes (i.e. put the episodes in order).

1   Stranger enters the room, sits quietly, talks to caregiver, tries to interact with infant.

2   Caregiver returns, comforting infant if needed. Stranger leaves.

3   Caregiver returns, comforting infant as needed. Stranger leaves.

4   Caregiver leaves infant alone with stranger, who tries to comfort infant if needed.

5   Caregiver, experimenter, and infant enter room. Caregiver sits. Experimenter leaves while infant plays with toys.

6   Caregiver leaves infant alone.

7   Infant explores while caregiver responds but does not initiate contact.

8   Stranger returns, greets infant, trying to comfort infant if needed.

17. During the strange situation task, what does the experimenter pay particular attention to?

18. An instrument called the Attachment Q-sort can be used in a _____ situation.

19. How does the Attachment Q-sort work?

20. Because its results are _____, the Attachment Q-sort is considered to be a reliable and versatile alternative to the strange situation task.

21. Describe secure attachment.

22. Describe insecure/resistant attachment.

23. Describe insecure/avoidant attachment.

24. Describe disorganized/disoriented attachment.

25. How are children, adolescents, and adults who were securely attached as infants different than those who were insecurely attached?

Emotional Development More Generally

1. As an infant's attachment to her primary caregiver grows, her fear of _____ becomes evident.

2. True or False: Separation anxiety typically emerges a bit after stranger anxiety.

3. True or False: Infants only smile at people, not at objects.

4. True or False: Even in the first couple of months of life, the infant experiences distress, pain, and anger as distinct emotions.

Parents, Alloparents, Siblings, and Peers

1. Parental-investment theory stresses _____.

2. Define 'parental investment'.

3. What are some differences in parenting styles between parents with high socio-economic status (SES) and parents with low SES?

4. With regard to the above differences, it can be said that the psychological mechanisms that calibrate _____ are responsive to resource levels in contemporary societies.

5. What is the inherent conflict between parent and offspring described by Robert Trivers?

6. In terms of inclusive fitness, one gets _____ credit for oneself, _____ credit for offspring or siblings, and _____ credit for nieces or nephews.

7. Parent–offspring conflict results from the fact that _____.

8. Define 'Hamilton's rule'.

9. In terms of genetic relatedness, four sisters equal how many nieces?

10. Genetic relatedness for cousins = _____.

11. True or False: Offspring should adopt their parents' wishes for allocating resources.

Differences in Parenting Make Little Difference

1. True or False: Parenting (within a broad range of 'normal' parenting) makes little difference in a child's development.

2. Why is the above finding to be expected?

3. Define 'good-enough parenting'.

4. Through socialization, the child acquires the _____ of his parents.

5. What do adoption and twin studies tell us about the effects of differences in parenting characteristics?

6. Parents don't seem to be the agents of socialization. How does that make sense following Triver's idea of parent–offspring conflict?

7. Judith Harris argues that knowledge about relative status and relative attractiveness can be more reliably given by _____ than _____.

8. What are some differences between early and late maturing boys?

9. According to a longitudinal study on the relationship between height and personality traits of males, the critical period for development of personality traits associated with dominance is _____.

Peer Influence

1. Harris suggests that (assuming physical and nutritional needs are covered) the absence of peers would be a greater challenge to normal development than the absence of parents. Outline some support for that idea.

2. Describe Harris' 'group socialization theory'.

3. Define 'alloparents'.

4. In traditional societies today, mothers rely on the help of _____ and _____ in particular to provide children with consistent childcare.

5. Several theorists have proposed that _____ is an adaptation that allows for an extended lifespan and increased reproductive success via grandparental investment.

6. How do Hadza grandmothers contribute to the success of grandchildren?

Step-Parents

1. True or False: Step-parents would have been uncommon in the EEA.

2. Step-parents would not be expected to (and indeed do not) invest in stepchildren to the extent that children's biological parents invest because _____.

3. True or False: Children are more likely to be murdered by stepfathers than biological fathers.

4. True or False: Abusive step-parents are just as likely to be abusive to their biological children as well.

5. Daly and Wilson do not propose that humans have any adaptations that are designed for harming stepchildren. What, instead, is their explanation for abuse by step-parents?

6. Newborns are more often said to resemble the father than the mother. The purpose of this is to _____.

7. True or False: In response to positive questions (e.g. 'Which child would you be more likely to adopt?'), men, but not women, were found to be biased toward choosing children who resemble them.

Birth Order

1. Frank Sulloway proposes that _____ has an enduring and formative effect on the developing personality.

2. How would Sulloway explain the fact that many presidents and heads-of-state are first-born children and many revolutionaries are later-born children?

3. _____ can lead to siblings that are more different than strangers.

Practice Test 1

1. The link between nutritional deprivation and glucose intolerance is an example of

    a. a negative correlation.
    b. a detrimental relationship.
    c. an insignificant association.
    d. a facultative adaptation.

2. Which of the following is *not* true regarding the !Kung, who live in a harsher climate than the Hadza?

    a. They are less attentive to their children than the Hadza.
    b. They have shorter birth intervals than the Hadza.
    c. They use more discipline with their children than the Hadza.
    d. Their children are expected to work more and at an earlier age than the Hadza.

3. In a society in which men spend considerable time on courtship and raising children, a man's worst-case scenario is to

    a. waste resources that he could use for himself on his biological children.
    b. be promiscuous.
    c. be cuckolded.
    d. be in a committed relationship.

4. When men had fathers who were present throughout their childhood, they _____ than if their fathers were absent.

    a. are more competitive
    b. are more manipulative
    c. are more likely to live in a low-investing society
    d. have more stable romantic relationships

5. Harlow found that baby rhesus monkeys prefer to spend time with a surrogate mother who

    a. was capable of movement.
    b. provided soft contact.
    c. provided nutrition.
    d. had a stylized face.

6. Attachment theory was developed by

    a. John Bowlby.
    b. Harry Harlow.
    c. Mary Ainsworth.
    d. B. F. Skinner.

7. Bowlby thought about attachment in terms of

    a. function.
    b. emotions.
    c. sociability.
    d. memory.

8. A baby greylag goose imprints on

    a. its littermates.
    b. its mother.
    c. the first thing that moves.
    d. none of the above

9. Which of the following did Ainsworth believe to be a key factor in assessing attachment quality?

    a. how the infant reacts to the presence of a stranger
    b. how the infant behaves when separated and reunited with the caregiver
    c. how the infant reacts to a stranger's attempt to comfort
    d. how the infant reacts when the caregiver fails to initiate contact

10. In the strange situation task, Roberto is clingy and unwilling to separate from his mother to explore the room. Roberto's attachment type will most likely be

    a. secure.
    b. insecure disorganized.
    c. insecure avoidant.
    d. insecure resistant.

11. Infants who are securely attached

    a. have more stable peer relationships as children.
    b. are more socially skilled as children.
    c. have more secure adult relationships.
    d. all of the above

12. Which of the following statements is *not* true regarding early smiles in infants?

    a. Infants tend to smile when they have an effect on their environment.
    b. Infants smile at people but not objects.
    c. Social smiles are evident in 1-month-old infants.
    d. They have an effect on adults.

13. Parental-investment theory stresses the _____ basis of aspects of parental behaviour.

    a. emotional
    b. behavioural
    c. evolutionary
    d. biological

14. Inclusive fitness =

    a. number of viable offspring + number of viable relatives, discounted by relatedness
    b. number of viable offspring + number of viable relatives
    c. number of viable offspring – number of viable relatives, discounted by relatedness
    d. number of viable offspring – number of viable relatives

15. In Hamilton's rule, the B stands for

    a. behaviour.
    b. brother.
    c. biology.
    d. benefit.

16. Which of the following statements is true of good-enough parenting?

    a. Although it is considered to be 'good enough' by the parent, it is not sufficient to bring up a healthy, functional child.
    b. It reflects the resiliency of children.
    c. It requires quite extraordinary parental contributions.
    d. It does not require anything of the parent.

17. Judith Harris

    a. argues that children are open to internalizing parental values.
    b. proposed that parenting style is more important for socialization than schools or neighbourhoods.
    c. argues that social information is more reliably delivered from peers than family.
    d. has made claims that are inconsistent with Triver's parent–offspring conflict theory.

18. The case of six Jewish children who lived together for years with no stable adult caregiver suggests that

    a. peers are preferable to parents for development.
    b. childhood peers can provide the stability required to grow into a functional adult.
    c. parental investment is necessary for normal development.
    d. in the absence of adults, one peer is better for development than a group of peers.

19. Trivers argued that it was unlikely that children receive their personality traits and values from their parents because

    a. children and parents have somewhat conflicting goals.
    b. personality is innate.
    c. children invent their own sets of values.
    d. parents and children do not spend sufficient time together.

20. According to the 'group socialization theory', socialization takes place

    a. at a very young age.
    b. in peer groups.
    c. between parent and child.
    d. individualistically.

21. Which of the following comes first?

    a. Separation anxiety begins to be evident.
    b. The Attachment Q-sort is an effective assessment of attachment style.
    c. Infants smile more at familiar than unfamiliar people.
    d. A father's presence or absence can inform developing life strategy.

22. Which of the following is *not* true of social-networking sites?

    a. Hundreds of millions of people use social-networking sites.
    b. Time spent socializing online predicts loneliness, social anxiety, and depression.
    c. The best use of social-networking sites seems to be in support of real social connections.
    d. Facebook time has been found to be correlated with greater social confidence when interacting in person.

23. Which of the following is *not* an alloparent?

    a. a neighbour
    b. a grandmother
    c. a friend of the father
    d. a parent

24. Who is more likely to assert that a newborn looks like the father?

 a. the mother
 b. the maternal relatives
 c. neither *a* nor *b*
 d. both *a* and *b*

25. Frank Sulloway proposes that birth order has an enduring and formative effect on

 a. personality.
 b. socialization.
 c. peer influence.
 d. attachment.

Practice Test 2

1. Only humans have cumulative culture because only humans

 a. have the cognitive machinery to permit the evolution and transmission of culture.
 b. are able to communicate.
 c. have the cognitive adaptations to learn from one another.
 d. can design cultural artifacts (e.g. tools).

2. Paternal investment

 a. is obligatory.
 b. is constant across cultures.
 c. does not occur in all species.
 d. is greater in communities that are extremely impoverished.

3. Strategically, if a woman lives in a society in which men are willing and able to invest in offspring, she *should not*

 a. reassure her mate of her sexual fidelity.
 b. be choosy in selecting a mate.
 c. secure an investing mate.
 d. stray from her marriage.

4. When a woman has a father present throughout her childhood, she may _____ than if her father was absent.

 a. have more sexual partners
 b. go through puberty later
 c. be a better liar
 d. be more dominant

5. According to life history theory, decisions to delay reproduction and invest in growth are affected by

   a. local mortality rates.
   b. level of societal paternal investment.
   c. rates of monogamy in the society.
   d. all of the above

6. According to Bowlby's theory, attachment was selected for because

   a. it discourages the infant from exploring the environment.
   b. it promotes cognitive development.
   c. it ensures that the infant will be fed.
   d. it keeps the infant safe.

7. Which of the following statements is *not* true of the Attachment Q-sort?

   a. It requires collecting data in the laboratory.
   b. It makes more families accessible to research on attachment.
   c. It is a reliable alternative to the strange situation task.
   d. It involves sorting cards into piles.

8. Insecure disorganized infants

   a. are indifferent to the return of the caregiver.
   b. are easily comforted by a stranger.
   c. do not seem to have a strategy for dealing with being separated from their mothers.
   d. explore the toys in an unfamiliar room while the caregiver is present.

9. The earliest evidence of fear in infants appears at

   a. 6 or 7 months.
   b. 2 or 3 months.
   c. birth.
   d. 10 or 12 months.

10. In the first year of life, negative emotions of distress, pain, and hunger

    a. are not functional in eliciting parental responses.
    b. are undifferentiated.
    c. do not exist.
    d. are not associated with a particular facial expression.

11. Compared to those with low socio-economic status, parents with high socio-economic status are more likely to

    a. act in a putative way toward their children.
    b. be less accepting of their children's behaviour.
    c. be more authoritarian.
    d. use more language with their children.

12. Parent–offspring conflict results from the fact that

    a. parents are concerned with maximizing the fitness of their offspring.
    b. parents and offspring do not have the same point of view regarding the point for decreasing parental investment.
    c. parents tend to invest in some offspring more than others.
    d. none of the above

13. The genetic relatedness of an uncle is

    a. 0.5
    b. 0.35
    c. 0.25
    d. 0.125

14. Hamilton's rule is

    a. $rC < B$
    b. $rB < C$
    c. $rC > B$
    d. $rB > C$

15. An example of a proxy measurement for the cost of altruistic behaviour is

    a. calories expended by the actor.
    b. genetic relatedness.
    c. reproductive success.
    d. food delivered to the recipient.

16. Maccoby & Martin propose that, in terms of socialization,

    a. adoptive siblings are more alike than strangers.
    b. biological siblings raised in the same home are very much alike.
    c. parents don't really matter.
    d. identical twins raised together are more alike than identical twins raised apart.

17. It has been found that early maturing boys

    a. are more anxious than their peers.
    b. score lower on measures of dominance than their peers.
    c. are, as men, more likely to have executive positions in their professions than men who were late maturing boys.
    d. none of the above

18. According to the group socialization theory, peer groups tend to be segregated by

    a. interests.
    b. sex.
    c. age.
    d. all of the above

19. The strange situation task is an effective assessment of attachment style for

    a. 9- to 18-month-old infants.
    b. 6- to 9-month-old infants.
    c. 3- to 6-month-old infants.
    d. all infants.

20. The contributions of Hadza grandmothers

    a. increase the chance of miscarriage.
    b. are aimed at reducing inclusive fitness.
    c. are negligible.
    d. reduce the birth interval of the mother.

21. Which of the following statements is true of step-parents?

    a. They have evolutionary adaptations designed to harm stepchildren.
    b. They very often report not having any 'parental feelings' for their stepchildren.
    c. They are equally likely to abuse their biological children as their stepchildren.
    d. They would have been very rare in the EEA.

22. Children under the age of 2 have been found to be _____ times more likely to be murdered if they live in a home with a step-parent compared to children living with two biological parents.

    a. 2
    b. 10
    c. 40
    d. 100

23. When photographs of children are digitally altered to look more like the experimental participant,

    a. men are relatively likely to identify the child as one they would punish severely for misbehaving.
    b. women are relatively likely to identify the child as one they would punish severely for misbehaving.
    c. men are relatively likely to identify the child as one they would be likely to adopt.
    d. women are relatively likely to identify the child as one they would be likely to adopt.

24. According to Sulloway, first-born children are more likely to be _____ and later-born children are more likely to be _____.

    a. traditionalists; risk-takers
    b. liberal; conservative
    c. revolutionaries; loyal to institutions
    d. controversial; adherent to the status quo

25. Effects of birth order can be seen to illustrate the power of _____ on development.
    a. the shared environment
    b. the non-shared environment
    c. genetics
    d. parenting style

Study Questions: Answer Key

Learning about One's Own Context

1. Learning might allow us
   - to take advantage of reliable information that is 'stored' in the environment.
   - the opportunity to assess the circumstances before choosing a strategy. (p. 339)

2. A social facultative adaptation is one that is designed to respond to specific cues in the social environment, allowing one to pursue the most advantageous social strategy. (p. 339)

Psychological Adaptations for Culture

1. The following are some examples of social learning in non-human species
   - Some vervet monkeys learned to soften an Acacia pod in water.
   - Some chimpanzees learned to use stones to open nut shells.
   - Some chimpanzees learned to use twigs to extract and eat termites.
   - Songbirds learn songs. (p. 340)

2. True—Only humans have cumulative culture because only humans have the cognitive machinery to permit and support the evolution and transmission of culture. (p. 340)

3. more complex (they require several individual accumulation innovations) (p. 340)

4. The !Kung live in a relatively harsher climate. They have to spend more time finding food and drinkable water. (pp. 341–342)

5. It implies that !Kung women either devote more resources to each child or they simply have fewer resources to devote to child rearing. (p. 342)

6. Consider the following in you response:
   - !Kung have fewer interactions between parent and child.
   - !Kung parents are less responsive to children's behaviour, speech, and bids for attention.
   - !Kung parents are more likely to use physical punishment and child-directed commands and prohibitions. (p. 342)

7. divorce; leave a single mother to raise the children; have an extramarital affair (p. 342)

8. Consider the following in your response:
   - The Hadza live in an environment in which food and water are easier to find.
   - A Hadza woman can use her resources to refuel her body and begin her next pregnancy. The environment is fertile enough to allow children to forage as well.
   - The fertile environment means that it is not as devastating for fathers to desert their families.
   - The fertile environment can thus explain the relatively smaller parental investment. (pp. 342–343)

Life History Theory

1. the timing of major life events across development (p. 343)

2. physical growth; physical and energetic maintenance; reproduction (p. 343)

3. Two broad reproductive strategies are
   - to mate relatively later in life, commit to monogamy, and raise children in partnership with one's mate.
   - to mate relatively early and more frequently. (p. 344)

4. what everyone else is doing (p. 344)

5. False—Paternal investment varies across human cultures. (p. 344)

6. Hamilton's rule states that paternal investment can occur only in situations in which a father can deliver enough resources to his mate and children to make a difference. (p. 344)

7. secure an investing mate (p. 345)

8. True—In a high-paternal-investment society, a woman needs to have a mate who believes in her sexual fidelity and thus believes that her children are his children. (p. 345)

9. not wait for a committed partner to begin reproducing (if she waited she would squander her reproductive opportunities) (p. 345)

10. cuckolded (p. 345)

11. Being cuckolded means that the man is squandering his resources to promote someone else's genetic interests. (pp. 345–346)

12. relative promiscuity (p. 346)

13. critical period (p. 346)

14. 1. Father Absent
    - f) low-investing society
    - i) sexually active earlier
    - c) more sexual partners
    - g) more dominant
    - a) better liar

    2. Father Present
    - j) high-investing society
    - d) later puberty
    - b) more securely attached
    - h) smiles more frequently
    - e) lower androgen levels (p. 347)

15. 1. Father Absent
    - e) low-investing society
    - c) more manipulative
    - d) more competitive

    2. Father Present
    - a) high-investing society
    - b) more stable romantic relationships (p. 347)

16. promiscuous sexual strategy (p. 347)

17. growth; reproductive years (p. 348)

18. False—The earlier her father leaves, the earlier her puberty. (p. 349)

19. The three factors are
    - family dynamics
    - father presence
    - quality of the parent–child relationship (p. 349)

20. sexual behaviour; pair-binding; parenting skills; timing of first menarche (p. 349)

21. Some stressors include
    - frequency or unpredictable scarcity of food
    - coercive family relationships
    - absence of the father (either because he does not live at home or because he works long hours) (p. 349)

22. True—The risk of delaying reproduction is greater if mortality rate is high. (p. 350)

23. a woman having her first baby before the age of 30 (pp. 350–351)

24. a shorter expected lifespan (p. 351)

Attachment

1. nutritional contribution; comforting features (p. 351)

2. False—They preferred to spend time with the terry-cloth mother, regardless of the source of nutrition. (p. 352)

3. Some signs of the monkeys' attachment include the following:
    - The monkeys would run to the terry-cloth mother if a frightening stimulus was introduced.
    - Placed in a novel environment, the monkeys would cling to the terry-cloth mother until they felt secure enough to explore. (p. 352)

4. The monkeys with only a wire mother
    - had trouble digesting what they ate.
    - frequently had diarrhea. (p. 352)

5. empiricist/behaviourist (p. 352)

6. comfort/social contact (p. 352)

7. Attachment refers to the emotional bond a young child feels with another specific person. (p. 352)

8. evolutionary (p. 352)

9. Consider the following in your response:
    - Bowlby was a British psychoanalyst after World War II.
    - A great number of children in England had been orphaned or separated from their parents because of the war.
    - Bowlby observed that these children were depressed, listless, emotionally disturbed, and cognitively delayed. They did not have normal attachments to anyone. (pp. 352–353)

10. False—It is designed to imprint on the first thing that moves (usually, that is the baby's mother). (p. 353)

11. functional; evolutionary (p. 354)

12. The two functions of attachment are the following:
    1. It keeps the infant safe.
    2. It allows for exploration. (p. 354)

13. This means that
    - with the caregiver present, the infant feels secure and can explore the environment.
    - the infant will return to the caregiver if he is hurt, scared, or disoriented. (p. 354)

14. John Bowlby (p. 354)

15. The two factors are
    1. how effectively the infant used his caregiver as a home base.
    2. how the infant behaved when the caregiver was separated from and then reunited with the infant. (pp. 354–355)

16. 1 Caregiver, experimenter, and infant enter room. Caregiver sits. Experimenter leaves while infant plays with toys.
    2 Infant explores while caregiver responds but does not initiate contact.
    3 Stranger enters the room, sits quietly, talks to caregiver, tries to interact with infant.
    4 Caregiver leaves infant alone with stranger, who tries to comfort infant if needed.
    5 Caregiver returns, comforting infant if needed. Stranger leaves.
    6 Caregiver leaves infant alone.
    7 Stranger returns, greets infant, trying to comfort infant if needed.
    8 Caregiver returns, comforting infant as needed. Stranger leaves. (p. 354)

17. The experimenter observes
    - whether the infant uses the parent as a secure base
    - the infant's reaction to the stranger
    - whether the infant is distressed when the caregiver leaves and how she reacts to the separation and to the stranger's attempts to comfort her
    - how the infant reacts to being reunited with the caregiver
    - how the infant reacts to the separation (without the stranger present)
    - how the infant reacts to the stranger trying to comfort her
    - how the infant reacts to the final reunion (p. 355)

18. home observational (p. 355)

19. The researcher has a set of cards that describe behaviours associated with secure attachment and behaviours associated with insecure attachment. During the observation, the cards are sorted into piles ranging from 'most like' to 'least like'. (p. 355)

20. concordant with the results from the strange situation task (p. 355)

21. In secure attachment,
    - there is a high-quality, positive relationship with caregiver.
    - the infant is upset when caregiver leaves and is quickly comforted on her return.
    - the infant uses the caregiver as secure base for exploring a new environment. (p. 356)

22. In insecure/resistant attachment,
    - the infant is clingy, and stays close to the caregiver rather than exploring a new environment.
    - the infant is very upset when left alone with a stranger and is not easily soothed when the caregiver returns. (p. 356)

23. In insecure/avoidant attachment,
    - the infant is indifferent to the caregiver and may avoid the caregiver.
    - the infant does not use the caregiver as a secure base.
    - the infant is not upset when the caregiver leaves and is indifferent when the caregiver returns.
    - the infant is comforted by the caregiver and a stranger equally. (p. 356)

24. In disorganized/disoriented attachment,
    - the infant has no consistent way of coping with novelty or with separation from the caregiver.
    - the infant may appear confused or disoriented (p. 356)
25. Answer:
    - As children, they tend to have more stable peer relationships.
    - As adolescents, they tend to have better peer and romantic relationships.
    - As adults, they tend to have more secure adult relationships and be more socially skilled. (p. 356)

Emotional Development More Generally

1. strangers (p. 356)

2. True—The earliest evidence of stranger anxiety appears at 6 or 7 months and separation anxiety emerges at about 8 months. (p. 356)

3. False—Although they smile more at people than at objects, they will smile at objects that capture their interest. (p. 357)

4. False—Researchers in the area tend to believe that those three emotions are not distinct early on. They seem to be expressed and perhaps experienced as the same. (p. 357)

Parents, Alloparents, Siblings, and Peers

1. the evolutionary basis of many aspects of parental behaviour (including parental investment) (p. 358)

2. Parental investment refers to an investment by a parent in an individual offspring that increases that offspring's chance of surviving and reproducing at the cost of the parent's ability to invest in other offspring. (p. 358)

3. Answer:
    - Low SES parents are more likely to use an authoritarian and putative child-rearing style.
    - High SES parents are more likely to use a style that is accepting and democratic. As well, they use more language with their children. (p. 358)

4. the level of parental investment (p. 358)

5. Consider the following in your response:
    - A parent is equally related to each offspring and would like to share resources equally among them.
    - Conflicts arise because the child's relatedness to siblings is only 0.5. Therefore the offspring would rather keep more resources for himself and share less with the sibling (or potential future siblings).
    - At some point, the parent would like to stop investing in the existing child and start working on the next child. The existing child may not be ready to forgo parental resources. (p. 358)

6. full; half; quarter (p. 358)

7. the ideal point for decreasing parental investment is not the same from the point of view of the parent and the point of view of the child (p. 358)

8. Hamilton's rule states that altruistic behaviour toward close family members is favoured by natural selection when the benefit, B, to the recipient (discounted by the relatedness, r, between the recipient and the actor) is greater than the cost, C, to the actor:

$$rB > C \quad \text{(p. 360)}$$

9. Answer:
   - Relatedness to sisters is 0.5.
   - Relatedness to nieces is 0.25 (half as much as sisters).
   - Therefore, four sisters are equal to 8 nieces. (p. 359)

10. 0.125 (p. 359)

11. False—Parents wish to further their own interests and those interests are different from the child's. (pp. 361–362)

Differences in Parenting Make Little Difference

1. True—Aside from extreme circumstances of abuse and neglect, parenting makes little difference in a child's development of personality traits, political views, and language, among other things. (p. 362)

2. It is to be expected because
   - evolution should not allow environmental factors to have an effect on traits that are important for survival and reproductive success.
   - as long as parenting is more-or-less normal, the child should, thanks to natural selection, be resilient to the effects. (p. 362)

3. Good-enough parenting is sufficient to rear viable children. According to Sandra Scarr, extraordinary parenting makes little difference to the child's outcome compared to good-enough parenting. (p. 362)

4. 'culture' (beliefs, values, language, skills) (p. 363)

5. Consider the following in your response:
   - Adoptive siblings are no more similar than strangers.
   - Biological siblings reared in the same home, while not very similar, will be more similar than adoptive siblings.
   - Identical twins raised together will not be more similar than identical twins raised apart.
   - In other words, adoption and twin studies tell us that parenting characteristics make little, if any, difference. (p. 363)

6. A child's aspirations are different from his parents; therefore, rather than internalizing parental values, the child is better to have cognitive mechanisms that preserve her self-interest. (p. 363)

7. peers; family (p. 363)

8. Early maturing boys
   - are less anxious and more poised than their peers.
   - score higher on measures of dominance than men who matured late as boys, regardless of ultimate adult height. (p. 363)

9. adolescence (p. 363)

Peer Influence

1. Consider the following in your response:
   - The social behaviour of rhesus monkeys raised without peers is more abnormal than that of monkeys raised without parents.
   - There is a case, documented by Anna Freud, of six Jewish children who spent their first three years in a concentration camp with no stable adult caregiver. They grew up to be typical adults, leading functional lives. (p. 364)

2. The group socialization theory proposes the following:
   - Peers and siblings, especially acting in groups, have a measurable effect on the personality development of children.
   - Socialization takes place in peer groups, especially sex- and age-segregated peer groups formed from middle childhood through adolescence.
   - Once children identify with the peer group, they adopt the group's attitudes and norms of behaviour.
   - Behaviours learned at home will only be transmitted to the group if the behaviour is shared by and approved of by most of the group members.
   - The child's culture is ultimately created by the peer group. Elements of adult culture are selected and rejected. Novel elements are invented.
   - Traditions may be passed on for generations from older children to younger children. (p. 365)

3. Alloparents are all of the people who contribute to the upbringing of a child other than the child's parents. (p. 366)

4. female family members; close female friends (p. 366)

5. menopause (p. 366)

6. Consider the following in your response:
   - A grandmother's foraging provides crucial nutrition for young children who are no longer nursing but not yet eating adult food.
   - A grandmother's contribution reduces the birth interval of the mother. She is free to wean her older child at a younger age, trusting that the grandmother will contribute to his nutrition. (p. 367)

Step-Parents

1. False—The EEA was dangerous; mortality rates were high due to famine, war, and disease. Loss of a parent during childhood would not, therefore, have been uncommon. For a parent who loses his or her mate, finding a new mate would have been a good strategy. (p. 367)

2. investment in unrelated children does not advance their reproductive interests (p. 368)

3. True—In fact, children are hundreds of times more likely to be murdered by stepfathers than biological fathers. (p. 368)

4. False—Abuse is more often directed toward the stepchildren. (p. 368)

5. Consider the following in your response:
   - Step-parents may be triggered by the demands, complaints, and ingratitude that all children manifest.
   - Biological parents have an adaptation that compels nurturing parenting behaviours and therefore do not act aggressively. Step-parents do not have this adaptation. (p. 368)

6. convey to the father than he is not a cuckold (pp. 369–370)

7. True—This may be due to evolved psychological processes in men that are designed to protect them against cuckoldry. (p. 370)

Birth Order

1. birth order (p. 370)

2. Consider the following in your response:
   - Oldest children are likely to inherit the parents' home as well as their status. First-borns, therefore, identify most strongly with authority figures. They are more likely to grow up to be conservative supporters of tradition and the status quo.
   - Later-born children have a different optimal strategy because they must seek their fortunes elsewhere. Out of necessity, they must be bigger risk-takers. (p. 371)

3. Non-shared environmental factors (p. 373)

Practice Test 1: Answer Key

1. **d** (p. 339)
2. **b** (p. 342)
3. **c** (p. 345)
4. **d** (p. 347)
5. **b** (p. 352)
6. **a** (p. 352)
7. **a** (p. 352)

8. **c** (p. 353)
9. **b** (p. 355)
10. **d** (p. 356)
11. **d** (p. 356)
12. **b** (p. 357)
13. **c** (p. 358)
14. **a** (p. 358)

15. **d** (p. 360)
16. **b** (p. 362)
17. **c** (p. 363)
18. **b** (p. 364)
19. **a** (p. 364)
20. **b** (p. 365)
21. **c** (p. 364)

22. **b** (p. 365)
23. **d** (p. 366)
24. **d** (p. 370)
25. **a** (p. 370)

Practice Test 2: Answer Key

1. **a** (p. 341)
2. **c** (p. 344)
3. **d** (p. 345)
4. **b** (p. 347)
5. **d** (p. 350)
6. **d** (p. 354)
7. **a** (p. 355)

8. **c** (p. 356)
9. **a** (p. 356)
10. **b** (pp. 357–358)
11. **d** (p. 358)
12. **b** (p. 359)
13. **c** (p. 359)
14. **d** (p. 360)

15. **a** (p. 360)
16. **c** (p. 363)
17. **c** (p. 363)
18. **d** (p. 365)
19. **a** (p. 364)
20. **d** (p. 367)
21. **b** (pp. 367–368)

22. **d** (p. 368)
23. **c** (p. 370)
24. **a** (pp. 370–371)
25. **b** (p. 372)

Chapter 11
Sex and Gender

Chapter Summary

Why Look at Gender?

The study of gender is useful for three reasons: first, sexual dimorphism in humans provides a good natural control group for examining cognitive adaptations; second, it provides an opportunity to test our commitment to viewing nature and nurture as interacting forces; and third, it allows us to consider the fit between adaptations and the adaptive problems they solve.

Gender Roles in the EEA

Division of labour in the EEA was probably the source of the selection pressures that led to the biggest sex differences. Women in the EEA were foragers; they needed to be able to make fine perceptual discriminations to find ripe fruit and they needed to remember the locations of fruit-bearing plants. Men in the EEA were hunters; they needed to work in coalitions, use projectile weapons, and travel across a large geographical range.

Adaptive Sex Differences

Variation in human genomes is usually accounted for by genes that have little or no affect on the phenotype or by genes that are relatively recent mutations. To some extent, the sexes are an exception to this rule. Men and women each have a broad set of adaptations that are designed to optimize their respective reproductive strategies.

Females contribute the larger gamete and, as such, make a larger investment in offspring than males. Because they make a larger investment, females are choosier in mate selection.

The Development of Sex and Gender

The 23rd pair of chromosomes is responsible for development of one sex or the other. Unlike the *autosomes*, this 23rd pair of sex chromosomes may not match. Females receive two X chromosomes (one from each parent) but males receive one X chromosome from the mother and one Y chromosome from the father. If the offspring has a Y chromosome, the *SRY gene* will, when transcribed, lead to the creation of the *testis determining factor*. This factor will trigger development of testes, which will produce and release androgens and masculinize the body. Without a Y chromosome, the offspring will develop into a female. The above description of sex development applies to humans; it does not apply to all species.

From the moment of conception, there are sex differences. Males are more likely than females to be spontaneously miscarried, to have physical and mental abnormalities, to be more active in utero, and to die shortly after birth.

Postnatally, there are a wide variety of sex differences that reflect reproductive advantages for each sex. Physically, boys tend to be somewhat larger and stronger. In terms of motor skills, girls tend to be more coordinated, with superior fine motor skills and balance, and boys tend to have superior gross motor skills and strength. Girls tend to be somewhat more advanced in language development and social skills. In terms of quantitative skills, boys and girls have different strengths: boys tend to do better on tests of mathematical reasoning and girls tend to do better on computational problems. Boys tend to be superior in many spatial skills, including mental rotation and navigation. However, girls tend to do better on tasks that require remembering object locations. Boys tend to be more physically aggressive and girls tend to be more relationally aggressive. Both boys and girls tend to prefer same-sex playmates. Girls tend to prefer quieter toys associated with fine motor skills and boys tend to prefer more active and constructive toys. These sex-based differences in toy preferences can be seen in monkeys as well as humans. Early sex differences are seen cross-culturally. In general, boys and girls are attracted to different types of play and those different types of play contribute to adaptive sex differences in cognitive development. This points to an interaction between genes and environment.

Between the ages of 2 and 4, children have formed some gender-related expectations about male- and female-associated objects and activities. They come to know which gender group they belong to and begin to categorize and label their own and others' sex. Gender stereotypes become stronger and children come to expect gender-appropriate behaviours. In middle childhood, there tends to be more tolerance of girls crossing gender lines than boys.

Puberty

Puberty refers to a series of dramatic body transformations in early adolescence. In addition to *menarche* in girls and *spermarche* in boys, there is development of numerous primary and secondary sex characteristics.

Views of Gender Development

According to gender socialization theory, gender development is a result of general, associationist psychological processes. Children are said to observe and imitate role models of one sex or the other. Parents are thought to explicitly and implicitly convey expectations regarding gender-appropriate behaviour. Boys are thought to be rewarded for masculine behaviour and girls are thought to be rewarded for feminine behaviour. There is laboratory research that supports these ideas.

Thoughts on the development of sex differences tend to be politically charged. Gender feminism arose in reaction to discrimination against women. This school of thought contends that almost all differences between men and women are socially constructed; infants are thought to be transformed into males and females by those around them. Such opinions aside, it is important to keep scientific issues separate from political issues. Of course, justice involves equality for all, regardless of sex. That does not mean that we should ignore empirical sex differences.

The Reimer Twins: A Natural Test of the Socialization Theory of Gender

Bruce and Brian Reimer were typical, healthy, identical twin boys. At the age of 8 months, Bruce's penis was destroyed during an attempted circumcision. At the time, it was widely believed that gender identity was completely dependent on socialization, so Bruce's parents were convinced that it was best to raise him as a girl. Bruce's genitalia was reconstructed to appear female and, at puberty, he was given estrogen treatments. Bruce (called Brenda) never felt like a girl and hated being raised as one. The attempted sex reassignment was a complete failure and, at 13, Brenda changed her name to David and lived as a male.

Intersex

Intersex people are those who have some combination of chromosomal, genital, and brain development that is not typically male or female. One example of an intersex condition is *5-alpha-reductase deficiency*, which affects males and is caused by the failure of the body to produce sufficient levels of 5-alpha-reductase. Without sufficient levels of 5-alpha-reductase, testosterone is not converted to a form that is useable in the body. Individuals with this condition have male internal reproductive organs but female-appearing external genitalia. At puberty, they may produce sufficient concentrations of testosterone to have some masculinization and some choose to assume male identities. Another intersex condition is *congenital adrenal hyperplasia* (CAH). Individuals with CAH have an XX karyotype but produce an unusually large concentration of androgens, sometimes resulting in masculinized external genitalia. Most individuals with CAH think of themselves as girls but they do show significant masculinization of play activities, playmate preference, spatial ability, aggression, and adolescent activities. They tend to have less interest in female-typical behaviour. Androgen insensitivity syndrome (AIS) is another intersex condition. Individuals with AIS have an XY karyotype but do not respond to androgens. They do not develop external male genitalia and may be identified as female at birth. Because they do not respond to androgens at all, an individual with complete AIS (there are varying degrees) may appear more female than the average woman. *Turner's Syndrome* is an intersex condition in which females have only one X chromosome. Individuals with Turner's syndrome do not have typical female development and may not produce normal level of estrogen.

Genetic imprinting involves chemical alteration of an allele that alters the likelihood that it will be expressed in the phenotype. Through genetic imprinting, an X chromosome that comes from a father is one made for a girl and an X chromosome that comes from a mother is one made for a boy. Since individuals with Turner's syndrome only have one X chromosome (that may come from either parent), it matters whether it comes from the mother or the father. If it is a girl-optimized X chromosome from the father, the individual will be better at cognitive skills that females are typically better at.

The Transgender Experience

Gender identification begins around the age of 3 years. The gender identity of most children is consistent with their parents' gender views but, for some children, it is inconsistent. Transgender expression is extremely resistant to therapy and may lead to a decision to live as the gender they identify with.

Relative Life Expectancy

Human females, on average, live five years longer than human males. Because there is greater variance in reproductive success for males, there is greater potential payoff for sometimes risky male strategies to attract a mate. Males, therefore, are more likely than females to die accidentally. As well, because males have more to gain from a pleiotropic gene at a young age, they are more vulnerable to dangers of pleiotropic genes later on.

Cultural Differences in Mating and Parenting

Compared to monogamous societies, in polygynous societies there is relatively greater male variance in reproductive success. Polygyny has been found to correlate with boy versus girl training differences. It has been found that boys in polygynous societies are taught to exhibit aggressiveness, fortitude, industriousness, and competitiveness, while girls in polygynous societies are taught to exhibit sexual restraint, industriousness, and responsibility.

Learning Objectives

After reading this chapter, you should be able to:

- Evaluate what we can learn from examining the development of sex and gender (pp. 380–381)

- Explain the different roles of men and women in the EEA (pp. 381–383)

- Demonstrate how adaptations differ in males and females (pp. 383–384)

- Explain how genes and chromosomes influence male and female development (pp. 385–388)

- Understand how boys and girls are different in terms of physical size and strength, motor skills, verbal skills, quantitative skills, social skills, spatial skills, aggression, and interests (pp. 389–394)

- Track children's understanding of gender throughout childhood (pp. 395–397)

- Review the changes that take place in boys and girls at puberty (p. 398)

- Summarize the tenets of gender socialization theory (pp. 399–401)

- Appreciate what happened in the case of David Reimer, a boy who was raised as a girl (pp. 401–402)

- Define four of the known intersex conditions: 5-alpha-reductase deficiency, congenital adrenal hyperplasia, androgen insensitivity syndrome, and Turner's syndrome (pp. 402–407)

- Appreciate the robustness of gender identity (pp. 407–408)

- Explain why men tend to die younger than women (pp. 408–409)

- Examine cross-cultural differences in mating (pp. 409–410)

Suggested Readings

Simmons, R. (2003). *Odd Girl Out: The Hidden Culture of Aggression in Girls*. San Diego, CA: Houghton Mifflin Harcourt.

Simmons takes a unique approach by exploring the ways in which girls are aggressive toward one another.

Bussey, K., and Bandura, A. (1999). Social cognitive theory of gender development and differentiation. *Psychological Review, 106*, 676–713.

Bussey and Bandura present a gender socialization theory account of the construction of gender conceptions.

Colapinto, J. (2006). *As Nature Made Him: The Boy Who Was Raised As A Girl*. New York: Harper Perennial.

John Colapinto tells the story of David Reimer.

Study Questions

1. Define 'androgen insensitivity syndrome'.

2. People with androgen insensitivity syndrome are not masculinized by _____.

Why Look at Gender?

1. Sexual dimorphism in humans provides a good _____ for examining interesting cognitive adaptations.

2. In navigation, men tend to use _____ and women tend to rely on _____.

3. True or False: It is important to set aside the nature–nurture issue when discussing gender development.

4. True or False: Adaptive problems differ for men and women.

Gender Roles in the EEA

1. In the EEA, how did men's and women's specialties differ when it came to providing?

2. What skills did women in the EEA need to do their jobs?

3. What skills did men in the EEA need to do their jobs?

4. True or False: Modern girls tend to stay closer to home than boys.

5. True or False: Navigational talent is inherently masculine.

Adaptive Sex Differences

1. True or False: Complex adaptations are expected to be universal.

2. Variation in human genomes can be accounted for by genes that _____ or are _____.

3. What does it mean to say that men and women are two 'morphs' of the human species?

4. True or False: Men have all of the genes that direct development of female reproductive organs.

5. Biologically, sex is defined in terms of _____ size.

6. True or False: Males produce a larger gamete than females.

7. In species that have males and females, and especially when a female's fertilization is internal, females are the choosier sex. Why?

8. Males only need to make a very small investment (producing sperm) in reproduction. How does that affect their reproductive strategies?

9. True or False: Sets of adaptations for males and females are a package deal.

The Development of Sex and Gender

1. Of the 23 pairs of chromosomes, 22 of them are called _____.

2. A developing offspring receives a/an _____ sex chromosome from the mother and a/an _____ sex chromosome from the father.

3. True or False: A conceptus with the XY chromosome begins to develop into a girl.

4. True or False: Female external genitalia are the developmental default.

5. What does the Y chromosome do?

6. True or False: For genes on the male's X chromosome, there is no such thing as dominant or recessive.

7. The _____ gene on the Y chromosome starts the cascade of events that leads to masculine development.

8. Define 'testes determining factor'.

9. What do the testes produce?

10. Sex hormones can affect neurons by manipulating the onset and rate of growth of _____ and _____.

11. Where in the brain can you find receptors for androgens and estrogens?

12. True or False: The Y chromosome determines sex.

13. True or False: In all species, males have different chromosomes than females.

14. What are some sex differences that exist between conception and birth?

15. The masculinization of the genitals occurs in the middle of the _____ trimester. The masculinization of the brain occurs around the time of _____. Both are caused by surges of _____.

16. When playing, boys are more likely to engage in _____ and girls are more likely to engage in _____.

17. Why is there a difference in the types of play that boys and girls engage in?

18. What are some sex differences in terms of size and strength that are present from birth?

19. True or False: At birth, girls are generally less coordinated than boys.

20. What are some sex differences in terms of motor skills in 5-year-old boys and girls?

21. In middle childhood, girls have better _____ motor skills and boys have better _____ motor skills.

22. How do girls and boys differ in verbal skills?

23. True or False: Girls receive higher grades in mathematics than boys.

24. From early to middle childhood, girls tend to do better on math problems that involve _____ and boys tend to do better on math problems that involve _____.

25. How do girls and boys differ in social skills?

26. True or False: Boys' advantage on spatial tasks increases though adolescence and into adulthood.

27. What kinds of spatial tasks are performed better by boys?

28. Girls are better than boys at recalling the identity and location of an object in an array of objects. Why does this make sense when you consider the selection pressures faced by females in the EEA?

29. Boys tend to engage in more _____ aggression and girls tend to engage in more _____ aggression.

30. Define 'relational aggression'.

31. True or False: Both boys and girls tend to spend much more time with same-sex playmates compared to opposite sex playmates.

32. Imagine that you fill a room with different kinds of toys—some that human boys prefer to play with, some that human girls prefer to play with, and some gender-neutral toys. You then let loose a group of young male and female vervet monkeys in the room. What is likely to happen?

33. Hazen (1982) equalized exposure to spatial play for boys and girls. This resulted in _____ sex differences in spatial-cognitive abilities.

34. Evolved mechanisms are not simply a 'nature' force. They can involve _____.

35. What do children learn about gender between the ages of 2, 3, and 4?

36. True or False: Infants can make male–female categorizations.

37. True or False: Boys are particularly intolerant of cross-gender behaviour.

38. Girls have a relatively large amount of gender freedom until _____.

Puberty

1. Define 'menarche'.

2. Define 'spermarche'.

3. In girls, at puberty, androgens released from the adrenal glands lead to _____ and _____.

4. The typical girl is taller than the typical boy between the ages of _____ and _____.

5. During the growth spurt, how do body proportions change in the two sexes?

6. Menstruation does not occur until the girl's body is large enough to _____.

7. True or False: Girls are able to get pregnant immediately after they start menstruating.

8. How does relative performance on cognitive tasks change over the course of a woman's menstrual cycle?

9. True or False: For boys, the growth spurt is followed by the development of primary sexual characteristics.

10. True or False: Boys are able to impregnate a female immediately after they start producing semen.

Views of Gender Development

1. According to the gender socialization theory, gender roles, norms, and behaviours are learned via _____.

2. Describe some laboratory research that supports the idea that gender develops as a result of 'socialization' from observations and imitation.

3. How do parents (explicitly and implicitly) convey their expectations regarding gender-appropriate behaviour?

4. The topic of how sex differences develop is different from topics such as the development of visual perception, language, or animacy perception in that it is _____.

5. _____ believe that gender is entirely plastic, and that newborn infants are 'bi-sexual'.

The Reimer Twins: A Natural Test of the Socialization Theory of Gender

1. How did the Reimer twins provide an ideal test of the socialization theory of gender?

2. Bruce Reimer was renamed Brenda. How did Brenda fare as a girl?

Intersex

1. Define 'intersex'.

2. Define '5-alpha-reductase deficiency'.

3. Internal male reproductive structures are called _____.

4. Define 'congenital adrenal hyperplasia (CAH)'.

5. What are some non-physical differences between girls with CAH and other girls?

6. Most often, the first sign that a child with androgen insensitivity syndrome (AIS) is experiencing unusual development is _____.

7. True or False: Women with AIS tend to appear more feminine than women without the syndrome.

8. The chromosomal configuration of an individual with Turner's syndrome is _____.

9. Why does a person who has Turner's syndrome look female?

10. What are some abnormalities associated with individuals with Turner's syndrome?

11. True or False: A second X chromosome is necessary for typical female development.

12. In Turner's syndrome, the _____ of the X chromosome makes a difference due to a process called genomic imprinting.

13. Define 'genomic imprinting'.

14. An X chromosome that comes from the mother is an X chromosome made for a _____. An X chromosome that comes from the father is an X chromosome made for a _____.

15. What are some differences between individuals with Turner's syndrome who have an X chromosome from the mother and those who have an X chromosome from the father?

The Transgender Experience

1. Children begin to identify with one gender or the other at around _____ years of age.

2. True or False: Gender identity can be modified with therapy.

Relative Life Expectancy

1. True or False: On average, human males die at an earlier age than females.

2. True or False: There is more variance in the number of offspring males have than the number of offspring females have.

3. What does the above finding mean for reproductive strategies and risk-taking behaviour?

4. Males with higher testosterone levels are more attractive to females, but testosterone _____, leaving them open to the risk of exposure to pathogens.

5. Men are more vulnerable than women to the senescent effects of _____.

Cultural Differences in Mating and Parenting

1. In cultures that are more polygynous versus monogamous, sex differences measured behaviourally are _____.

2. In polygynous societies, girls are taught to _____.

Practice Test 1

1. The biggest sex differences in terms of selection pressures in the EEA are related to

   a. health.
   b. division of labour.
   c. nutritional needs.
   d. vulnerability to environmental toxins.

2. Navigational abilities

   a. are not related to mental rotation.
   b. are inherently masculine.
   c. were selected for in human women.
   d. are related to range of exploration

3. Which of the following statements is true of gametes and reproductive investment?

   a. Whichever sex makes the larger gamete is likely to be choosier in selecting a mate.
   b. Male and female strategies are constant across species.
   c. Human males must make a large mandatory investment in offspring.
   d. In humans, the male gamete is larger than the female gamete.

4. The gene on the Y chromosome that starts the chain of events that leads to masculine development is called the _____ gene.

   a. MRY
   b. Y
   c. SRY
   d. SR2

5. There are receptors for androgens and estrogens in all of the following brain structures *except*

   a. the cerebral cortex.
   b. the cerebellum.
   c. the hypothalamus.
   d. the amygdala.

6. Compared to female fetuses, male fetuses

   a. are less active in utero.
   b. are more likely to be spontaneously miscarried.
   c. are less likely to suffer from a physical abnormality.
   d. are not significantly different on any measurable characteristic.

7. In terms of growth rates during childhood,

    a. boys grow earlier than girls.
    b. boys are more variable than girls.
    c. girls' growth is more gradual than boys'.
    d. boys and girls are similar.

8. For which of the following do young boys have the biggest advantage over young girls?

    a. spatial skills
    b. social skills
    c. verbal skills
    d. quantitative skills

9. Gossiping, spreading rumours, and ostracism are all forms of

    a. associative aggression
    b. male-typical aggression.
    c. relational aggression.
    d. physical aggression.

10. Which of the following statements is true regarding early sex differences in interests and free time?

    a. They are seen only in certain cultures.
    b. Boys tend to be interested in quieter activities.
    c. Young girls show no preference for same-sex versus opposite-sex playmates.
    d. Young male non-humans have been found to be more interested in human male-preferred toys than human female-preferred toys.

11. In an experiment by Serbin, Poulin-Dubois, & Eichstedt (2002), 2-year-old children watched a man (wearing a shirt and tie) and a woman (wearing a blouse and skirt) perform masculine or feminine activities. Which did they look longest at?

    a. a man performing feminine actions
    b. a woman performing feminine actions
    c. a man performing masculine actions
    d. a woman performing masculine actions

12. The onset of menstruation is called

    a. menses.
    b. menarche.
    c. spermarche.
    d. none of the above

13. Ovaries do not cyclically produce eggs until _____ after menstruation begins.

    a. 2 to 3 weeks
    b. 4 to 6 months
    c. 12 to 18 months
    d. 2 to 3 years

14. Gender socialization theory is a/an _____ theory of gender.

    a. perceptual
    b. biological
    c. evolutionary
    d. social learning

15. Which of the following was *not* true of Bruce Reimer?

    a. He had an identical twin.
    b. He was born with some physical abnormalities.
    c. He provided a unique test of gender identity.
    d. His case suggested that the mind is a blank slate for gender development.

16. When some body tissues have XY chromosomes and some tissues have XX chromosomes, there is said to be a genetic _____ pattern.

    a. mosaic
    b. blending
    c. fusion
    d. mixture

17. Individuals with 5-alpha-reductase deficiency have a _____ that normally functions to produce sufficient levels of 5-alpha-reductase.

    a. missing reproductive organ
    b. lower level of a hormone
    c. mutation in the gene
    d. missing chromosome

18. Girls with congenital adrenal hyperplasia are less likely than other girls to

    a. choose toys that boys typically prefer.
    b. perform well on spatial tasks.
    c. engage in rough-and-tumble play.
    d. be interested in infants.

19. Androgen insensitivity syndrome is associated with a _____ gene on the _____ chromosome.

   a. dominant; X
   b. recessive; X
   c. dominant; Y
   d. recessive; Y

20. The karyotype for individuals with Turner's syndrome is

   a. XX
   b. XY
   c. X
   d. Y

21. Which of the following is *not* typical of individuals with Turner's syndrome?

   a. lack of development of secondary sex characteristics
   b. heart problems
   c. typical female genitalia
   d. above-average height

22. The average lifespan for human females is _____ than human males.

   a. 5 years longer
   b. 5 years shorter
   c. 2 years longer
   d. 2 years shorter

23. Which of the following statements is *not* true regarding the offspring of human males and females?

   a. Risk-taking in reproductive strategies is worth it for males but not for females.
   b. There is a positive correlation between the number of mates a male has and the number of offspring he has.
   c. There is more variance in the number of offspring males have than the number of offspring females have.
   d. Variance in the number of offspring in males and females does not differ cross-culturally.

24. Polygynous species are those in which

   a. couples mate for life.
   b. males have the potential of mating with many females.
   c. female variance in reproductive success is greater than male variance in reproductive success.
   d. females die younger than males.

25. An ambitious cross-cultural survey found that the more polygyny in a culture, the more the girls were taught to exhibit

    a. risk-taking.
    b. aggression.
    c. fortitude.
    d. sexual restraint.

Practice Test 2

1. Foraging by women in the EEA required

    a. making fine perceptual discriminations.
    b. working in coalitions.
    c. dealing extensively with rival groups.
    d. great physical strength.

2. Men and women are two _____ of the human species, meaning that they are two phenotypes with the same genes that underlie universal complex adaptations.

    a. mutations
    b. genotypes
    c. morphs
    d. adaptations

3. Of the 46 human chromosomes, _____ are autosomes.

    a. 22
    b. 44
    c. 23
    d. 42

4. Transcription of the SRY gene leads to creation of

    a. a Y chromosome.
    b. androgens.
    c. testosterone.
    d. the testis determining factor.

5. If you remove the gonadal tissue of a fetal rabbit, the rabbit

    a. develops a visibly female body.
    b. develops a visibly male body.
    c. develops a visibly female body roughly 50 per cent of the time.
    d. does not develop.

6. Which of the following statements is, in general, *not* true regarding motor skills during childhood?

    a. Girls have better fine motor skills than boys.
    b. Boys can run faster than girls.
    c. Boys have a better sense of balance than girls.
    d. Girls are more coordinated than boys.

7. Compared to young boys, young girls

    a. use words earlier.
    b. have larger vocabularies.
    c. produce more speech sounds.
    d. all of the above

8. On which of the following spatial skills do girls typically out-perform boys?

    a. map interpretation
    b. memory for object location
    c. map making
    d. mental rotation

9. Which of the following sex and gender milestones comes last?

    a. Children identify themselves as 'girl' or 'boy'.
    b. Boys are more active than girls.
    c. Girls show evidence of more empathy than boys.
    d. Masculinization of the brain takes place.

10. Spermarche is the onset of

    a. secondary sex characteristics.
    b. adolescence.
    c. ejaculation.
    d. menstruation.

11. At puberty, _____ in girls lead to increased height.

    a. estrogens
    b. androgens
    c. both estrogens and androgens
    d. neither estrogens nor androgens

12. In boys, the first sign of puberty is

    a. masculinization of the voice.
    b. emergence of pubic hair.
    c. growth of the penis.
    d. growth of the testes.

13. Gender feminism is a school of thought that contends that

    a. biology is destiny.
    b. parents have no control over gender identity formation.
    c. differences between men and women are almost entirely socially constructed.
    d. differences between men and women do not exist.

14. If an individual has a combination of chromosomal, genital, or brain development that is not typically male or female, he or she is said to be a(n) _____ person.

    a. intersex
    b. unisex
    c. bisexual
    d. transexual

15. Guevedoche is also known as

    a. Turner's syndrome.
    b. 5-alpha-reductase deficiency.
    c. androgen insensitivity syndrome.
    d. congenital adrenal hyperplasia.

16. Wolffian structures are _____ reproductive structures.

    a. external female
    b. internal female
    c. external male
    d. internal male

17. The most common form of intersex in XX people is

    a. Turner's syndrome.
    b. 5-alpha-reductase deficiency.
    c. androgen insensitivity syndrome.
    d. congenital adrenal hyperplasia.

18. Which of the following is *not* typical of individuals with androgen insensitivity syndrome?

    a. a failure to menstruate
    b. an XY karyotype
    c. a masculine appearance
    d. breast development

19. Genomic imprinting involves the tagging of a(n) _____ that alters the likelihood of expression in the phenotype.

    a. autosome
    b. allele
    c. gene
    d. sex chromosome

20. An individual with Turner's syndrome who has a _____ X chromosome from her _____ is better at reading body language and facial expressions than those who don't.

    a. girl-optimized; father
    b. boy-optimized; mother
    c. girl-optimized; mother
    d. boy-optimized; father

21. Transgender individuals demonstrate that gender identity

    a. is consistent with parental views.
    b. fluctuates.
    c. is best explained by gender socialization theory.
    d. is resistant to intense therapy.

22. Mitochondrial DNA comes to you from

    a. your father.
    b. your mother.
    c. either your mother or your father.
    d. the Y chromosome.

23. Examination of maternal DNA and paternal DNA has revealed that

    a. not everyone has maternal DNA.
    b. females sometimes contribute a Y chromosome.
    c. humans have more grandmothers than grandfathers.
    d. there is greater variance in reproductive success in females than males.

24. Compared to females, males are more resistant to the _____ of deleterious effects of genes that occur after the age of reproduction.

    a. addition
    b. weeding out
    c. pleiotropy
    d. none of the above

25. An ambitious cross-cultural survey found that the more polygyny in a culture, the more the boys were taught to exhibit

    a. responsibility.
    b. submissiveness.
    c. aggression.
    d. intellect.

Study Questions: Answer Key

1. Androgen insensitivity syndrome is a condition in which a person has a mutation in the gene associated with the development of androgen receptors. Without functioning androgen receptors, a person with an XY karyotype can develop a female phenotype. (p. 379)

2. testosterone (p. 379)

Why Look at Gender?

1. natural control group (p. 380)

2. cognitive maps; landmarks (p. 380)

3. True—Although some people may be politically motivated to refer to sex differences as 'learned' or 'cultural', a nature–nurture debate is just as futile when discussing gender as any other developmental issue. (p. 381)

4. True—Men and women have different adaptations that work to maximize fitness. (p. 381)

Gender Roles in the EEA

1. Consider the following in your response:
   - Hunting was done mostly by men.
   - Foraging of fruits and vegetables was done mostly by women.
   - Women, through breast-feeding, were the exclusive source of calories for newborn babies. (p. 382)

2. In the EEA, women needed to
   - find fruit-bearing plants.
   - remember the locations of fruits when they were in season.
   - make fine perceptual discriminations using colour and texture in order to select ripe fruit from the unripe. (p. 382)

3. In the EEA, men needed to
   - hunt in coalitions because hunting game is challenging, leading to a coalitional psychology.
   - be able to throw things at moving targets.
   - be able to travel across a large range, leading to sophisticated spatial-cognition and navigational skills. (p. 382)

4. True—Cross-cultural data support the idea that boys have a larger range of exploration than girls. (p. 382)

5. False—Navigational abilities will be greater in males only in species in which navigational abilities were selected for. (p. 382)

Adaptive Sex Differences

1. True—Adaptations complex enough to involve multiple genes will spread throughout the species. (p. 383)

2. have little or no effect on the phenotype; are relatively recent mutations (p. 383)

3. It means that there are two different phenotypes (man and woman). Each phenotype displays a coherent set of complex adaptations. Men and women both have the complete set of human genetic information. (p. 383)

4. True—Those genes are part of the complete set of human genetic information, which all humans have. (p. 384)

5. gamete (p. 384)

6. False—Male sperm is smaller than female eggs. (p. 384)

7. Females are choosier because making the larger gamete means making a larger investment and internal fertilization leads to a larger investment in offspring. Since females are more invested, they are less willing to take risks on a mate. (p. 384)

8. Males aim to maximize their number of offspring. They will invest if necessary (i.e. if the female bargains for more investment). They are very motivated to avoid accidentally investing in another male's offspring. (p. 384)

9. True—Cognitive adaptations and morphological adaptation cannot be arbitrarily selected and packaged with gamete size. (p. 384)

The Development of Sex and Gender

1. autosomes (p. 385)

2. X; X or Y (p. 385)

3. False—With an XY genome, the conceptus begins developing into a boy. Girls are XX. (p. 385)

4. True—Without androgens influencing development, external appearance will be female. (p. 385)

5. The Y chromosome is too small to hold many genes. Its primary responsibility is to put the developing fetus on the path to masculine development. (pp. 385–386)

6. True—In genes on the male X chromosome, there are no complimentary alleles (because there is no other X chromosome). As such, there is nothing to which a gene can be dominant or recessive. (p. 386)

7. SRY (p. 386)

8. A testes determining factor is a protein that will trigger the development of the fetus's testes in typical male development. (p. 386)

9. The testes produce androgens (including testosterone) that masculinize the body, leading to the development of male external genitalia. Androgens also masculinize the brain. (p. 386)

10. axons; dendrites (p. 387)

11. Receptors for androgens and estrogens are found in
    - the hippocampus
    - the hypothalamus
    - the amygdala
    - the limbic system
    - the cerebral cortex (p. 387)

12. False—The Y chromosome's SRY gene starts the series of events leading to masculinization but many genes on many chromosomes are involves in the development of male characteristics. (p. 387)

13. False—There are different schemes of sexual development in different species. (p. 387)

14. Between conception and birth, males are
    - more likely to be spontaneously miscarried.
    - more vulnerable to developmental abnormalities (both physical and mental).
    - more active in utero.
    - more likely to die shortly after birth. (pp. 387–388)

15. second; birth; androgens (p. 388)

16. rough-and-tumble play; pretend parenting (p. 389)

17. Boys and girls play in ways that allow them to practise the sex-specific skills they are developing. (p. 389)

18. Girls tend to be measurably smaller, lighter, healthier, more mature, and less muscular. (p. 389)

19. False—Girls are generally more coordinated than boys. (p. 389)

20. Some differences include the following:
    - Boys have an advantage on measures that require strength and power. They can jump farther, run faster, and throw a ball farther.
    - Girls have an advantage on measures that require fine motor skills and balance. They are better at skipping and hopping. (p. 389)

21. fine; gross (p. 389)

22. Some differences include the following:
    - Infant girls produce more speech sounds.
    - Young girls perform better on tests of verbal skills.
    - Girls use words earlier, have larger early vocabularies, and show more grammatical complexity.
    - Girls have superior verbal memory. (p. 390)

23. True—But boys do out-perform girls on high stakes tests of mathematics (e.g. the SAT). (p. 390)

24. computations; mathematical reasoning (p. 390)

25. In contrast to boys, girls
    - orient more toward people by turning toward faces and voices.
    - smile more at other people.
    - maintain eye contact longer participate in more face-to-face communication.
    - show more empathy. (p. 390)

26. True—Boys out-perform girls on spatial tasks and, especially for spatial rotation tasks, sex differences increase through adolescence and into adulthood. (p. 390)

27. Boys performed better on the follow spatial tasks:
    - Spatial transformation/rotation
    - Navigation of real and virtual environments
    - Map-making
    - Map-interpretation (pp. 390–392)

28. In the EEA, females were gatherers. They have to make fine perceptual discriminations and remember the location of objects they had observed. (p. 392)

29. physical; relational (p. 392)

30. Relational aggression refers to the attempt to harm others by damaging social relationships (e.g. gossiping, spreading rumours, ostracizing, etc.). (p. 392)

31. True—At age 4, they spend four times as much time with same-sex playmates and at age 6, they spend 11 times as much time with same-sex playmates. (p. 393)

32. Consider the following in your response:
    - Findings from past research suggests that the vervet females will spend more time playing with the girl-preferred toys and the vervet males will spend more time playing with the boy-preferred toys.
    - There will be no sex difference in playing time for the neutral toys.
    - This can be taken as evidence that sex differences in toy preferences are not dependent on human cultural influences. (p. 393)

33. reduced (p. 394)

34. environmental and experiential input (learning) (p. 394)

35. Between the ages of 2, 3, and 4, children
    - come to know which gender group they belong to.
    - come to use gender terms in their speech.
    - become better able to categorize and label their own, and others', sex.
    - learn to categorize the gender cues (toys, tools, activities, etc.) of their local culture. (pp. 395–396)

36. True—At 6 months of age, infants can discriminate between male and female voices and between 9 and 12 months of age, infants can discriminate between male and female faces. (p. 396)

37. True—A boy who repeatedly engages in cross-gender behaviour is eventually excluded from social activities. (p. 396)

38. adolescence (p. 397)

Puberty

1. Menarche is the point in female puberty at which the first menstrual bleeding occurs. (p. 398)

2. Spermarche is the point in male puberty at which sperm is first ejaculated. (p. 398)

3. increased height; the growth of pubic and underarm hair (p. 398)

4. 10; 14 (p. 398)

5. During a growth spurt, the following changes take place:
   - Boys' shoulders grow wider than their hips.
   - Girls' hips grow wider than their shoulders.
   - Body fat decreases in boys.
   - Body fat increases in girls, depositing on the arms, legs, and trunk. (p. 398)

6. carry a pregnancy (p. 398)

7. False—There is a 12- to 18-month period of sterility following first menstruation. During that time, ovaries are not producing eggs with each cycle. (p. 398)

8. During a woman's cycle, when estrogen levels are
   - highest, women perform better on cognitive tasks that are typically associated with superior female performance (e.g. verbal fluency tasks).
   - lowest, women perform better on cognitive tasks that are typically associated with superior male performance (e.g. spatial rotation tasks). (p. 398)

9. False—The growth spurt begins after the development of primary sexual characteristics is complete. (p. 398)

10. False—For several months after spermarche, the semen contains no sperm. (p. 398)

Views of Gender Development

1. general learning principles (the same principles that underlie other types of social learning) (p. 399)

2. Studies have shown that children watching adult models perform various activities will watch a same-sex model more, will better remember the actions of a same-sex model, and will be more likely to imitate a same-sex model. (pp. 399–400)

3. Parents tend to
   - provide gender-appropriate toys (even before children are old enough to verbally request those toys).
   - assign different household chores to boys and girls.
   - express their own gender expectations in conversation (e.g. one study conducted at a science museum found that parents were three times more likely to explain science exhibits to their sons than their daughters). (p. 400)

4. politically charged (p. 400)

5. Gender feminists (pp. 400–401)

The Reimer Twins: A Natural Test of the Socialization Theory of Gender

1. Consider the following in your response:
   - Bruce Reimer was born a completely healthy, typical boy. His penis was destroyed during an attempted circumcision and after that he was raised as a girl. His genitals were believably female and he (and everyone else) was told he was a girl. In other words, his biology was completely male but his socialization was completely female.
   - Bruce had an identical twin, Brian, who was completely male and whose socialization was completely male. Brian, therefore, provided a control for comparison. (p. 401)

2. After the sex-reassignment surgery, Brenda
   - was miserable.
   - never felt like a girl and hated being raised as a girl.
   - was rejected as a girl by her peers and she was ostracized and bullied.
   - was far too aggressive to fit in socially as a girl. (p. 402)

Intersex

1. Intersex is an umbrella term describing conditions in which an individual has some combination of chromosomal, genital, and brain development that is not typically male or female. (p. 403)

2. 5-alpha-reductase deficiency is a developmental condition caused by the failure of the body to produce sufficient levels of 5-alpha-reductase. Babies with an XY chromosomal configuration will be born with typical internal male reproductive organs but female-appearing external genitalia. (p. 403)

3. Wolffian structures (p. 403)

4. CAH is a condition resulting from a mutation in genes associated with cortisol production. Excessive production of androgens results in the masculinization of secondary sex characteristics in developing girls. (p. 403)

5. Compared to other girls, CAH girls
   - are more likely to engage in rough-and-tumble play.
   - are more likely to choose male-preferred toys.
   - show significant masculinization of play activities, playmate preference, aggression, spatial ability, and adolescent activities.
   - have less interest in typically-female activities.
   - have less interest in infants. (p. 404)

6. failure to menstruate (p. 404)

7. True—Women with AIS respond to estrogens and therefore develop breasts and hips. Because they do not respond to androgens in their system, women with AIS have less hair on their arms, legs, and upper lips and less hair on their heads than non-AIS women, which may result in a more feminine appearance. (pp. 404–405)

8. X (p. 405)

9. The female body plan is the default. Two X chromosomes are not necessary for female body development; all that is necessary for a person to look female is lack of a Y chromosome. (p. 405)

10. Individuals with Turner's syndrome
    - are shorter than the average woman.
    - may have abnormal levels of sex hormones.
    - may experience degeneration of their ovaries and a failure to produce normal levels of estrogen.
    - may not develop their secondary sex characteristics without exogenous estrogen therapy.
    - may have heart problems. (p. 405)

11. True—We know that from people with Turner's syndrome who have only one X chromosome. Individuals with Turner's syndrome are female but do not develop as typical females. (p. 405)

12. parental source (p. 405)

13. Genomic imprinting refers to the chemical tagging of an allele that alters the likelihood that it will be expressed in the phenotype. (p. 405)

14. boy; girl (p. 406)

15. Consider the following in your response:
    - Those with an X chromosome from the father are better at cognitive skills that females are typically better at (e.g. reading body language and facial expressions, recognizing faces, verbal fluency, social skills, etc.).
    - These differences cannot be due to associative learning since no one was aware of whether the individual had the father's or the mother's X chromosome. (p. 407)

The Transgender Experience

1. 3 (p. 407)

2. False—Gender identity is extremely resilient and resistant even to intensive therapy. (pp. 407–408)

Relative Life Expectancy

1. True—Females live, on average, five years longer than males. (p. 408)

2. True—Compared to women, more men have a greater number of children and more men have none. Women are closer to the average. (p. 408)

3. Consider the following in your response:
   - Because men run more of a risk of having no offspring at all, risk-taking is worth it for them.
   - There is, therefore, a greater potential payoff for any male strategy that might attract a mate.
   - These strategies may involve potentially dangerous behaviours that are meant to be attractive to females (physical derring-do). (p. 409)

4. suppresses the immune system (p. 409)

5. pleiotropic genes (p. 409)

Cultural Differences in Mating and Parenting

1. greater (pp. 409–410)

2. be responsible and show sexual restraint (p. 410)

Practice Test 1: Answer Key

1. **b** (p. 382)
2. **d** (p. 382)
3. **a** (p. 384)
4. **c** (p. 386)
5. **b** (p. 387)
6. **b** (pp. 387–388)
7. **d** (p. 389)
8. **a** (pp. 390–392)
9. **c** (p. 392)
10. **d** (p. 393)
11. **a** (p. 397)
12. **b** (p. 398)
13. **c** (p. 398)
14. **d** (p. 399)
15. **b** (pp. 401–402)
16. **a** (p. 403)
17. **c** (p. 403)
18. **d** (p. 404)
19. **b** (p. 404)
20. **c** (p. 405)
21. **d** (p. 405)
22. **a** (p. 408)
23. **d** (p. 408)
24. **b** (p. 409)
25. **d** (p. 410)

Practice Test 2

1. **a** (p. 382)
2. **c** (p. 383)
3. **b** (p. 385)
4. **d** (p. 386)
5. **a** (p. 388)
6. **c** (p. 389)
7. **d** (p. 389)
8. **b** (p. 390)
9. **a** (p. 392)
10. **c** (p. 396)
11. **b** (p. 398)
12. **d** (p. 398)
13. **c** (p. 398)
14. **a** (p. 400)
15. **b** (pp. 402–403)
16. **d** (p. 403)
17. **d** (p. 403)
18. **c** (p. 403)
19. **b** (p. 404)
20. **a** (p. 405)
21. **d** (p. 407)
22. **b** (pp. 407–408)
23. **c** (p. 408)
24. **b** (p. 409)
25. **c** (pp. 409–410)

Chapter 12
Moral and Prosocial Development

Chapter Summary

Morality and Prosocial Behaviour

Morality, our intuitive sense of right and wrong, guides our behaviour and our judgment of others. The nice things that we do for others (e.g. altruism, friendship) can be categorized as *prosocial behaviour*.

Traditional Views on Moral Development

Traditionally, the discussion of moral development has been framed in terms of nature and nurture. George Edward Moore, in 1903, pointed out that we have a tendency to equate what is natural with what is good. In fact, natural behaviours are often not 'good'.

Piaget described three stages of moral development: the *morality of constraint stage, the transitional period*, and the *autonomous morality stage*. He believed that the developing child first understands rules as rigid and unchangeable. Largely through struggles and interactions with peers, the child eventually comes to understand rules as social contracts.

Lawrence Kohlberg is the best-known name in the field of moral development. He presented children with dilemmas and listened to their thoughts on right and wrong. Kohlberg proposed six stages:

- Stage 1, morality involves obeying authority figures
- Stage 2, morality involves bargaining to mitigate punishment
- Stage 3, morality involves fulfilling the expectations of a social role
- Stage 4, morality involves upholding social systems
- Stage 5, morality involves ensuring individual rights
- Stage 6, morality involves upholding universal principles

Kohlberg believed that all children progress through the same stages in the same order but that most do not make it past Stage 4. Kohlberg's research has been criticized for failing to consider girls' perspectives on morality and for failing to generalize cross-culturally. Richard Alexander has interpreted Kohlberg's stages from an evolutionary standpoint; he emphasizes that morality at each stage of life (and at each of Kohlberg's stages) is essentially self-serving in terms of reproductive investments.

What Evolutionary Thinking Adds to Moral and Prosocial Development

Evolutionary thinkers view morality as an adaptive solution to the challenge of living in groups. Specialized learning mechanisms have evolved to allow children to 'learn' their culture and become socialized.

The Function of Morality

The function of moral psychology is not to allow us to learn the objective truth about good and bad in the world; rather, morality allows us to behave in the world in a way that maximizes our evolutionary fitness. More specifically, it is social cognitive adaptations that apply to morality that allow us to live in large groups.

Social Behaviour and Fitness

People could not have lived alone in the EEA; the risks of food and water depletion and attack from other groups would have been too great. A human social psychology was necessary to allow for the social skills that were needed to form alliances and friendships.

Getting Altruism off the Ground

Survival of the fittest usually involves 'winning' resources so as to produce more and healthier offspring than your competitors. Altruism at first seems to fly in the face of the logic of natural selection. In fact, there are evolutionarily-sound reasons for the existence of altruism.

Kin-Selected Altruism

Kin-selected altruism refers to helping genetic relatives, thus increasing the frequency of shared alleles. Benefits, costs, *and* relatedness are considered when assessing the probability of altruistic behaviour; all else being equal, you are more likely to go out of your way for a brother than a cousin and more likely to go out of your way for a cousin than a stranger.

Co-Operation among Non-Kin

Individuals may altruistically help non-kin if they have reason to expect that the favour will someday be returned. This is referred to as *reciprocal altruism*. People tend to use a *tit-for-tat strategy* in which they start out nice, re-paying favours, but exclude cheaters from further exchanges. This strategy can be demonstrated in the iterated *prisoner's dilemma* where people test relationships and will respond to exploitation. Once people have become friends, they continue to exchange resources but in a very casual, inexact way. Friendship can lead to *by-product mutualism* where benefits may be conferred simply by hanging around with someone who has helpful knowledge or status. In a *runaway friendship*, one friend's great sacrifice may prove her value and result in extraordinary aid when she needs it.

Moral Intuition or Rational Moral Decision-Making?

We tend to think that moral reasoning precedes moral decision-making but that is not necessarily the case. Moral reasoning may often function to justify moral verdicts that were made very quickly and automatically. Mark Hauser has suggested that humans have a *moral grammar* (not unlike Chomsky's universal grammar for language) that is part of our psychology and that allows for quick, automatic moral decisions.

Specialized Cognitive Machinery Underlying Morality

Antonio Damasio studied a group of patients who sustained orbitofrontal brain damage as adults. In a game that involved choosing from 'winning' and 'losing' decks of cards, control subjects, but not patients, learned to avoid losing decks. Further, patients, unlike controls, did not show emotional responses to losing decks. Patients did not seem to be able to make decisions that optimized long-term consequences. Performance on Kohlberg's moral dilemma tasks was equivalent for patients and control subjects, suggesting that patients had intact slow, deliberate moral reasoning. In contrast, individuals with *early* frontal lobe damage performed abnormally on Kohlberg's tasks.

Piaget and Kohlberg assumed that right and wrong exist as objective entities. More recent thinkers see morality as situational; it is something the mind creates as an adaptive response to the environment.

The Development of Social Exchange Reasoning

Performance on Wason's four-card selection task is better if the rule to be evaluated involves a social contract. When the same essential problem is made abstract, people often make mistakes, even though the logic is the same. It seems we are very effective cheater detectors in a social situation. This shouldn't be surprising as cheater detection is necessary for reciprocal altruism to take hold. Even young children have the cognitive machinery to detect cheaters.

The Development of Sexual Morals

Incest leads to a greater chance of maldevelopment in offspring due to pairings of harmful recessive alleles. It seems that, in order to avoid such problems, humans have kin-recognition mechanisms that inhibit sexual interest. The *Westermarck effect* prevents sexual attraction between individuals who lived together as young children. Sexual disinterest between couples in minor marriages and between children raised together in Israeli kibbutzim provides support for the existence of this effect.

Universal Rules vs. Conventions

There is a meaningful distinction to be made between universal rules (that cross cultural lines) and conventions. Conventions are dependent on culture. They seem to have a critical or sensitive period for acquisition and are often framed in terms of politeness. Psychopaths do not make a distinction between universal rules and conventions; typical children do make that distinction.

Teaching Morals: Over-Reward or Internalize?

A supportive and constructive parenting style seems to be best for internalization of prosocial values in children. Punishment and coercion seems to have the opposite effect. It may be that, more so than parents, peers are the agents of socialization.

Learning Objectives

After reading this chapter, you should be able to:

- Conceptualize morality and prosocial behaviour (p. 416)
- Summarize how moral development has historically been perceived (pp. 417–419)
- Explain how Piaget viewed moral development (pp. 419–420)
- Discuss the work of Lawrence Kohlberg, the biggest contributor to the foundations of the field of moral development (pp. 421–425)
- Examine how our understanding of moral development can be guided by evolutionary thinking (pp. 425–428)
- Start solving the evolutionary puzzle of altruism (pp. 428–430)
- Explain how individuals behave altruistically without being exploited (pp. 430–436)
- Evaluate which comes first, moral intuition or moral decision-making (pp. 436–438)
- Understand morality as a product of the mind (pp. 439–441)

- Appreciate our impressive ability to detect cheaters (pp. 441–444)

- Explain the adaptive function of sexual morals (pp. 444–446)

- Distinguish between universal and conventional rules (pp. 446–449)

- Discuss how morals are best taught (pp. 449–451)

Suggested Readings

Piaget, J. (2010). *The Moral Judgment of the Child.* Whitefish, MT: Kessinger Publishing.

This recent reprint is Piaget's seminal account of children's beliefs about right and wrong.

Gilligan, C. (1982). New maps of development: New visions of maturity. *American Journal of Orthopsychiatry, 52,* 199–212.

Gilligan presents an account of the contrasting moral perspectives of males and females.

Poundstone, W. (1993). *Prisoner's Dilemma.* New York: Anchor.

An introduction to the principles and history of game theory.

Study Questions

Morality and Prosocial Behaviour

1. Define 'morality'.

2. True or False: Morality is unique to humans.

3. Altruism, friendship, coalitional behaviours, and parental behaviours can all be classified as _____ behaviours.

Traditional Views on Moral Development

1. True or False: Thomas Hobbes believed that morality was learned.

2. British philosopher _____ proposed a view on morality called utilitarianism.

3. Define 'utilitarianism'.

4. George Edward Moore's naturalistic fallacy is the error of equating what is _____ with what is _____.

5. Contemporary philosopher Wolfgang Wickler argues that what is good for _____ is good ethically.

6. _____ and _____ laid the groundwork for contemporary understanding of moral development.

7. How did Piaget view moral development?

8. What methods did Piaget use to study moral development?

9. Name Piaget's three stages of moral development and the ages they cover.

10. According to Piaget, what does a child in the morality of constraint stage think about rules and punishments?

11. True or False: Intentions matter to a child in the morality of constraint stage.

12. According to Piaget, what are two reasons why a child at the morality of constraint stage accepts rules as unalterable?

13. What happens during Piaget's transitional period?

14. Autonomous morality is also called _____.

15. According to Piaget, how do children understand morality in the autonomous morality stage?

16. True or False: Kohlberg, like Piaget, believed that moral development occurs in stages.

17. Describe Kohlberg's method for studying moral development.

18. Name Kohlberg's three levels of moral reasoning.

19. True or False: According to Kohlberg, most individuals eventually reach the sixth stage.

20. In pre-conventional reasoning, the focus is on _____.

21. In conventional reasoning, the focus is on _____.

22. In post-conventional reasoning, the focus is on _____.

23. Match Kohlberg's stage with the brief description on the right.
    1. Stage 1   a) Law and Order
    2. Stage 2   b) Universal Moral Principles
    3. Stage 3   c) Social Contracts and Individual Rights
    4. Stage 4   d) Exchange
    5. Stage 5   e) Obedience
    6. Stage 6   f) Relationships

24. True or False: Kohlberg believed that moral stages were always achieved and completed in the same order.

25. According to Kohlberg most people reach Stage _____ and stay there.

26. How well does moral reasoning (as measured by Kohlberg's methods) predict moral behaviour?

27. True or False: When people are in their mid-20s, more are in Stage 4 than Stage 3.

28. True or False: Kohlberg's subjects included both boys and girls.

29. Carol Gilligan suggested that, morally, boys are taught to value _____ and girls are taught to value _____.

30. Are Kohlberg's stages truly universal?

31. Match Kohlberg's stage with the child's priority, according to Richard Alexander.

   1. Stage 1   a) concern with cultivating relationships
   2. Stage 2   b) consideration of the welfare of the group
   3. Stage 3   c) focus on ideal principles
   4. Stage 4   d) focus on own growth and development
   5. Stage 5   e) indirect efforts employed to engage other people to fulfill needs
   6. Stage 6   f) concern for the greatest good for the greatest number of people

32. Alexander believes that Kohlberg's stages are functional; they reflect changes with age in the _____ that children and adults face.

What Evolutionary Thinking Adds to Moral and Prosocial Development

1. Summarize the view of moral development put forward by evolutionary psychology.

2. The implication of an evolutionary view of moral development is that moral learning is constrained by _____, which were designed by _____.

The Function of Morality

1. The *function* of our moral psychology is to _____.

2. How does the above perspective differ from Piaget's and Kohlberg's views of morality?

Social Behaviour and Fitness

1. True or False: Social cognition was not very important to our ancestors.

2. Why couldn't people in the EEA live alone?

Getting Altruism off the Ground

1. Why was it so difficult for evolutionary psychologists to account for altruistic behaviour?

2. How does group selection theory explain altruism?

3. Once evolutionary thinkers re-discovered _____'s work, it became clear that groups were not the relevant unit of selection

4. Eventually, it became clear that the _____, and not the group or even the individual, was the relevant unit of selection.

Kin-Selected Altruism

1. Define 'kin-selected altruism'.

2. Behaviours that enhance the reproductive success of genetic relatives can enhance _____.

3. When a ground squirrel sees a predator approaching, instead of immediately heading for cover, the squirrel will conspicuously stand on its hind legs and emit a loud alarm call. What is the classic explanation for this?

4. According to the inclusive fitness theory, the probability of prosocial behaviours increases with _____.

5. True or False: Kin-selected altruism is expected in cases in which rB< C.

Co-Operation among Non-Kin

1. Define 'reciprocal altruism'.

2. Altruism can be selected for if altruistic behaviour causes _____.

3. Reciprocal exchange can be beneficial to both parties. However, to avoid exploitation, what must be done?

4. The tit-for-tat strategy for reciprocal altruism involves _____.

5. Define 'evolutionarily stable strategy'.

6. What is the prisoner's dilemma?

7. When you play the prisoner's dilemma game with a given partner once, the best strategy is to _____.

8. In the iterated prisoner's dilemma, the best strategy is _____.

9. The iterated prisoner's dilemma can be taken as a model for _____.

10. Why do vampire bats practise reciprocal altruism?

11. According to Tooby and Cosmides, what factors influence the selection of friends?

12. Define Tooby and Cosmides' notion of 'runaway friendship'.

13. What perplexing observation does the theory of runaway friendship explain?

14. Friends prefer to return favours in a _____ way.

Moral Intuition or Rational Moral Decision-Making?

1. Which comes first, moral thought or moral decision-making?

2. Define 'moral grammar'.

3. Marc Hauser proposes that a moral grammar is acquired by specialized cognitive machinery, analogous to _____.

Specialized Cognitive Machinery Underlying Morality

1. In the real world, patients with orbitofrontal brain damage find it difficult to _____.

2. True or False: In Damasio's card game, 'winning' decks award and cost small amounts and 'losing' decks award and cost large amounts. Patients with orbitofrontal brain damage learn to draw from the winning decks.

3. As indexed by _____, control subjects, but not patients with orbitofrontal damage, show an emotional response when picking from the losing decks.

4. True or False: Control subjects and patients with orbitofrontal damage show no differences in performance on Kohlberg's moral dilemma tasks.

5. Responses to the card game show that, unlike control subjects, patients with orbitofrontal damage ignore information about _____.

6. Individuals whose frontal lobe damage occurred when they were _____ seemed to have developed neither the quick, automatic component nor the slow, deliberate component of moral decision-making.

7. How do we know this (above)?

8. What are the dictator game and the ultimatum game?

9. _____ has been found to be a better predictor of dictator proposals than gender.

10. In contrast to Piaget and Kohlberg, more recent thinkers see morality as a creation of _____.

The Development of Social Exchange Reasoning

1. In order for reciprocal altruism to evolve in a population, it is necessary that individuals be able to recognize and exclude _____.

2. Studies employing Wason's four-card selection task support the idea that detection of rule violation is easier when the rule involves a _____ than when it doesn't.

3. True or False: Responses to the Carol problem show that children as young as 3 years of age perform better in the cheater condition than the control condition even though the logic of the two problems is the same.

The Development of Sexual Morals

1. Why is incest a bad evolutionary strategy?

2. Define 'inbreeding depression'.

3. Define the 'Westermarck effect'.

4. How does 'minor marriage' provide evidence for Westermarck's ideas?

5. Also in support of Westermarck's ideas is the finding that unrelated children reared together in _____ rarely marry each other.

6. It has been found that the length of time spent in the same household with an opposite-sex sibling predicted the strength of the _____ judgment regarding sibling sex.

Universal Rules vs. Conventions

1. What are some examples of cross-cultural prohibitions?

2. What is the difference between universal and conventional moral rules?

3. True or False: Conventional moral rules are usually explained in terms of harm done to others.

4. _____ make no distinction between universal and conventional rules.

Teaching Morals: Over-Reward or Internalize?

1. True or False: Greater parental punishment and authoritarianism are associated with greater maturity in terms of moral reasoning and moral behaviour.

2. A _____ parenting style is most effective in encouraging internalization of prosocial values.

3. Benjamin's dad, Eli, wants to encourage prosocial behaviour in his son. What should Eli say to Benjamin the next time Benjamin misbehaves?

4. What are three parenting styles described by Diana Baumrind?

5. Children who are subjected to authoritarian parenting may not have the freedom to develop _____.

6. Permissive parenting is associated with _____ later in childhood.

7. Judith Harris argues that morality comes from _____, not parents.

8. A study of criminality in adopted men in Denmark found that, if the biological father had a criminal record, there was a significant relationship between criminality of adoptive parent and child only if the child grew up in _____.

9. According to Harris, the above finding suggests that _____ turns the biological son of a criminal into a criminal, not the criminal adoptive parent.

Practice Test 1

1. Altruism and friendship are best described as
   a. moral behaviours.
   b. prosocial behaviours.
   c. natural behaviours.
   d. autonomous behaviours.

2. Utilitarianism is the view that

   a. moral decisions should be made based on what is best for the greatest number of people.
   b. the human mind does not need to provide anything in order for a person to develop morally.
   c. what is good is what is natural.
   d. rewards and punishments are an integral part of moral development.

3. Piaget found that when children under the age of 6 are judging the seriousness of a 'crime', they fail to take into account

   a. the details of what happened.
   b. the rules being broken.
   c. the damage done.
   d. the intentions of the actor.

4. Which of the following is *not* one of Piaget's stages of moral development?

   a. the stage of autonomous morality
   b. the moral intuition stage
   c. the transitional period
   d. the morality of constraint stage

5. An understanding that rules are social contracts open to negotiation comes in which of Piaget's stages?

   a. the stage of autonomous morality
   b. the moral intuition stage
   c. the transitional period
   d. the morality of constraint stage

6. All of Kohlberg's vignettes ended with

   a. a 'crime'.
   b. a statement on morality.
   c. a dilemma.
   d. a rule.

7. In Kohlberg's Stage 5, the focus is on

   a. relationships.
   b. bargaining to mitigate punishment.
   c. the greatest good for the greatest number.
   d. universal principles.

8. According to Carol Gilligan, girls, unlike boys, are taught to value

   a. societal rules.
   b. independence.
   c. ideal principles.
   d. responsibility for others.

9. The risk of depleting food and water supplies and the risk of attack from other human groups meant that individuals in the EEA could not

   a. follow rules.
   b. live alone.
   c. maintain friendships.
   d. judge anything as morally forbidden.

10. Which of the following is *not* relevant in explaining why one individual would accept a cost in order to benefit another?

    a. group selection theory
    b. rB > C
    c. reciprocal altruism
    d. kin-selected altruism

11. Reciprocal altruism is the phenomenon of

    a. exploiting others.
    b. favouring those who are genetically related.
    c. helping another individual and then having the favour returned.
    d. incurring a benefit for one individual but not another.

12. Juliana is initially nice to Gabriela but when Gabriela starts to cheat her, Juliana stops sharing things with Gabriela. Juliana is using a _____ strategy.

    a. balanced
    b. tit-for-tat
    c. kin selection
    d. mutualism

13. When a strategy _____, it becomes predominant in the population.

    a. is dependent on genetics
    b. is reciprocal
    c. involves give and take.
    d. is evolutionarily stable.

14. If you play the prisoner's dilemma game with one person, one time, your best strategy is to

    a. defect.
    b. agree.
    c. cooperate.
    d. none of the above

15. Which of the following is an example of runaway friendship?

    a. Peter has Amir over for dinner and, a month later, Amir has Peter over for dinner.
    b. Bert and Ernie spend the whole weekend talking about their goals in life.
    c. Deigo gives John his last $500 as an investment to John's company and, when his company becomes successful, John buys Deigo a house.
    d. none of the above

16. Mark Hauser believes that people may make quick, automatic moral judgments based on

    a. carefully thought out moral principles.
    b. a moral grammar.
    c. an idiosyncratic moral philosophy.
    d. language processing.

17. Damasio's patients had damage to the _____ lobe.

    a. temporal
    b. parietal
    c. occipital
    d. frontal

18. Which of the following statements is true of the decision-making of Damasio's patients?

    a. They do not show an emotional response to losing decks.
    b. They consider the long-term consequences of their behaviour.
    c. They perform abnormally on Kohlberg's moral dilemma tasks.
    d. They learn to avoid the losing decks.

19. Which of the following was found to be a good predictor of proposal amounts for the dictator game?

    a. height
    b. age
    c. gender
    d. race

20. Pairing your genetic contribution with someone unrelated is referred to as

    a. deleterious breeding.
    b. incest.
    c. inbreeding depression.
    d. genetic avoidance.

21. Children raised together in Israeli kibbutzim

    a. typically discontinue any sexual play as soon as they become fertile.
    b. are genetically related.
    c. are likely to marry each other.
    d. are likely to be romantically involved without getting married.

22. Which of the following is the strongest predictor of the 'moral wrongness' judgment regarding sibling sex?

    a. genetic relatedness
    b. the number of years of co-residence with an opposite-sex sibling
    c. gender
    d. age

23. Which of the following statements is *not* true of conventional moral rules?

    a. 'Do not walk around naked' is one example.
    b. They seem to have critical periods for acquisition.
    c. They reflect ideas regarding politeness.
    d. They are seen cross-culturally.

24. Which of the following is the best parenting style if the goal is internalization of prosocial values?

    a. casual
    b. punishing
    c. supportive
    d. cohersive

25. Which of the following parenting styles involves high demand and rigid regulation?

    a. permissive
    b. strict
    c. authoritative
    d. authoritarian

Practice Test 2

1. Who was *not* an empiricist with regard to morality?

    a. John Locke
    b. Thomas Hobbes
    c. Jean Piaget
    d. They were all empiricists with regard to morality.

2. The existence of widespread violence in humans and other species argues against

    a. utilitarianism.
    b. ethology.
    c. the naturalistic fallacy.
    d. coalitional behaviour.

3. According to a child in Piaget's morality of constraint stage, why is a rule a rule?

    a. Because it is the result of a negotiation.
    b. Because an authority figure said it is.
    c. Because it is part of a social contract.
    d. Because it is in everyone's best interest.

4. Piaget's transitional period covers which age range?

    a. 2 to 4 years
    b. 4 to 7 years
    c. 7 to 10 years
    d. 10 to 12 years

5. Which of Kohlberg's stages is focused on social systems?

    a. Stage 2
    b. Stage 3
    c. Stage 4
    d. Stage 5

6. Kohlberg's Stage 6

    a. is mostly hypothetical.
    b. is relevant to social relationships.
    c. involves obedience.
    d. is the most important stage.

7. Kohlberg's Stage 5 is attained by

    a. late adulthood.
    b. more females than males.
    c. more than 40 per cent of people.
    d. less than 10 per cent of people.

8. Which of the following is *not* a shortcoming of Kohlberg's work on morality?

    a. His results cannot be generalized cross-culturally.
    b. All of Kohlberg's subjects were males.
    c. His theory is not flexible enough to account for differences between groups that value individual rights and groups that value obedience.
    d. His theory focused only on very young children.

9. Richard Alexander interpreted Kohlberg's stages in terms of evolutionary priorities. Unlike Kohlberg, he sees moral thoughts as

    a. a means to an end.
    b. a way to promote good feelings.
    c. a way to establish good relationships.
    d. a way of helping others.

10. Our moral psychology is what allows us to

    a. recognize inherent goodness and badness.
    b. develop culture.
    c. live independently.
    d. make rules.

11. For evolutionary thinkers, altruistic behaviour was hard to account for because

    a. 'nice' designs are so rare.
    b. resource allocation is unimportant in evolution.
    c. a generosity allele would seem likely to be weeded out by natural selection.
    d. none of the above

12. Group selection theory does not work as an explanation for altruism (or anything else) because

    a. human beings in the EEA didn't always live in groups.
    b. group welfare does not benefit the individual.
    c. the unit of selection is particulate.
    d. the individual is the important level for natural selection.

13. A ground squirrel emits an alarm call to warn of a predator because

    a. squirrels are quite advanced, morally.
    b. emitting the call involves no cost.
    c. squirrels are very social creatures.
    d. its genetic relatives are likely close by.

14. A downside of reciprocal altruism is

    a. the risk of exploitation.
    b. its evolutionary instability.
    c. the fact that receiving benefits requires a kin relationship.
    d. it is not favoured by natural selection.

15. The _____ prisoner's dilemma is a model for reciprocal altruism.

    a. single
    b. iterated
    c. complex
    d. simple

16. Steve learns how to navigate the social scene in high school by hanging out with Dylan. This is an example of

    a. intuition.
    b. prosocial behaviour.
    c. by-product mutualism.
    d. runaway friendship.

17. People do better on Wason's four-card selection task when

   a. the cards have letters and numbers printed on them.
   b. the rule is abstract.
   c. they are forced to make a quick decision.
   d. the rule involves a social contract.

18. The above finding is to be expected if humans have

   a. tit-for-tat strategies.
   b. embodied morality.
   c. specialized cognitive processes for detecting cheaters.
   d. all of the above

19. Feng and Lian are brother and sister. The thought of developing an attraction to each other is horrifying to both of them. Their horror is part of the _____ effect.

   a. Winkelmeyer
   b. Westermarck
   c. Weiss
   d. Wortenburg

20. Compared to average married couples, couples who are part of a minor marriage

   a. have more extramarital affairs.
   b. have fewer children.
   c. have higher divorce rates.
   d. all of the above

21. _____ make no distinction between universal and conventional rules.

   a. Psychopaths
   b. People in some cultures
   c. Children
   d. Adolescents

22. Which of the following comes first?

   a. Children solve the 'cheater detection' problem
   b. Children believe in negotiation in rule formation
   c. Piaget's transitional period
   d. Sensitive period for culture-specific rules

23. Young Giovanna hit her brother. To encourage more prosocial behaviour from Giovanna, her parents would be wise to say what to her?

   a. 'Your brother is going to hit you back'.
   b. 'Think about how your brother felt when you hit him'.
   c. 'Go to your room'.
   d. 'You are grounded for a week'.

24. Which of the following parenting styles has been described as 'just right'?

    a. permissive
    b. strict
    c. authoritative
    d. authoritarian

25. Judith Harris believes that _____ can have a large impact on criminality.

    a. parental rewards and punishments
    b. socialization by parents
    c. genetics
    d. neighbourhood

Study Questions: Answer Key

Morality and Prosocial Behaviour

1. Morality is the intuitive sense of right and wrong that guides our behaviour and leads us to judge and possibly condemn others' behaviours. (p. 446)

2. True—Other animals may have some sense of right and wrong and they may have prosocial and altruistic behaviours, but only humans hold some behaviours as obligatory and others as prohibited. (p. 446)

3. prosocial (p. 446)

Traditional Views on Moral Development

1. True—Hobbes believed that our minds were blank slates in terms of morality. (p. 417)

2. John Stuart Mill (p. 417)

3. Utilitarianism contends that one could and should make deliberate moral decisions based on what is best for the greatest number of people. (p. 417)

4. good; natural (p. 417)

5. evolution (p. 417)

6. Jean Piaget; Lawrence Kohlberg (p. 418)

7. With regards to moral development, Piaget believed
   - that morality developed in stages.
   - that children's understanding of morality changes from a concrete acceptance of rigid, unchangeable rules to an understanding of rules as part of a negotiable, changeable, social contract.
   - that struggles and interactions with peers, rather than adults, facilitate this change in moral understanding. (p. 418)

8. When studying moral development, Piaget
   - observed children playing games together and watched how they negotiated and how they dealt with the creation and violation of rules.
   - interviewed children about their reactions to rules being broken or followed. He was interested in whether it mattered whether a rule was broken intentionally or accidentally. He was also interested in children's thoughts on appropriate punishments.
   - developed a standardized interview method in which he told children a short story and had them choose the more serious of two transgressions. For example, if one child spills a large glass of juice while trying to be helpful and another child spills a small glass of juice which being naughty, who has committed the bigger 'crime'? (pp. 418–419)

9. Piaget's three stages of moral development are
   - the morality of constraint stage, younger than 7 or 8 years.
   - the transitional period, 7 to 10 years.
   - the stage of autonomous morality, older than 10 years. (pp. 419–420)

10. At this stage, the child views rules as unchangeable and non-negotiable. Following the rules is good and breaking the rules is bad. Punishments are justified if an authority figure says they are. (p. 419)

11. False—To a child at this stage, the consequence of the action matters; intention does not. (p. 419)

12. A child accepts rules as unalterable because
    1. Children in this stage are at an early stage of cognitive development and can only understand rules as 'things'. 'Things' are objects whose existence cannot be disputed.
    2. Children are smaller and less powerful than parents; they are not in a position to negotiate. (p. 419)

13. During Piaget's transitional period,
    - children spend an increasing amount of time with peers. Peer relationships are likely to be (roughly) equal with respect to power status and therefore there are opportunities to negotiate and to contribute to rule-making and rule-enforcement. It becomes apparent to children that rules can change.
    - Also in this stage, children learn to appreciate (and take into account) another person's perspective. Intentions become relevant in deciding on punishments. (p. 420)

14. moral relativism (p. 420)

15. In the autonomous morality stage, children
    - believe that rules are social contracts that can be negotiated and re-negotiated.
    - understand that rules must meet the needs of multiple people.
    - can consider multiple perspectives when proposing fair rules.
    - believe that punishment is a product of social agreement and should be fair to everyone involved.
    - believe that rules and punishments dispensed from authority figures can be unfair. (p. 420)

16. True—Both Kohlberg and Piaget were stage theorists. (p. 421)

17. Kohlberg presented children with stories that involved some sort of moral dilemma. He listened to each child's thoughts on what was right and wrong with regard to the dilemma and encouraged the child to explain his answer. (p. 421)

18. Kohlberg's three levels of moral reasoning are
    - Pre-conventional
    - Conventional
    - Post-Conventional (p. 421)

19. False—Kohlberg believed it was extremely rare for an individual to reach Stage 6. He eventually stopped scoring that stage. (p. 421)

20. punishments (p. 422)

21. social relationships and social order (p. 422)

22. ideals or moral principles (p. 422)

23. 1. Stage 1   e) Obedience
    2. Stage 2   d) Exchange
    3. Stage 3   f) Relationships
    4. Stage 4   a) Law and Order
    5. Stage 5   c) Social Contracts and Individual Rights
    6. Stage 6   b) Universal Moral Principles (p. 422)

24. True—He believed the order was universal (although not all people reach the same stage). (p. 422)

25. 4 (p. 422)

26. Consider the following in your response:
    - Not very well.
    - People with a higher stage of moral reasoning are somewhat more likely to provide assistance to others in need and somewhat less likely to engage in immoral behaviours. These relationships, though, are small.
    - In practice, people tend to use moral reasoning to justify decisions rather than guide them. (pp. 422–423)

27. True—Beginning in the mid-20s, the percentage of people in Stage 4 is greater than the percentage in Stage 3. (p. 423)

28. False—Kohlberg's subjects were boys. Therefore, his theory is skewed toward a male idea of morality. (p. 424)

29. ideal principles and societal rules; responsibility to others and avoiding hurting others (p. 424)

30. Consider the following in your response:
    - They do not seem to be truly universal.
    - Children in non-Western cultures do not usually climb to levels as high as Western children do. In traditional, non-Western cultures, conflicts are likely to be worked out face to face among people with lifelong relationships. In that situation, ideal principles may not be highly valued or useful.
    - There are also cross-cultural differences in terms of the balance between individual rights and obedience to authority. Kohlberg's theory does not allow for flexibility in that regard. (p. 424)

31. 1. Stage 1   d) focus on own growth and development
    2. Stage 2   e) indirect efforts employed to engage other people to fulfill needs
    3. Stage 3   a) concern with cultivating relationships
    4. Stage 4   b) consideration of the welfare of the group
    5. Stage 5   f) concern for the greatest good for the greatest number of people
    6. Stage 6   c) focus on ideal principles (pp. 424–425)

32. adaptive problems (p. 425)

What Evolutionary Thinking Adds to Moral and Prosocial Development

1. Evolutionary psychology has proposed that
    *   the learning mechanisms of humans include learning mechanisms specialized for solving the adaptive problems of the EEA.
    *   these specialized learning mechanisms include content that led to learning that would have been adaptive in the EEA.
    *   developing children can 'learn' their culture or become specialized to the extent that these specialized learning mechanisms were designed for this purpose. (pp. 425–426)

2. cognitive learning mechanisms; natural selection (p. 426)

The Function of Morality

1. allow us to behave in ways that maximize our evolutionary fitness (p. 427)

2. Thinking of morality as evolutionarily functional means setting aside absolute ideas of morality. Piaget and Kohlberg believed that there were ideal moral judgments that wouldn't change across situations. (p. 427)

Social Behaviour and Fitness

1. False—Living conditions in the EEA were brutal and so being a member of a group was critical. The importance of social cognition could not be over-stated. (p. 428)

2. People in the EEA were completely at risk of
    *   the depletion of food, water, and other resources. Relationships with other people helped to guard against the fluctuations of resources availability.
    *   attack and exploitation by other human groups. Relationships with other people provided protection. (p. 428)

Getting Altruism off the Ground

1. It was difficult to account for because
    *   the general view of evolutionary psychology is that alleles spread if they lead to the individual acquiring more resources and, in turn, producing more and healthier offspring than other members of the population.
    *   altruistic behaviour means giving resources to competitors. These resources come at a cost to the individual and give the competitor an edge. This would seem to go against the principles of survival of the fittest. (p. 428)

2. According to group selection theory, altruistic behaviour occurs so that weaker members of the group will not drag down the whole group. The group, rather than the individual, is thought to be the unit of selection. (pp. 429–430)

3. Mendel (pp. 429–430)

4. gene (pp. 429–430)

Kin-Selected Altruism

1. Kin-selected altruism is altruism that was shaped by the fitness advantage provided by increasing the frequency of one's genes via the fitness success of genetic relatives. (p. 430)

2. inclusive fitness (p. 346430

3. The classic explanation is that those who would benefit from the alarm call would be individuals who likely share genes with the squirrel making the call. (p. 430)

4. the relatedness between the actor and the recipient (p. 430)

5. False—It is expected when rB > C. (p. 431)

Co-Operation among Non-Kin

1. Reciprocal altruism involves helping another individual and then having the favour returned. (p. 432)

2. reciprocation (p. 433)

3. To avoid exploitation, one must only give away resources to those who will reciprocate. (p. 433)

4. starting out nice and repaying others' kindnesses but excluding cheaters from further exchanges (p. 433)

5. An evolutionarily stable strategy is one in which, if played by a number of individuals in a population, can not be invaded via natural selection by an alternative strategy that is introduced at a low frequency. (p. 433)

6. The prisoner's dilemma is a game in which a player assumes the role of a prisoner and selects his best strategy in the following situation:
    * Two prisoners are in police custody, held in separate rooms and without a line of communication.
    * The police do not have enough evidence for a conviction unless one prisoner testifies against the other.
    * Each prisoner is offered the same deal: If you testify against the other prisoner ('defect') and the other prisoner keeps the secret ('co-operates'), then you will go free and the other prisoner will get the maximum 10-year sentence. If you and the other prisoner remain silent, you will both get 6-month sentences. If you and the other prisoner testify against each other, you will both get 5-year sentences.
    * What do you do? (pp. 433–434)

7. defect (your sentence will be lighter whether your partner defects or cooperates) (p. 434)

8. continuous cooperation, a tit-for-tat strategy (p. 434)

9. reciprocal altruism (p. 434)

10. They do so because they live in stable social groups for up to 20 years and therefore have multiple opportunities to interact with the same individual. (pp. 434–435)

11. Factors that influence the selection of friends include
    * by-product mutualism (there may be benefits to hanging around with others, sharing in their status and knowledge).
    * mind reading, goal similarity, and reciprocation. (p. 435)

12. Runaway friendship refers to the situation in which one person values another to the extent that he is willing to make great sacrifices for her. This, in turn, makes him a more valuable friend who is likely to benefit from extraordinary aid when he needs it. (p. 435)

13. It explains the finding that, in closer and more intimate relationships, people are less likely to ensure that exchanges are equal. (p. 435)

14. casual, inexact (p. 435)

Moral Intuition or Rational Moral Decision-Making?

1. The classic view is that thought comes first and informs decision-making. Alternatively, it has been suggested that moral decisions are made very quickly and intuitively and that moral thought is used to justify the decisions we have already made. (p. 437)

2. Moral grammar refers to the rules, heuristics, and intuitions that are a part of our human psychology and that allow us to make moral decisions fast and automatically. (p. 438)

3. language acquisition (p. 438)

Specialized Cognitive Machinery Underlying Morality

1. make and implement socially acceptable plans of behaviour (p. 439)

2. False—Control subjects learn to draw from winning decks but the patients do not. (p. 439)

3. a sweat response (p. 439)

4. True—Kohlberg's tasks involve deliberate, slow, logical moral reasoning and patients do not differ from control subjects in this regard. (p. 439)

5. danger (p. 439)

6. infants or young toddlers (p. 440)

7. Consider the following in your response:
   - Damasio and colleagues found that people whose frontal lobe damage occurred at a very young age were relatively likely to have been repeatedly convicted of minor crimes, suggesting a deficit in considering consequences (quick, automatic moral decision-making).
   - As well, they showed abnormal performance on Kohlberg's tests, suggesting a deficit in slow, deliberate moral decision-making. (p. 440)

8. Answer:
   - In the dictator game, a player is given tokens that can be exchanged for cash. The player gets to decide how the tokens are shared with a partner.
   - In the ultimatum game, a player is given tokens. The player gets to propose a division of the tokens, which may be accepted or rejected by a partner. If the partner rejects the division, neither player gets anything. (p. 440)

9. Height (p. 440)

10. the human mind (p. 441)

The Development of Social Exchange Reasoning

1. cheaters (pp. 441–442)

2. social contract, or agreement between two parties (p. 442)

3. True—In fact, they performed twice as well in the cheater condition as the control condition, suggesting that already they have sophisticated 'cheater detection' cognitive machinery. (p. 443)

The Development of Sexual Morals

1. Incest leads to a greater chance that resulting offspring will inherit the same harmful recessive alleles that could lead to maldevelopment. (p. 444)

2. Inbreeding depression refers to the strategy of pairing your genetic contribution with someone who is not closely related to you, thus reducing the risk of pairing deleterious recessive genes in your offspring. (p. 444)

3. The Westermarck effect is a psychological process that makes sexual attraction unlikely between two people who lived together as young children. This process is thought to be designed to avoid incest. (p. 444)

4. Consider the following in your response:
   - Minor marriages are those in which the parents of a young son select his bride early in life and then bring that girl into their home, raising her from infancy.
   - These couples have been found to have higher divorce rates, produce fewer children, and have more extramarital affairs than couples who were not raised together. (p. 445)

5. Isreali kibbutzim (p. 446)

6. 'moral wrongness' (p. 446)

Universal Rules vs. Conventions

1. Some examples of cross-cultural prohibitions include the following:
   - Cheating
   - Stealing
   - Harming
   - Murdering (p. 446)

2. Answer:
   - Universal moral rules seem to be important moral guidelines in all known cultures. These rules were probably important to all EEAs. The cognitive processes that underlie these rules do not require information about specific ecological or cultural conditions to develop reliably.
   - Conventional moral rules may be very serious in some cultures but are not universal (e.g. age of sexual consent, polygamy, the treatment of animals, etc.) Cognitive processes underlying these rules seem to need input for development. As well, there seem to be critical periods for receiving that input. (pp. 447–448)

3. False—Conventions are usually explained in terms of social acceptability (politeness). (p. 448)

4. Psychopaths (p. 448)

Teaching Morals: Over-Reward or Internalize?

1. False—In fact, that parenting style is associated with less maturity in moral reasoning and moral decision-making, suggesting that strong-arm tactics do not work. (p. 449)

2. supportive and constructive (p. 449)

3. Eli should encourage Benjamin to reflect on the effect Benjamin's behaviour had on others. (p. 449)

4. Diana Baumrind's parenting styles are
   1. Authoritarian: parenting is rigid, harsh, and demanding
   2. Permissive: children are indulged; rules are not enforced
   3. Authoritative: parents are relatively responsive but not indulgent; rules are enforced consistently but not rigidly, with exceptions made when necessary (p. 450)

5. their own moral directions (p. 450)

6. delinquency and aggression (p. 450)

7. peers (p. 450)

8. an urban area (the capital city of Copenhagen) (p. 451)

9. neighbourhood (p. 451)

Practice Test 1: Answer Key

1. **b** (p. 416)
2. **a** (p. 417)
3. **d** (p. 419)
4. **b** (pp. 419–420)
5. **a** (p. 420)
6. **c** (p. 421)
7. **c** (p. 422)

8. **d** (p. 424)
9. **b** (p. 428)
10. **a** (pp. 430–432)
11. **c** (p. 432)
12. **b** (p. 433)
13. **d** (p. 433)
14. **a** (p. 434)

15. **c** (p. 435)
16. **b** (p. 438)
17. **d** (p. 439)
18. **a** (p. 439)
19. **a** (p. 440)
20. **c** (p. 444)
21. **a** (p. 445)

22. **b** (p. 446)
23. **d** (pp. 447–448)
24. **c** (p. 449)
25. **d** (p. 450)

Practice Test 2

1. **d** (pp. 417–418)
2. **c** (p. 418)
3. **b** (p. 419)
4. **c** (p. 420)
5. **c** (p. 422)
6. **a** (p. 422)
7. **d** (p. 422)

8. **d** (pp. 423–424)
9. **a** (p. 424)
10. **b** (p. 425)
11. **c** (p. 429)
12. **c** (pp. 429–430)
13. **d** (p. 430)
14. **a** (p. 433)

15. **b** (p. 434)
16. **c** (p. 435)
17. **d** (p. 442)
18. **c** (p. 443)
19. **b** (p. 444)
20. **d** (p. 445)
21. **a** (p. 448)

22. **a** (p. 448)
23. **b** (p. 449)
24. **c** (p. 450)
25. **d** (p. 457)

Practice Mid-Term

Multiple Choice Questions

1. Biologically, sex is defined in terms of _____ size.

    a. gamete
    b. genital
    c. sperm
    d. chromosome

2. Jean Piaget's developmental psychology career began when

    a. he was accepted to graduate school.
    b. he was hired to administer intelligence tests on school-aged children.
    c. he became an elementary school teacher.
    d. he became a father.

3. The results of Piaget's 'out of sight' experiment would have been different if he had

    a. turned out the lights.
    b. made the object smaller.
    c. watched the infant's body positioning.
    d. made the object more attractive to the infant.

4. Ethologists discovered the phenomenon of

    a. altruism.
    b. natural selection.
    c. critical periods.
    d. recessive alleles.

5. Categories help us to

    a. build memory capacity.
    b. prevent information overload.
    c. prevent neuronal overload.
    d. make inferences.

6. How would B. F. Skinner have explained prepared learning?

    a. with reference to reinforcements and punishments
    b. with reference to innate biological processes
    c. with reference to classical conditioning
    d. He couldn't have.

7. All genes really do is

    a. produce codons.
    b. 'read' mRNA molecules.
    c. determine outcomes.
    d. store the information that codes for proteins.

8. Which of the following statements would *not* be grounds for rejecting a hypothesis?

    a. It is not consistent with what we know from fields other than psychology.
    b. It does not allow for definitive conclusions.
    c. Experimental results do not support it.
    d. They are all grounds for rejecting a hypothesis.

9. In the strange situation, Nikolai is not upset when his mother leaves and is indifferent when she returns. Nikolai would most likely be classified as

    a. secure.
    b. insecure resistant.
    c. insecure avoidant.
    d. insecure disorganized.

10. The _____ assumes that infants will look longer at events that are impossible.

    a. psychophysical
    b. violation of expectation paradigm
    c. preferential-looking paradigm
    d. habituation

11. Children with autism spectrum disorder do *not* have

    a. communication delays.
    b. deficits in joint attention.
    c. deficits in imitation.
    d. deficits in logical thought.

12. When some aspect of the environment is constant across many generations, it makes sense for the organism to rely on the information in the environment rather than taking up precious genetic space. This can be referred to as

    a. a generalized learning mechanism.
    b. associationism.
    c. a norm of reaction.
    d. storing information in the environment.

13. Which of the following statements is *not* true about twins?

    a.   There are more dizygotic twins than monozygotic twins.
    b.   They are always more closely genetically-related than ordinary siblings.
    c.   They are more common in older mothers.
    d.   They may have different placentas.

14. Inbreeding depression reduces the risk of _____ in your offspring.

    a.   infertility
    b.   genetic mutation
    c.   pairing deleterious recessive genes
    d.   dominance of deleterious genes

15. The fact that we have a very strong intuition that we should be able to identify a single cause for any event is referred to as

    a.   the fallacy of exclusive determinism.
    b.   the myth of causality.
    c.   the SSSM.
    d.   the nature–nurture fallacy.

16. Gossiping, spreading rumours, and ostracism are all

    a.   forms of associative aggression.
    b.   more common in boys than girls.
    c.   forms of relational aggression.
    d.   non-aggressive acts.

17. Which of the following is an example of experience-dependant learning?

    a.   skilled fingering in violinists.
    b.   vertical/horizontal line perception in cats
    c.   mealworm detection in chicks
    d.   language comprehension in humans

18. According to Sandra Scarr, parenting is 'good enough' as long as

    a.   it fits within a fairly narrow range of normal.
    b.   it is responsive.
    c.   it is not abusive or neglectful.
    d.   it includes explicit attempts at socialization.

19. Which of the following tasks was Sidney Bradford (who regained his sight relatively late in life) able to do?

    a.   recognize faces
    b.   perceive depth
    c.   resolve the Necker cube
    d.   read the time from a clock

20. Richard Alexander interpreted Kohlberg's stages in terms of evolutionary priorities. Unlike Kohlberg, he sees moral thoughts as

   a. self-serving.
   b. a way to promote good feelings.
   c. a way to establish good relationships.
   d. a way of helping others.

21. _____'s influence on child-rearing can be seen to this day in parents' use of 'time-outs'.

   a. Ivan Pavlov
   b. John B. Watson
   c. B. F. Skinner
   d. Albert Bandura

22. The classic view of category membership involves no

   a. sufficient features.
   b. mental representations.
   c. natural-kinds.
   d. ambiguity.

23. Which of the following parenting styles involves inconsistency with regard to feedback?

   a. permissive
   b. strict
   c. authoritative
   d. authoritarian

24. Which of the following statements is true of child-basic categories?

   a. They are organized immaturely.
   b. They are more specific than adult's basic-level categories.
   c. They change mostly between early childhood and adolescence.
   d. all of the above

25. Concepts

   a. are not lexicalized.
   b. are not as powerful as categories.
   c. do not have agreed-upon definitions.
   d. cannot be applied to events.

26. Which of the following is *not* a good match between Piaget's sub-stage and the description?

   a. Sub-stage 5—can deal with 'visible displacement' but not 'invisible displacement'
   b. Sub-stage 3—immediately loses interest in an object that disappears from view
   c. Sub-stage 6—can search systematically through a series of possible hiding places for a hidden object
   d. Sub-stage 4—commits the A-not-B error

27. In boys, the first sign of puberty is

    a. masculinization of body proportions.
    b. growth of the testes.
    c. increased height.
    d. spermarche.

28. Harvey, a 4-year-old child, is shown pictures of a bat with wings outstretched, a hummingbird with wings outstretched, and a flamingo. He is asked which two go together. How would Piaget have predicted Harvey would respond?

    a. 'the bat and the hummingbird'
    b. 'the hummingbird and the flamingo'
    c. 'the bat and the flamingo'
    d. 'I don't know'

29. Harvey, a 4-year-old child, is shown pictures of a bat with wings outstretched, a hummingbird with wings outstretched, and a flamingo. He is asked which two go together. How is Harvey *actually* likely to respond?

    a. 'the bat and the hummingbird'
    b. 'the hummingbird and the flamingo'
    c. 'the bat and the flamingo'
    d. 'I don't know'

30. What did Piaget and Vygotsky have in common?

    a. Their work was not appreciated when it first came out.
    b. They were both very interested in language.
    c. They were from the same country.
    d. They both believed in the strong influence of culture.

31. Moral grammar refers to the rules, heuristics, and intuitions that are a part of our human psychology and that allow us to make moral decisions

    a. fast and automatically.
    b. that conform to objective rightness and wrongness.
    c. without emotional processing.
    d. that help us avoid dangerous situations.

32. What were the results of partial isolation in Harlow's monkeys?

    a. pacing
    b. catatonia
    c. self-mutilation
    d. all of the above

33. Which of the following is *not* a good match between reflex and description?

    a. Babinski—in response to stroking sole of foot, toes fan out and foot twists
    b. sucking—infant sucks what is placed in its mouth
    c. rooting—infant lifts its head when touched on the forehead
    d. grasping—closes hand to grasp what's there

34. A lengthy period of _____ seems to have evolved as a way to acquire social knowledge expertise.

    a. infancy
    b. early childhood
    c. adolescence
    d. middle age

35. Genomic imprinting matters for

    a. Turner's syndrome.
    b. 5-alpha-reductase deficiency.
    c. androgen insensitivity syndrome.
    d. congenital adrenal hyperplasia.

36. 'The man took a nap.' and 'He went to sleep.' have

    a. similar deep structures and dissimilar surface structures.
    b. dissimilar deep structures and similar surface structures.
    c. similar deep structures and similar surface structures.
    d. dissimilar deep structures and dissimilar surface structures.

37. Which person does *not* prefer to look at faces over non-faces?

    a. 9-minute-old infants
    b. 1-month-old infants
    c. 2-month-old infants
    d. adults

38. Which of the following *is not* a cognitive advantage of bilingualism?

    a. better control of attention
    b. more attention to irrelevant stimuli
    c. greater executive control
    d. buffer against cognitive declines in old age

39. All of the following are social cognitive skills *except*

    a. social referencing.
    b. joint attention.
    c. holistic processing.
    d. imitation.

40. Harlow's experimental findings with monkeys suggest that the driving force behind attachment is _____

   a. facial responsiveness.
   b. nutrition.
   c. comfort.
   d. reliability.

41. Piaget was influential in the field of developmental psychology for all of the following reasons *except*

   a. he was active in the field for almost 60 years.
   b. his work covered a very broad age range.
   c. his methodology was very strong.
   d. he incorporated a broad range of topics into his theories.

42. What is the inherent conflict between parent and offspring described by Robert Trivers?

   a. They have different fitness interests.
   b. They both want resources for themselves.
   c. Only the parents follow Hamilton's rule.
   d. They are likely to differ personality-wise.

43. Broca's area is located near the _____ cortex.

   a. auditory
   b. sensory
   c. visual
   d. motor

44. Which of the following is true of a chromosome?

   a. It is too small to be seen under a microscope.
   b. It is composed of a large DNA helix.
   c. It cannot be replicated.
   d. It contains millions of genes.

45. At 5 years of age, children apply counting principles with a consistency of about _____ per cent.

   a. 30
   b. 50
   c. 75
   d. 95

46. Girls with congenital adrenal hyperplasia are more likely than other girls to

   a. choose typically girl-preferred toys.
   b. perform poorly on spatial tasks.
   c. engage in rough-and-tumble play.
   d. be interested in infants.

47. Who conducted the first large systematic study of development in North America?

   a. G. Stanley Hall
   b. Jean Piaget
   c. Charles Darwin
   d. Arnold Gesell

48. Fast mapping requires _____ encounter(s) for word learning to occur.

   a. 0
   b. 1
   c. 3
   d. 6

49. Chimps who get extensive language training

   a. take conversational turns.
   b. acquire a modest vocabulary.
   c. use language spontaneously.
   d. none of the above

50. It is not until the age of 5 years that _____ reaches adult levels.

   a. depth perception
   b. colour vision
   c. acuity
   d. shape constancy

Fill-in-the-Blanks Questions

1. Whether the relationship between the variables is positive or negative and the strength of the relationship can be revealed by the _____.

2. In Kohlberg's stage 3, the focus is on _____.

3. Using a _____ involves grouping items based on their use together or their prior association in a story rather than on category membership.

4. Sandra Scarr's niche-picking theory proposes that _____.

5. Other animals communicate but only human language has a _____.

6. Pierre is 1 week old. When presented with the smell of rotten eggs, he will likely _____.

7. Children with ASD perform well on false-photo tests but not on _____ tests.

8. An adaptation is a trait that is designed and preserved by the process of natural selection because that trait confers a _____ in the environment in which it evolved.

9. Infants who do not seem to have a strategy for dealing with being separated from their mothers are classified as _____.

10. In occlusion events, an object becomes invisible as it _____.

Short Answer Questions

1. Give an example of how environment can affect genes.

2. Why would it be difficult for associationists to explain essentialism?

3. Outline 'group socialization theory' proposed by Judith Harris.

4. Describe newborns' hearing abilities.

5. Why are human females the choosier sex?

6. What are the advantages and disadvantages of using a longitudinal design?

7. What happens when a kitten is deprived of visual input to the one eye?

8. List children's counting principles.

9. What is the heritability statistic and how is it calculated?

10. Describe the symptoms of Broca's aphasia and Wernicke's aphasia.

Multiple Choice Questions: Answer Key

1. **a** (p. 384)
2. **b** (p. 12)
3. **a** (p. 225)
4. **c** (p. 43)
5. **d** (p. 194)
6. **d** (p. 137)
7. **d** (p. 82)
8. **b** (p. 4)
9. **c** (p. 356)
10. **b** (p. 53)
11. **d** (p. 231)
12. **d** (p. 131)
13. **b** (p. 91)
14. **c** (p. 444)
15. **a** (p. 110)
16. **c** (p. 392)
17. **a** (p. 134)
18. **c** (p. 362)
19. **d** (p. 172)
20. **a** (p. 425)
21. **c** (p. 38)
22. **d** (p. 189)
23. **a** (p. 450)
24. **a** (p. 201)
25. **c** (p. 184)
26. **b** (p. 234)
27. **b** (p. 398)
28. **a** (p. 244)
29. **b** (p. 244)
30. **a** (pp. 12–14)
31. **a** (p. 438)
32. **d** (pp. 258–259)
33. **c** (p. 162)
34. **c** (p. 264)
35. **a** (p. 405)
36. **c** (p. 302)
37. **b** (p. 275–276)
38. **b** (p. 320)
39. **c** (p. 279)
40. **c** (p. 352)
41. **c** (p. 30)
42. **a** (p. 358)
43. **d** (p. 303)
44. **b** (p. 69)
45. **d** (p. 248)
46. **c** (p. 404)
47. **a** (p. 10)
48. **b** (p. 311)
49. **b** (p. 329)
50. **c** (p. 158)

Fill-in-the-Blanks Questions: Answer Key

1. correlation coefficient (p. 50)

2. relationships (p. 422)

3. thematic association (p. 192)

4. a child determines her environment (at least to some extent) (p. 87)

5. generative grammar (p. 327)

6. frown and turn his head away (p. 164)

7. false-belief (p. 288)

8. reproductive advantage (p. 6)

9. insecure disorganized (p. 356)

10. moves behind a nearer object (p. 231)

Short Answer Questions: Answer Key

1. Consider the following in your response:
   - Social status can affect gene expression.
   - Burmeister et al. (2007) found that an individual fish's rank in the social hierarchy affects the expression of the gene that codes for androgen and estrogen receptors. The higher the rank, the more receptors produced by DNA. More receptors lead to more dominant behaviour. (pp. 85–86)

2. The associationist perspective relies heavily on perceptual similarity and in essence does depend on perceptual characteristics. (p. 204)

3. The theory proposes that
   - peers and siblings, especially acting in groups, have a measurable effect on the personality development of children.
   - socialization takes place in peer groups, especially sex- and age-segregated peer groups formed from middle childhood through adolescence.
   - once children identify with the peer group, they adopt the group's attitudes and norms of behaviour.
   - behaviours learned at home will only be transmitted to the group if the behaviour is shared and approved of by most of the group members.
   - the child's culture is ultimately created by the peer group. Elements of adult culture are selected and rejected. Novel elements are invented.
   - traditions may be passed on for generations from older children to younger children. (pp. 365–366)

4. Compared to adults, newborns
   - have an auditory system that is quite well developed.
   - prefer to listen to voices over pure tones. They may be particularly adept at discriminating human speech sounds.
   - have higher thresholds for loudness and for low pitch (i.e. they don't hear those sounds as well).
   - are better at hearing high-pitched sounds. (p. 162)

5. In species that have males and females, and especially when fertilization is internal to the female, females are choosier because making the larger gamete means making a larger investment and internal fertilization leads to a larger investment in offspring. Since females are more invested, they are less willing to take risks on a mate. (p. 384)

6. Advantages
   - It measures change within individuals.
   - Cohort effects can be eliminated.

Disadvantages
- It takes a long time.
- There may be attrition (a loss of participants over time).
- There may be practice effects (because the task is completed more than once). (pp. 46–47)

7. Eventually, the ocular dominance columns that would be devoted to the that eye start to process information from the other eye instead. This setup is irreversible. (p. 169)

8. Children's counting principles are as follows:
- The one-to-one principle: each item gets a unique number label
- The stable-order principle: number labels should be spoken in the same order every time
- The cardinal principle: the last number label assigned is the total
- The abstraction principle: *anything* can be counted
- The order-irrelevant principle: counting order doesn't matter; the total should be the same regardless of order (p. 248)

9. The heritability statistic is the estimate of the proportion of the measured variance in a trait among individuals in a given population that is attributable to genetic differences among those individuals.

$$\text{Heritability} = \frac{V(genes)}{V(genes) + V(environment) + V(g*e)}$$

(pp. 114–115)

10. Broca's aphasia
- They can produce only 'telegraphic speech'—single-word, halting, laboriously-produced word strings—with little grammatical organization.
- Language comprehension remains largely intact.

Wernicke's area
- They are unable to understand other people's speech.
- Their own speech is fluent and largely grammatical, but nonsensical. (pp. 303–304)

Practice Final Exam

Multiple Choice Questions

1. Flavell's Level 1 understanding of perspective

   a. includes the understanding that another person might see an object but see it differently.
   b. includes the understanding that, in order to see something, a person's eyes must be open and there must be a clear line of sight to the object.
   c. is present by the age of 4 or 5.
   d. is present in newborns.

2. Compared to those raised in a deprived environment, rats raised in a complex environment have

   a. more synapses.
   b. a thicker cortex.
   c. more dendritic extensions.
   d. all of the above

3. Which of the following statements is *not* true of IRBs?

   a. They consist of a panel of objective and knowledgeable individuals.
   b. They may deny permission to conduct an experiment.
   c. The acronym stands for Institutional Review Board.
   d. They exist only at universities.

4. Which of the following statements is true of John B. Watson?

   a. He believed humans have many specific mechanisms for learning.
   b. He believed in subjective methods of experimental design.
   c. His perspective was rooted in the work of Ivan Pavlov.
   d. He was interested in the study of cognition.

5. Preschoolers distinguish animate from inanimate objects based on an object's ability to

   a. breathe.
   b. respond to other animate objects.
   c. move by itself.
   d. eat.

6. _____ is the term used to refer to a shaping by natural selection such that reproductive success is maximized.

   a. Advancement
   b. Optimization
   c. Strategy
   d. Scheme

7. _____ conduct electrical signals away from the cell body.

    a. Dendrites
    b. Axons
    c. Synapses
    d. Neurons

8. In the _____ game, a player is given tokens that can be exchanged for cash. The player gets to decide how the tokens are shared with a partner.

    a. director
    b. ruler
    c. ultimatum
    d. dictator

9. Pretend play

    a. indicates a developing theory of mind.
    b. becomes less sophisticated with age.
    c. is also called 'literal play'.
    d. emerges before 1 year of age.

10. Which of the following is an example of a sleeper effect?

    a. A lack of activation in the face-processing part of the brain after lifelong blindness
    b. A lack of depth perception in individuals with monocular vision
    c. Plasticity in the visual cortex.
    d. Individuals who had cataracts removed in the first year of life later show deficits in holistic face processing.

11. Prepared learning can take place after

    a. a single exposure.
    b. several exposures.
    c. many exposures.
    d. zero exposures.

12. Which of the following comes last?

    a. Children believe in negotiation in rule formation.
    b. Children solve the 'cheater detection' problem.
    c. Piaget's transitional period.
    d. Sensitive period for culture-specific rules.

13. Developmental systems theory does *not* propose that

    a. small initial changes in the system can have far-reaching effects.
    b. genes play a special role in development.
    c. the whole of a complex system is more than the sum of its parts.
    d. influences are bidirectional.

14. Development begins when the _____ of a new individual is complete.

    a. genome
    b. egg
    c. cellular specialization
    d. gametes

15. _____ refers to our failure to appreciate the uniformity and the usefulness of our concepts.

    a. Imperfect taxonomy
    b. Instinct blindness
    c. Essentialism
    d. Perceptual loss

16. Reliability is

    a. a measure of how well the conditions of the study allow for measurement of the phenomenon of interest.
    b. the extent of generalizability outside of the research situation.
    c. the consistency in repeated measures of the same variable using the same measurement method.
    d. the extent to which a measuring technique measures the attribute that it is designed to measure.

17. We know that 3-month-old infants have an appreciation of _____ because they will express surprise when part of an object remains when another part is lifted.

    a. support
    b. continuity
    c. contact
    d. cohesion

18. Which of the following factors did Ainsworth believe was one of the keys in assessing the quality of the child's attachment?

    a. how effectively the infant used his caregiver as a home base
    b. how the infant reacts to first seeing the stranger
    c. how the infant reacts when the stranger leaves the room
    d. how the infant responds when scared

19. Which of the following is *not* true of experience-expectant learning?

    a. it is largely universal.
    b. it continues throughout the lifespan.
    c. it relies on what the genome 'expects'.
    d. it has a critical period.

20. Which of the following is *not* true regarding typicality ratings?

    a. Findings regarding typicality ratings can be accounted for by the classic view of categorization.
    b. People are faster to affirm category membership for more typical items.
    c. The number of shared features predicts the typicality rating.
    d. Typicality ratings are quite stable between individuals.

21. The link between high testosterone levels and prostate cancer in middle-age men can be explained with reference to

    a. interactionism.
    b. transcription.
    c. pleiotropy.
    d. bidirectional influences.

22. Which of the following is *not* a factor that influences the selection of friends, according to Tooby and Cosmides?

    a. reciprocation
    b. shared interests
    c. mind reading
    d. by-product mutualism

23. According to research described in the textbook, early and late maturing boys have been found to differ in terms of

    a. intelligence.
    b. risk-taking.
    c. poise.
    d. neuroticism.

24. Which of the following is *not* a good match?

    a. Meiosis I—includes crossover
    b. Meiosis II—produces two haploid daughter cells
    c. Meiosis II—results in a chromotid that is ready to pair up in mating
    d. Meiosis I—reductive division

25. Which of the following variables would be best investigated using a within-subjects design?

    a. age
    b. training effects
    c. education level
    d. gender

26. Infant-directed speech *does not* tend to include

    a. exaggerated intonation.
    b. high pitch.
    c. grammatical errors.
    d. focus on concrete and current topics.

27. Compared to female fetuses, male fetuses are *not*

    a. more active in utero.
    b. as likely to be carried to term.
    c. as likely to suffer from a physical abnormality.
    d. significantly different on any measurable characteristic.

28. Which of the following is a good match?

    a. left hemisphere of the brain—controls the right side of the body
    b. right hemisphere of the brain—more active for language processing
    c. right hemisphere of the brain—receives sensory information from the right side of the body
    d. left hemisphere of the brain—more active for visual imagery

29. Which of the following is *not* a good match?

    a. 5 months—will manually search for a previously-seen object in a dark room
    b. 8 months—appreciates that height is important in a covering event
    c. 4 months—expects continuity if a partly occluded object moves behind a screen
    d. 7 ½ months—appreciates that height is important in a containment event

30. A genetic 'mosaic' pattern occurs when

    a. some body tissues have XY chromosomes and some tissues have XX chromosomes.
    b. there is blending of the X and Y chromosomes.
    c. an individual has neither XY or XY chromosomes.
    d. none of the above

31. Which of the following have high heritability estimates?

    a. adaptations
    b. number of fingers and toes
    c. human universals
    d. none of the above

32. The difference between a critical period and a sensitive period is

    a. timing.
    b. that humans have sensitive periods and other animals have critical periods.
    c. that critical periods exist for perceptual abilities and sensitive periods exist for cognitive abilities.
    d. the difference between 'has to happen then' and 'is best to happen then'.

33. Which of the following is *not* true of stranger anxiety?

    a. It emerges somewhat before separation anxiety.
    b. It is measured by the strange situation task.
    c. It first appears at around 6 or 7 months.
    d. It decreases as infants' attachment to their primary caregiver grows.

34. Internal male reproductive structures are called _____ structures.

    a. androgen
    b. intersex
    c. reductase
    d. Wolffian

35. Which of the following is *not* one of the three constructs at the centre of naïve psychology?

    a. desires
    b. goals
    c. beliefs
    d. actions

36. Acuity reaches 20/40 by _____ months.

    a. 1
    b. 2
    c. 4
    d. 6

37. Parental-investment theory stresses the _____ basis of aspects of parental behaviour.

    a. social
    b. evolutionary
    c. genetic
    d. behavioural

38. The correlation statistic was modified to create the _____ statistic.

    a. regression
    b. mean
    c. heritability
    d. standard deviation

39. Who was an empiricist with regard to morality?

    a. George Edward Moore
    b. Thomas Hobbes
    c. John Stuart Mill
    d. They were all empiricists with regard to morality.

40. The speech sounds /ba/ and /pa/ differ in terms of

    a. VOT
    b. TOV
    c. STV
    d. VTS

41. A monkey emits an alarm call to warn of a predator because

    a. monkeys are closely related to humans and, therefore, have altruism genes.
    b. emitting the call involves no cost.
    c. monkeys are very social creatures.
    d. its genetic relatives are likely close by.

42. Hubel & Wiesel's 'complex' cells

    a. respond to vertical lines.
    b. respond to horizontal lines.
    c. receive input from a number of other cells and integrate the information received.
    d. all of the above

43. Michael May had a lack of activation in the _____ face area of the brain.

    a. lateral
    b. fusiform
    c. frontal
    d. holistic

44. For _____, language processing does *not* occur primarily in the left hemisphere.

    a. 90 per cent of people who are right-handed
    b. 10 per cent of people who are right-handed
    c. 70 per cent of people who are left-handed
    d. 10 per cent of people who are left-handed

45. When a feature did not arise as an adaptation for its present role but was subsequently co-opted for that function, it is called

    a. a by-product.
    b. genetic drift.
    c. a founder situation.
    d. an exaptation.

46. Piaget's autonomous morality stage covers which age range?

    a. 4 to 7 years
    b. 7 to 10 years
    c. 10 years and up
    d. 10 to 20 years

47. Concepts are like theories in all of the following ways *except*

   a. Both are generated in the same way by children.
   b. Both address a set of causal relationships that apply within, but not outside of, the domain.
   c. Both include a distinct set of items.
   d. Both address phenomena involving members of a set.

48. Of the following, which is the best example of a superordinate level category?

   a. weather
   b. blizzard
   c. sleet
   d. snow

49. Which of the following statements best describes what the inductive method can reveal?

   a. It reveals children's deductive reasoning.
   b. It reveals what categories children hold and what inferences are warranted within a category.
   c. It reveals the adaptiveness of psychological processes.
   d. It reveals the problem with similarity.

50. Which of the following statements is true of ocular dominance columns?

   a. They are, literally, columns.
   b. All of the left-eye ones are side-by-side and all of the right-eye ones are side-by-side.
   c. They are present in the visual cortex of newborns.
   d. They are of varying widths.

51. Privileged domains, core knowledge, and innate domains are all ways of referring to

   a. intuitive physics.
   b. informational priorities.
   c. specialized learning mechanisms.
   d. none of the above

52. The knowledge that height is an important factor comes first for _____ events.

   a. gravitational
   b. containment
   c. covering
   d. occlusion

53. Which sex and gender milestone comes first?

   a. Children identify themselves as 'girl' or 'boy'.
   b. Boys are more active than girls.
   c. Girls show evidence of more empathy than boys.
   d. Girls are more coordinated than boys.

54. Preschoolers do *not* accept the idea that

   a. food is a prerequisite for growth.
   b. very small animals can grow.
   c. growth is beyond intentional control.
   d. change can be quantitative.

55. Constancy refers to strategies used by the visual system so that a given object will appear to the be same size, shape, brightness, or colour despite enormous differences in

   a. the objective features.
   b. the characteristics of the image on our retina.
   c. our perceptions.
   d. motion.

56. At 10 months of age, infants are *not* capable of discriminating between items of a ratio of

   a. 2:1
   b. 1:2
   c. 2:3
   d. 3:4

57. The modern synthesis refers to

   a. the blending of DNA.
   b. the combined work of Darwin and Mendel.
   c. evolutionary processes that take place over time.
   d. particulate inheritance.

58. All of the following have been found to predict brain size among primates except

   a. deception rates.
   b. coalition size.
   c. amount of time spent in social activity during the day.
   d. size of the home range.

59. Cross-cultural moral prohibitions include all of the following *except*

   a. stealing.
   b. cheating.
   c. nudity.
   d. murder.

60. Which of the following demonstrates holistic processing?

   a. the inversion effect
   b. the three mountains task
   c. the false-photo task
   d. the composite face task

61. When two or more groups exist through no action of the experimenter, allowing for a comparison between these naturally occurring groups, it is called

    a. a correlation.
    b. an observational method.
    c. a natural experiment.
    d. a comparative experiment.

62. All of the following techniques are used for learning about children's understanding of biology *except*

    a. asking them.
    b. the transformation technique.
    c. the core knowledge technique.
    d. the method of induction.

63. _____ is the only learning theory that includes focus on personality.

    a. Operant conditioning
    b. Social learning
    c. Behaviourism
    d. Classical conditioning

64. Infants' responses to salty tastes

    a. shifts over the first 4 months.
    b. usually involve relaxation of facial muscles.
    c. usually involve frowning.
    d. are similar to adults'.

65. Which of the following statements is true regarding Piaget's theory of cognitive development?

    a. It proposes a set of continuous changes.
    b. It was devised using unplanned, unstructured interviews.
    c. It purports that experience gained from the environment is unimportant.
    d. It is an example of genetic epistemology.

66. According to Werker & Tees' (1984) findings on speech sound discriminations over the first year of life, at what age do infants lose speech sound discrimination abilities for languages other than their native language?

    a. 12 months
    b. 10 months
    c. 8 months
    d. 6 months

67. Humans are most likely to develop phobias to which kind of stimuli?

    a. dangerous
    b. poisonous
    c. evolutionarily relevant
    d. innocuous

68. Which of the following statements is *not* true of functional fixedness?

    a. It happens quite commonly in everyday life.
    b. It is related to problem-solving.
    c. It tends to decrease with age.
    d. It is demonstrated by Duncker's candle problem.

69. Which of the following is a good age–milestone match?

    a. 6 months—starts babbling
    b. 9 months—understands several words
    c. birth—perceives speech sounds categorically
    d. 1 month—uses voice to attract attention

70. Which of the following is true of infant colour vision?

    a. All photoreceptors develop at the same rate.
    b. Infants prefer pastel colours over bright colours.
    c. Newborns can discriminate between red and green.
    d. It is completely absent in newborns.

71. Which of the following is a specific family stressor during childhood that can lead to earlier puberty, earlier sexual relationships, and more sex partners?

    a. coercive family relationships
    b. frequent scarcity of food
    c. absence of the father
    d. all of the above

72. The effect that occurs only after training has taken place is the

    a. conditioned response.
    b. unconditioned response.
    c. conditioned stimulus.
    d. unconditioned stimulus.

73. The most successful treatment for the former isolates in Harlow's experiments involved

    a. a surrogate mother.
    b. pairing them with normally-reared, younger monkeys.
    c. having them adopt a baby monkey.
    d. leaving them alone.

74. Crossover results in

    a. genetic distance.
    b. dizygotic twins.
    c. genetic diversity.
    d. multiple zygotes.

75. The advantage of the Attachment Q-sort over the strange situation task is that it

    a. is more reliable.
    b. is more versatile.
    c. can be used with younger infants.
    d. can be used in the lab.

76. After the development of numerosity comes the development of

    a. multiplicity.
    b. magnitude.
    c. arithmetic.
    d. ordinality.

77. Garcia's and Mineka's findings with rats and monkeys were quite devastating to those who believed that the mind

    a. develops as it does because of genetics.
    b. is not a suitable topic of study.
    c. is a blank slate.
    d. is affected by nature more than nurture.

78. Wittgenstein dealt the first critical blow to

    a. Piaget's theory of child categorization.
    b. the idea of prototypes.
    c. the classic view of categories.
    d. the views of Eleanor Rosch.

79. Which of the following would be an example of a population bottleneck?

    a. A mother with both brown eye and blue eye alleles passes the blue eye allele to all of her children.
    b. White fur in rabbits becomes prevalent when the climate gets colder.
    c. A devastating disease wipes out all but 500 people, none of whom have or are carriers for colour-blindness.
    d. all of the above

80. Which of the following is *not* a 'pragmatic cue' that children use for word learning?

    a. adults' focus of attention
    b. adults' intentionality
    c. adults' statements
    d. adults' emotional reactions

81. Animism is

    a. the attribution of mental states to inanimate objects.
    b. the attribution of physical and mechanical characteristics to mental entities.
    c. the inability to appreciate other points of view.
    d. the preference for moving over stable objects.

82. Which of the following is *not* an alloparent?

    a. the parent
    b. an uncle
    c. a teacher
    d. a friend of the mother

83. Which of the following is *not* one of the three types of categories described in the textbook?

    a. nominal
    b. natural kinds
    c. artifacts
    d. conceptual

84. Of the 46 human chromosomes, _____ are *not* autosomes.

    a. 22
    b. 44
    c. 4
    d. 2

85. Having two copies of each chromosome is referred to as

    a. haploid.
    b. biploid.
    c. twoploid.
    d. diploid.

86. The _____ involves computing averages that represent typical development.

    a. method of averages
    b. normative approach
    c. standardized approach
    d. method of commonality

87. 'Home signs' can be taken as evidence for

    a. a universal grammar.
    b. very early language production.
    c. a critical period of language acquisition.
    d. surface structure.

88. Menarche is the onset of

    a. ejaculation.
    b. adolescence.
    c. menstruation.
    d. gender identity.

89. Which of the following describes Vygotsky's notion of a 'dialectical process'?

    a. applying a cultural context to learning
    b. a task that the child can complete with help from an adult
    c. establishing a relationship between language and thought
    d. the process of shared problem-solving

90. How are 'creole' languages different from established languages?

    a. They lack a grammatical structure.
    b. Word order varies from speaker to speaker.
    c. They were created relatively recently.
    d. They are less complex.

91. A cross-cultural survey found that the more polygyny in a culture, the more the boys were taught to exhibit

    a. responsibility.
    b. aggression.
    c. passivity.
    d. sexual restraint.

92. Following two or more groups longitudinally is called a _____ design.

    a. cross-sectional
    b. cross-sequential
    c. selective
    d. sequential

93. The first social smiles are usually seen at

    a. 1 week.
    b. 6 weeks.
    c. 12 weeks.
    d. 24 weeks.

94. Which of the following is *not* a good match?

    a.   John B. Watson—'Little Albert'
    b.   Jean-Jacques Rousseau—'noble savages'
    c.   G. Stanley Hall—'baby biography'
    d.   John Locke—'All children are created equal.'

95. For a child in Piaget's _____, a rule is a rule because an authority figure said it is.

    a.   moral judgment stage
    b.   autonomous morality stage
    c.   morality of constraint stage
    d.   transitional period

96. At Piaget's sensorimotor substage 4, the focus is on

    a.   intentional behaviour.
    b.   developing schemes.
    c.   discovering procedures.
    d.   mental representation.

97. The human zygote lasts for about

    a.   24 hours.
    b.   4 days.
    c.   2 weeks.
    d.   1 month.

98. Which of the following is a measurement of the slow, deliberate component of moral decision-making?

    a.   responses to Damasio's decks of cards
    b.   responses to Kohlberg's moral dilemmas
    c.   both *a* and *b*
    d.   neither *a* nor *b*

99. The genetic relatedness of a cousin is

    a.   0.5
    b.   0.35
    c.   0.25
    d.   0.125

100. Which of the following statements is *not* true regarding the evolution of human traits?

    a.   Complex systems take a very long time to evolve because they are reliant on many alleles.
    b.   Not all information that an individual needs is coded into his genes.
    c.   Progress brought on by evolution is thought to be slower today than it might have been in the past.
    d.   The current environment matches the EEA so closely that adaptations are never maladaptive.

Short Answer Questions

1. Inclusive fitness = _____ + _____ .

2. 'Norm of reaction' describes the relationship between a specific environmental factor and a _____ .

3. Transcription of the SRY gene leads to creation of the _____ .

4. Piaget proposed that the social cognitive limitation at the preoperational stage is _____ .

5. The _____ can be used to determine if infants reliably look at one stimulus more than another. If they do, researchers infer that the infants can tell the difference between the two.

6. In terms of morality, Carol Gilligan argues that boys, more so than girls, are taught to value _____ and _____ .

7. The function of perception is to _____ .

8. Relations between boys and girls in 'minor marriages' and Isreali kibbutzim provide evidence for the _____ effect.

9. The ability to continuously keep track of one's location relative to a starting point is referred to as _____ .

10. According to our definition, a gene is a functional sequence of DNA that remains across a large number of generations, potentially for long enough for it to _____ .

11. Adaptations that are designed to respond to specific cues in the environment are called _____ adaptations.

12. Piaget's stages, in the correct order, are _____, _____, _____, and _____.

13. When Garcia paired sweetened water with _____, the rats learned to avoid the sweet water.

14. _____ involves over-applying grammatical tools (e.g. 'goed' instead of 'went').

15. The karyotype for individuals with Turner's syndrome is _____.

16. Perceptual categories are implicit classifications of perceptual stimuli into discrete sets in spite of a lack of _____.

17. A nativist believes that development is the result of _____. An empiricist believes that development is the result of _____.

18. Boys seem to have the biggest advantage over girls on _____ skills.

19. Infants have a(n) _____ system for small numbers and a(n) _____ system for large numbers.

20. Synaptic pruning refers to the selective death of synapses based on _____.

Short Answer Questions

1. What is perceptual narrowing?

2. How is morning sickness adaptive?

3. According to John Bowlby, what is the purpose of attachment?

4. What is the A-not-B error and why does it occur?

5. In essence, what do experiments do?

6. How did the case of Bruce/David Reimer provide evidence against the socialization theory of gender?

7. What are three 'rules' that young children use for word learning?

8. What is the EEA?

9. According to Piaget, 5-year-old Juan does not have 'mature' categorization abilities. More specifically, how would Piaget describe Juan's categorization abilities?

10. What are some differences in moral decision-making abilities between individuals who had frontal lobe damage when they were very young and control subjects?

Multiple Choice Questions: Answer Key

1. **b** (p. 268)
2. **d** (p. 134)
3. **d** (p. 56)
4. **c** (p. 12)
5. **c** (p. 280)
6. **c** (p. 21)
7. **b** (p. 97)
8. **d** (p. 440)
9. **a** (p. 272)
10. **d** (p. 173)
11. **a** (p. 138)
12. **a** (p. 448)
13. **b** (pp. 39–40)
14. **a** (p. 6)
15. **b** (p. 186)
16. **c** (p. 55)
17. **d** (p. 228)
18. **a** (pp. 354–355)
19. **b** (p. 133)
20. **a** (p. 190)
21. **c** (p. 83)
22. **b** (p. 435)
23. **c** (p. 363)
24. **b** (p. 89)
25. **b** (p. 50)
26. **c** (p. 315)
27. **b** (pp. 387–388)
28. **a** (p. 99)
29. **b** (p. 244)
30. **a** (p. 403)
31. **d** (p. 128)
32. **d** (p. 133)
33. **d** (p. 355)
34. **d** (p. 403)
35. **b** (p. 283)
36. **d** (pp. 157–158)
37. **b** (p. 358)
38. **c** (p. 114)
39. **b** (p. 417)
40. **a** (p. 306)
41. **d** (p. 430)
42. **c** (p. 169)
43. **b** (p. 172)
44. **b** (p. 303)
45. **d** (p. 77)
46. **c** (p. 420)
47. **a** (p. 185)
48. **a** (p. 198)
49. **b** (p. 208)
50. **a** (p. 169)
51. **c** (p. 222)
52. **d** (p. 231)
53. **b** (p. 396)
54. **b** (p. 240)
55. **b** (p. 165)
56. **d** (p. 246)
57. **b** (p. 64)
58. **d** (pp. 262–263)
59. **c** (p. 446)
60. **d** (p. 274)
61. **c** (p. 172)
62. **c** (pp. 238–239)
63. **b** (p. 38)
64. **a** (p. 163)
65. **d** (p. 13)
66. **b** (p. 306)
67. **c** (p. 139)
68. **c** (p. 197)
69. **a** (p. 322)
70. **c** (p. 159)
71. **d** (p. 349)
72. **a** (p. 36)
73. **b** (p. 260)
74. **c** (p. 90)
75. **b** (p. 355)
76. **d** (p. 245)
77. **c** (p. 138)
78. **c** (p. 189)
79. **c** (p. 75)
80. **c** (p. 313)
81. **a** (p. 266)
82. **a** (p. 366)
83. **d** (pp. 201–202)
84. **d** (p. 385)
85. **d** (p. 89)
86. **b** (p. 11)
87. **a** (p. 302)
88. **c** (p. 398)
89. **d** (p. 14)
90. **c** (p. 323)
91. **b** (p. 409–410)
92. **b** (p. 48)
93. **b** (p. 357)
94. **c** (pp. 9–12)
95. **c** (p. 419)
96. **a** (p. 32)
97. **b** (p. 87)
98. **b** (p. 440)
99. **d** (p. 359)
100. **d** (p. 23)

Short Answer Questions: Answer Key

1. number of viable offspring; number of viable relatives, discounted by relatedness (p. 358)

2. measurable phenotypic expression (p. 135)

3. the testis determining factor (p. 386)

4. egocentrism (p. 265)

5. preferential-looking paradigm (p. 51)

6. societal rules; ideal principles (p. 424)

7. to aid us in surviving and reproducing (p. 147)

8. Westermarck (p. 444)

9. dead reckoning (p. 237)

10. function as a significant unit of natural selection (p. 70)

11. facultative (p. 130)

12. sensorimotor; preoperational; concrete operational; formal operational (pp. 31–32)

13. a nausea-inducing stimulus (p. 138)

14. Over-regularization (p. 321)

15. X (p. 405)

16. physical discontinuity in the stimuli (p. 183)

17. genetics; environment (pp. 7–8)

18. spatial (p. 390)

19. precise; approximate (p. 246)

20. experience (p. 169)

Short Answer Questions: Answer Key

1. Perceptual narrowing is the process of perceptual mechanisms becoming more specialized. (p. 278)

2. Consider the following in your response:
   - Women who experience morning sickness are less likely to have a miscarriage than women who do not.
   - Morning sickness is now understood to be a mechanism that protects the developing fetus. (p. 96)

3. According to Bowlby,
   - attachment has a functional, evolutionary purpose.
   - attachment keeps the infant safe and allows for exploration. (p. 354)

4. The A-not-B error occurs when an object is first hidden in the same spot again and again. Next, the infant watches as it is hidden in a different spot. When given a chance to search for the object, children in Piaget's sub-stage 4 will search for the object in the first location. No one is really sure why the A-not-B error occurs. (p. 234)

5. They isolate the contribution of a particular cause of an event statistically. (p. 110)

6. Consider the following in your response:
   - Bruce Reimer was born a completely healthy, typical boy. His penis was destroyed during an attempted circumcision and after that he was raised as a girl. His genitals were believably female and he (and everyone else) was told he was a girl. In other words, his biology was completely male but his socialization was completely female.
   - Bruce was renamed Brenda and was miserable. She never felt like a girl and hated being raised as a girl. Her peers rejected her as a girl and she was ostracized and bullied. She was far too aggressive to fit in socially as a girl. Once told she was a boy, Brenda immediately changed her name to David and lived as a boy.
   - The sex-reassignment was an unqualified failure, proving that socialization is not enough for gender identity. (pp. 401–402)

7. The three 'rules' are
   - The whole-object assumption
     - Children narrow the set of possible meanings that might be associated with a novel word by assuming that novel words will refer to whole objects.
   - The taxonomic assumption
     - Children assume that novel words will refer to object that are grouped conceptually or categorically rather than thematically.
   - The mutual exclusivity assumption

- Children assume that novel words applied to a new object will refer to a novel property rather than to the whole object or a known property. It is assumed that a novel word does not duplicate a known word but means something else. (pp. 311–313)

8. EEA stands for 'environment of evolutionary adaptedness'. It refers to the environment in which natural selection took place. (p. 20)

9. Juan cannot
   - identify which items are included and excluded in a category.
   - understand that membership in one category means that the item is not a member of another category at the same level.
   - organizes categories hierarchically. (p. 191)

10. Consider the following in your response:
   - Damasio and colleagues found that people whose frontal lobe damage occurred at a very young age were relatively likely to have been repeatedly convicted of minor crimes, suggesting a deficit in considering consequences. In other words, they had deficits in quick, automatic moral decision-making.
   - As well, these people showed abnormal performance on Kohlberg's tests, suggesting a deficit in slow, deliberate moral decision-making. (p. 439)

Notes